CLASSIC HINTS AND T

MOTORCYCLISTS

Patrick Stephens Limited, an imprint of Haynes Publishing, has published authoritative, quality books for enthusiasts for more than 25 years. During that time the company has established a reputation as one of the world's leading publishers of books on aviation, maritime, military, model-making, motor cycling, motoring, motor racing, railway and railway modelling subjects. Readers or authors with suggestions for books they would like to see published are invited to write to: The Editorial Director, Patrick Stephens Limited, Sparkford, Nr Yeovil, Somerset, BA22 7JJ.

CLASSIC HINTS AND TIPS FOR
MOTORCYCLISTS

IAN JOHNSON

Patrick Stephens Limited

First published 1994

A catalogue record for this book is available from the British Library

ISBN 1 85260 497 2
Library of Congress catalog card No. 94-77770

Patrick Stephens Limited as an imprint of
Haynes Publishing,
Sparkford, Nr Yeovil, Somerset
BA22 7JJ, England

Printed in Great Britain by J.H. Haynes & Co. Ltd.

Front cover illustration is from a photograph by Martyn Barnwell

CONTENTS

INTRODUCTION

Fifty-two years of effort have gone into the compilation of this book. All the hints and tips have been selected from *The Motor Cycle* between the dates 1908 and 1960 when it ran the 'Hints and Tips' column almost continuously. Most were submitted by readers who were generously rewarded with a guinea, and some emerged from the experts of the editorial body. Many ideas repeated themselves over the years, in which case the most appropriate version for modern times has been included. Indeed, some tips have been blatantly updated to suit the present day. A few are the result of my own experiences in the damp lay-bys of England.

THE MACHINE

Unsurprisingly, this is the largest section of the book. It has been divided roughly along the lines of the standard factory manual of the 50s and 60s, with considerable licence taken to accommodate the balance of hints and tips on offer. Hence there is a section for control cables, usually ignored by manuals, because there were a lot of good tips listed on the subject. The boundaries of each section have been crossed occasionally where there is a clash of interests (e.g. the special tool for removing a clutch centre could be in the clutch section or the special tool section), in which case the most logical place has been chosen.

The engine

1. Oil changes

It is difficult to remove all old oil from a system during an oil change. One answer is to start with a clean engine after a rebuild and change the oil more often. Don't try to economize as far as oil is concerned. Sludge can be scraped out of the bottom of tanks with long thin brushes, but only with limited success; flushing oil will also help. One suggestion was to weld a tube to the inside of the tank on the end of the supply pipe, raising the oil supplied above the level of sludge in the tank. This is all right if there is enough space at the top of the tank for the extra oil and the required air space. To clear all oilways and pipes of oil during a change, fit a length of rubber hose to the end of the return pipe inside the mouth of the oil tank, and run the engine until only clean oil is coming out of the tube. Top up the oil level again after the hose has been removed.

2. Which type of oil?

If possible use the oil recommended by the manufacturer in the handbook. If this information is not available, as a rule-of-thumb steer away from modern thin oils in older engines. Sixties twins will run happily on SAE 20W/50W; so will some singles. I prefer a monograde oil in single-cylinder engines because they are usually fitted with ball and roller bearings, and not plain journals. In which case I use SAE 50W in summer, and either SAE 40W or SAE 30W in winter. The former is thicker, and so will take longer to break down on a long hot run. The latter are thinner, and so will reach all moving parts quicker in cold weather.

3. Use of modern oils

Modern detergent oils can be used in old motor cycles if care is taken. Their disadvantage is their ability to clean the inside of an engine. If you haven't cleaned inside first, the oil is likely to block up oilways with debris it has collected from around the internals. If you have not stripped the engine and cleaned it yourself, and you are not sure of the engine's maintenance history, do not use detergent oil.

4. Castor oil

Ordinary mineral four-stroke oil and the vegetable-based castor oil used for racing do not mix. If a change is being made from one to another, all traces of the old oil must be removed completely from the inside of the engine. If you're not sure which type of oil has been used previously in a new acquisition or restoration project, play safe and clean thoroughly.

5. Flushing oil

Flushing oil can be used more than once. It makes a good external degreasing solution if it is brushed copiously over the engine and then washed off with warm, soapy water.

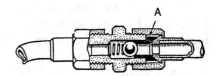

6. Filter by-pass

Improving factory lubrication systems, though beneficial, can lead to problems emerging elsewhere. An Ariel owner who fitted a fabric filter in the return pipe from the oil pump soon found that the return flow was too great for the filter. He made up a pressure relief by-pass valve as follows, and connected it across the filter. An ordinary union for ¼ in. bore pipe was drilled out to ⅜ in. for about three quarters of its length. For the ball seating (marked A in the sketch) a length of brass rod ½ in. long by ½ in. diameter was cut, and filed to ⅜ in. diameter for half its length. A ¼ in. hole was drilled out axially in the rod. Then both sides were countersunk; a large countersink on the ½ in. diameter side provided seating for the pipe nipple; a small countersink on the reverse formed the ball seat. The ball bearing was ⁵⁄₁₆ in. diameter, and a conical spring was wound to keep it on its seat.

As the pipe union nut is tightened, both the nipple and the ball seating are compressed onto the union (filed flat this end), so that a tight leakproof joint is assured. The valve blows at about 45 psi, the filter failing at 300 psi.

7. Wet sump oil change

After any oil change it is best to recheck the oil level straight after the first short run, to compensate for the take-up of oil in the system. This is more important on machines which store the oil in the crankcase. On Royal Enfield's single-cylinder four-stroke engines, for example, the timing case holds a considerable quantity of oil. When changing the oil the case should be drained by removing the oil-feed plug and leaning the machine over to the right. As the timing case will refill during the first five miles or so after the oil has been changed, it is important to check the level in the container and top up as necessary.

8. Dry sump oil return

On many machines, especially pre-war, the oil return pump has a larger capacity than the delivery pump, so as soon as the oil which has drained into the sump is pumped out, the sump becomes 'dry' and the return pump lifts a mixture of oil and air. So it is quite in order if, on a machine with dry sump lubrication, the oil spurts steadily from the return pipe into the tank when the engine is started, but after a few seconds the stream dies away to a few drips and bubbles.

9. Oil frothing tower

Some oil tanks fitted to dry-sump lubricated machines of early vintage are so designed that, should the tank be more than about half full, oil will leak out of the filler cap and distribute itself over the rear of the machine. To cure the trouble without reducing the amount of lubricant, a small cylinder, or frothing tower, a couple of inches high and about half-an-inch in diameter can be fitted to the top of the oil tank behind the filler cap.

If you don't wish to alter the original appearance of the tank, a simpler but not always effective method is to fit a perforated tin disc inside the filler cap. Cut from a piece of tin plate a disc that will just fit inside the filler and rest on the shoulder that is usually found in the neck of the filler. Punch a number of holes in the disc, and fix in its centre a small nut which will act as a handle for removing the baffle. With the handle in place, fit the disc with the rough side underneath.

10. Upper cylinder lubrication

Wear on engine components is heaviest immediately after starting the engine before the oil has circulated properly round the system. In an engine which is run constantly there will be enough residual oil left on parts such as valve stems to protect them over this crucial initial phase. But in a newly-rebuilt engine extra protection can be affected to the top end by adding a few tablespoonfuls of engine oil or two-stroke oil to the petrol tank.

11. Rocker box caps

Many twins in the early 60s were fitted with threaded rocker inspection caps which were liable to disappear during every other fast run. Some were retained by a spring clip fixed on the rocker box stud. If this is loose and no longer touching the cap, it should be replaced. For those without the spring retainer, one suggestion was to replace the standard thin gasket with the rubber O-ring used to seal the carburettor flange to the inlet tract. Not only does it keep the cap in place, but seals in the oil as well.

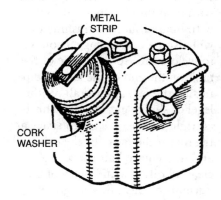

12. Rocker cap retainer

This home-made rocker cap retainer was fitted to an Ariel in 1949. A strip 2½ in. x 8⅛ in. mild steel was bent to shape and clamped onto the front bolt of the rocker box.

13. Cylinder head removal

One suggestion for removing the cylinder head is to loosen the holding down bolts and push on the kickstarter, allowing the force of compression to break the seal. In some cases this may work, but in most the necessary prior removal of carburettor and exhaust system may reduce compression by too much. Or, how about filling the combustion chamber with oil through the plug hole, and rolling the machine forward in gear? A bit messy for me.

More usually a soft mallet is used to tap the exhaust port, which should break the seal. It can be used in conjunction with a softwood drift if access is difficult. On no account hit the fins. On many later multi-cylinder models, the heads were provided with hitting points of stronger alloy, but make sure before you try it!

14. Leaking cylinder head joint

Should a cylinder head joint leak on a single-cylinder machine, and the gasket is in good condition, the cylinder head should be ground onto the barrel with fine valve-grinding paste. (Many early engines did not have a head gasket at all, but sealed the joint in this way.) Grind with a semi-rotary motion until both faces have a continuous bright ring, lifting and reseating to distribute the paste evenly. Be sure to clean every trace of paste off thoroughly with solvent before reassembly.

15.
On multi-cylinder heads, check the level of the face with the edge of a steel rule. Placed from end to end, the rule should touch each part of the head between combustion chambers. If it doesn't, the head will need skimming by a specialist.

16.
The simplest check of all is to ensure that the head bolts have been tightened down correctly. On 50s and 60s twins the manufacturer's handbook should give a tightening sequence and torque settings, and this should be followed. For most singles, torque settings aren't available, in which case the old rule-of-thumb of 'finger tight, tight and bloody tight' should be used. I always use 'bloody tight' on cylinder heads, but not with a socket set and long bar. A normal ring spanner is sufficient, and less likely to damage delicate alloy threads.

17. Cylinder head bolts

Cylinder head bolts should go back into the holes from which they came. One way to keep them in order on the workbench is to push them through a piece of cardboard to the same layout as the cylinder head.

18.
This tip is also useful for timing cover screws, which are usually of different lengths. A rough outline of the timing cover sketched on the card, with the screws pushed through in the correct position, will ensure correct replacement.

A TOOL FOR HOLDING A CYLINDER HEAD
FIRMLY DURING DE-CARBONIZING

19. Cylinder head tool

When decarbonizing a cylinder head, or grinding in valves, it's handy to be able to hold the cylinder head firmly. This tool is made from an 8 in. length of ½ in. steel bar (such as an old wheel spindle), and the bodies of 14 mm and 18 mm detachable sparking plugs. The plug bodies are welded at either end of the rod, the appropriate plug size can be screwed into the cylinder head spark plug hole, and the tool clamped in a vice.

20.
If you remove the rocker box, many post-war cylinder heads can be gripped vertically in a vice, as long as the vice jaws are lined with wood or aluminium packers and as long as the head is held across mating surfaces – keep well away from the fins!

21. Removing valve caps

If difficulty is experienced in removing the valve caps on a vintage side-valve engine, spray with penetrating oil or diesel and leave them overnight. Then obtain a long, well-fitting ring or socket spanner with which to grip the cap, and give a few sharp light taps on the extreme end of the spanner with a hammer. If this doesn't jar it free, try warming up the cylinder by running the engine, and then pouring cold water into the hollow of the valve cap, so causing it to contract.

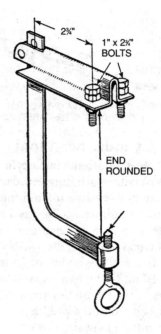

22. Valve compressor

It shouldn't be difficult or expensive to buy a professional valve compressor suitable for most overhead-valve engines, but in some cases they may not fit. This home-made suggestion comes from 1939, and the dimensions should be checked for your own requirements. The top was cut off a carpentry G-clamp, and an arm made up from flanged strip steel. The arm was cut at one end to accept the G-clamp, and drilled at the other to take the two spring-compressing bolts. The screw thread at the other end of the G-clamp was rounded to accommodate the valve head.

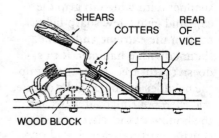

If this is too complicated you can always use the garden shears, though what this would do to the valve or the shears I'm not sure.

23. Another way of adapting a carpenter's G-clamp is as follows: Select a nut the same size as the valve's spring collar, and cut out a segment (say, two adjacent sides of the hexagon) with a hacksaw. Use the nut as a spacer between the clamp and the collar, and feed the collets in place through the missing segment.

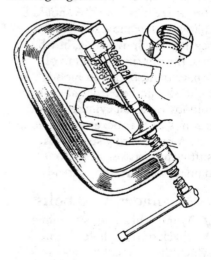

24. Valve grinding

Some valves have deep tulip heads which prevent the normal suction cup from gripping satisfactorily. A squash ball cut in half and turned by hand is an effective substitute.

25. Valve tool

Instead of grinding in valves by pushing down on the tulip head with a rubber sucker, many advocate pulling the valve up to the seat from the other side. This sketch shows how a small lathe carrier can be used to grip the end of the valve stem, packing it first

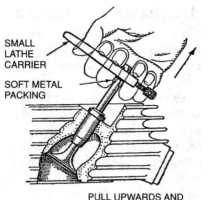

with copper shim to prevent scoring the stem. The main disadvantage with this method is the difficulty, while grinding, in keeping the valve square with the seat to provide a continuous even face. Modernists have been known to grip the valve stem in the chuck of an electric drill; not only does this suffer from the same problem, but it does it at high speed, causing considerable damage very quickly.

26. Valve collets

When replacing a valve in the cylinder head, ensure that the retaining collets are put back so that they are not touching on either side of the valve; ideally the gaps should be equal. Once the springs, collars and collets are in place, give the tip of the valve stem a firm and true tap with a hammer. This ensures that the collets bed down fully, and there is no chance of one coming adrift when the engine is restarted.

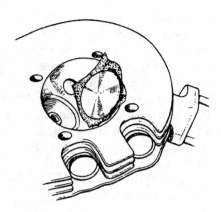

27. Pitted valves

Badly pitted valves can be re-faced without a special tool by punching a hole in a piece of fine emery cloth and putting it over the valve stem before grinding in the normal way.

28. Valve guide insertion

Fitting new valve guides is much easier if they are stored in the freezer overnight. The contraction they undergo will reduce the amount the cylinder head has to be heated up.

29. Valve guide removal

An ordinary socket head screw can be used successfully as a ready-made two-diameter drift for driving out worn valve guides. The screw has a round head which must be fractionally smaller than the outside diameter of the guide, whilst the screw shank must be a good sliding fit in the bore of the guide. With a soft metal drift applied to the head of the screw (preferably one that fits into the hexagon socket) the guide can be driven out in the normal way.

30. Valve guide fitting

That section of a valve guide which projects into a port is nearly always tapered, or reduced

in diameter. There is usually a sharp edge where the section changes; this can hinder fitting and, in time, the cylinder head hole may become enlarged; then the guide will be a sloppy fit. Chamfering off this change of section, fitting is made easier, and damage to a soft alloy head avoided. If you don't have access to a lathe, to chamfer the guide, mount it in a drill clamped in a vice, and take the sharp edge off with a file.

31. Screw-in valve guides

Before attempting to remove screw-in valve guides, soak the area in penetrating oil or diesel overnight, as the guide is certain to be at least partially rusted in. Use a well-fitting spanner to free the guide. When fitting a new guide, smear the threads with graphite grease to help its removal next time.

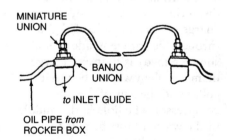

32. Valve guide lubrication

Valve guides suffered considerably in the days of exposed valve gear and lack of greasing. The 750 cc BSA V-twins of the late 30s were fitted with a valve lubrication system, but in one case it was found wanting when no oil could be persuaded to reach the front cylinder inlet valve guide. This modification cured the BSA's problem and increased greatly the subsequent life span of all the guides.

As the oil supply to the rear cylinder head was more than adequate, a pipe was connected from the rear to the front to feed that also. The oil pipe banjo union bolt heads were drilled through to the oil passage, and the holes tapped to take two miniature oil pipe unions. The coupling pipe was sweated into the miniature unions, with a coil in its length to cope with vibration. It was tinned for a weatherproof finish.

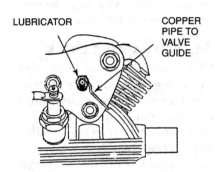

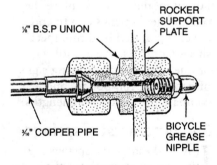

33. Valve guide lubrication – single-cylinder

This suggestion for automatic valve guide lubrication was designed for a 1928 Raleigh, but it is adaptable to most types of engines of that period which have the rocker gear carried between flat steel plates on each side of the cylinder head.

The nearside rocker plate was drilled .406 in. diameter in a convenient position to receive an ⅛ in. union body, which had one end coned out. The plain end was tapped out to receive a grease nipple. Next, the valve guide boss was drilled .187 in. diameter, and the valve guide itself drilled .125 in. diameter. A short length of .187 in. diameter copper tube was inserted into the boss and connected up to the union on the rocker plate. The ⅛ in. nut holding the union body was made by sawing off the shouldered end of a union nut. With this conversion the rocker gear only needs a shot of grease every 100 miles or so.

34. Valve spring check

The usual check for worn valve springs is to compare the free length of the suspect spring with a new one, and scrap it if it is shorter by more than one eighth. Yet a spring could have maintained length but lost energy. For an infallible check, place the old and new springs end to end in a vice, separated by a thin metal sheet. Compress them until they – or one of them – is showing signs of becoming coil-bound, and compare the compressed lengths.

35. Pattern valve springs

It is vital that valve springs are the correct strength for the engine. AMC offered this advice in 1956 for those who wanted to check the quality of pattern springs. This applies to any unmarked springs from an autojumble for most post-war machines:

'The pattern springs become coil bound when the valves are at full lift and cause serious wear on the apex of the cams. After adjusting both pushrods, check valve motion by turning the engine until each valve is exactly

at full lift. Apply a spanner to the rocker spindle nut to determine whether further valve movement is possible. If not, the springs are coil bound and should be discarded.'

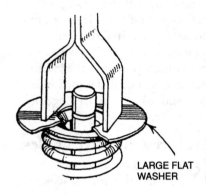

LARGE FLAT WASHER

36. Collet replacement

When replacing valve split collets, the legs of the spring compressor sometimes have a tendency to slide off one side or the other. If slip occurs, at best the collets disappear into the middle distance; at worst the valve springs charge off as from a loaded gun through the garage window. A simple remedy is to insert a large diameter plain washer between the collar and the legs of the compressor. The hole in the middle of the washer must be able to accept the collets.

37. Fitting hairpin valve springs

New hairpin valve springs can often be difficult to compress while their top collars and bottom washers are fitted, or they may form such a wide angle as to preclude the use of a valve spring compressor. To ease fitting, push the valve spring ends into the holes in the bottom washer and, fitting the top collars as you go, compress

the springs in a vice. With the complete assembly held in the vice, wire the springs securely to retain them in their compressed state once the vice grip is relaxed. Fit the spring assembly in the cylinder head, place the spring-retaining collets in position and, using a valve spring compressor as a safety catch, cut the wire. Release the spring compressor as normal to complete the operation.

38. Valve clearances

When setting valve clearances it is best to turn the engine by means of the back wheel with top gear engaged. This is far more sensitive than the kickstarter, and can turn the engine backwards as well as forwards.

39. Valve stretch

Assuming the adjuster locknuts are not slackening off, the need for frequent resetting of valve clearances is a danger sign. Clearances closing up is an indication of a stretching valve or a pocketing valve seat. A stretched valve will drop its head into the cylinder shortly, and should be replaced without delay.

Growing clearances without loss of compression can suggest rapid wear in the cam mechanism. Possibly the follower has worn through the case-hardening of the cam surface – and in time you will end up with a completely circular cam and no valve movement at all!

A common cause of difficulty in setting valve clearances is that the pushrod is not seated properly in the cup of the cam follower. This should be double-checked before the engine is turned over, or the result will be a bent or broken pushrod.

40. Valve gear clatter

Valve gear on high mileage OHV engines becomes noisy because of wear in the pushrods and rocker end cups. This modification to cure the rattle was applied to a Rudge. Two brass nuts of a size just capable of sliding over the pushrod were fashioned into collars, and soldered onto the rod one inch below the top.

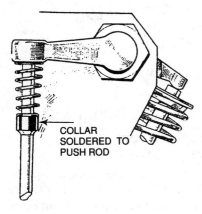

COLLAR SOLDERED TO PUSH ROD

The flats of the nut were removed for appearance. Two springs 1¼ in. long were fitted in such a way that they were in compression between the soldered collars and the rocker ends. These light springs kept the whole of the valve gear in firm contact, eliminating the rattle, without affecting valve clearance settings.

41. Inverted rocker end cups

Excessive wear in overhead valve rocker cups is usually attributable to wear in the hardened surface of the rocker cup which mates with the valve stem. A common remedy is to insert hardened steel pads into the rocker cups to replace this surface. These can either be a flat plate wedged tightly into the cups or, in cases

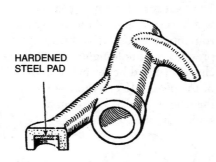

HARDENED STEEL PAD

where valve clearances are almost nil, a loose cup sitting on the end of the valve stem.

42. Cylinder head steady

Cylinder head steadies were not fitted to some earlier machines, much to their detriment. It is often easy enough to connect a head stud to a frame point with a stout strip of mild steel, and unobtrusively under the tank. This idea is designed for a 16H Norton, but demonstrates the general principle.

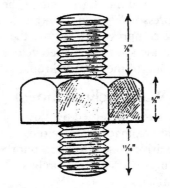

Replace the centrally positioned compression tap with a bolt cut and fitted with a locknut as shown. Twin strips of 1 in. x ⅛ in. mild steel were taken from this bolt to a clamp fitted to the bottom tank rail.

43. Engine vibration

General vibration over and above that expected can be because of drastic problems such

as flywheel imbalance. But before panic sets in, check the simple things. Is the head steady tight? Is it broken? (This usually happens right by the nut and is difficult to spot). Are the engine mounting bolts loose? Is the primary chain too tight or damaged, and is the engine shock absorber properly adjusted?

44. Piston tips

When lifting the cylinder barrel, stop halfway and pack a rag around the crankcase mouth to prevent broken piston rings from falling in the crankcase. Leave this in place until after the piston has been removed to avoid losing the gudgeon pin circlips the same way.

45. Carbon deposits

Cleaning the carbon deposits off both piston crown and combustion chamber is difficult without scratching the soft surface. An old penny was recommended in 1936 as being soft enough without bending under pressure, and the curved edge helped with the head. If an old penny isn't available, a modern coin should suffice, gently checking its hardness first. Perspex is also a good material for scraping alloy without scratching the metal. It is tempting today to speed up laborious cleaning tasks by using power tools with special attachments. Be careful. What appears to be a soft buffer or fine sander in the hand will be far more vigorous spun at speed in an electric drill.

46. Carbon trap

If decarbonizing is being done without removing the cylinder barrel, it is difficult to prevent carbon deposits from escaping down the bore. Lower the piston in the bore, insert an old piston ring smeared with grease, and bring the piston back up to top dead centre. Once the crown has been cleaned, lower the piston again, and remove the old ring with the carbon particles stuck to the grease.

47. Barrel, piston and ring wear

Carbon or black marks on the skirt of the piston, coupled with weak compression, usually indicate that gas is blowing past the piston rings. This may be because of worn rings, a worn piston or bore, or all three, or even a scored cylinder bore.

Unless the cylinder is badly worn or deeply scored, a new set of piston rings may be enough. Scores of one or two thousandths of an inch can be removed by lapping; any more and the cylinder should be rebored.

48. Cleaning piston ring grooves

Piston ring grooves can be scraped clean using the broken end of an old ring. To polish the corners of the grooves, hold one end of a piece of soft string in a vice, wind it one complete turn in the ring groove, and sprinkle with paraffin and metal polish. Hold the free end of the string, and polish the groove by moving the piston backwards and forwards.

49. Removing a gudgeon pin

It is usual to warm an alloy piston with a blow lamp to free a stiff gudgeon pin. This tip from

1950 suggests borrowing the wife's iron (don't tell me you're the romantic type and it's a birthday present), and holding it against the cleaned (it had better be!) crown of the piston. If you can't borrow the iron, wrap the piston in a cloth soaked in boiling water.

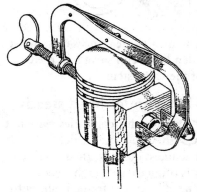

50. An overhead valve-spring compressor can be used to push out a gudgeon pin. Drill a hole bigger than the pin in a softwood block and use it to protect the piston from the clawed end of the compressor. Wind in the other end of the compressor to remove the pin, using a washer if need be over the point of the threaded rod.

51. Wire circlip removal

This tool was used by BSA fitters, made from an old screwdriver. Use it to hook out the circlip. Always replace circlips with the gap at 7 o'clock.

SCREWDRIVER GROUND TO A POINT

52. Circlip safety

One way of preventing piston circlips from dropping into

the crankcase is to pass a rod through the gudgeon pin so it projects a couple of inches either side. This is particularly useful for the type of circlips without 'ears' for circlip pliers, as it will probably stop them flying across the garage as well.

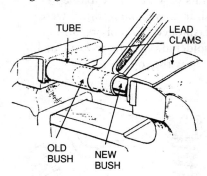

TUBE

LEAD CLAMS

OLD BUSH

NEW BUSH

53. Small-end bush replacement

Small-end bushes can be replaced using a vice as a press. Place the con-rod between the vice jaws with the new small-end bush on one side and a short tube on the other. The tube should be long enough and with sufficient inside diameter to accept the old small-end bush. By tightening the vice jaws the new bush will slide into place, forcing the old bush out into the tube. Protect the bush by lining the vice jaws with soft metal clamps before starting.

54. Cubic capacity

Where the bore and stroke dimensions of an engine are known (in mm) the exact cubic capacity equals:

$$\frac{3.142(\pi) \times R2H \times N}{1000}$$

where R is the radius (that is, half the diameter of the bore), H the length of stroke, and N the number of cylinders.

55. Measuring cylinder bore wear

Most people don't have access to a set of reverse callipers, so this method of bore measurement is useful. Cut a length of ¼ in. rod fractionally longer than the bore diameter and, by careful filing, make it an exact fit at the bottom of the cylinder bore, where the wear is negligible. Insert the rod across the thrust faces (in line with the rotation of flywheels) at the highest point of ring travel and, by measuring the gap with a feeler gauge, ascertain the amount of wear. On a 500 cc single-cylinder engine, wear should not exceed 0.008 in.

56. A piston ring can be used to measure bore wear. Insert the ring squarely into the bore at the bottom of piston travel, and measure the gap with a feeler gauge. Move the ring to the top of piston travel just below the top of the bore (underneath the lip, if there is one), and compare the gap here with the first reading.

57. Parallel twin-cylinder block removal

This tip is vital to all Triumph twin owners, and probably applies to many other parallel twins. Before removing a twin cylinder block the tappets must be secured, otherwise they will fall into the crankcase. If a tank rubber is pushed in between them they will be held safely.

58. V-twin cylinder angle

The simplest method of measuring the angle at which the cylinders of a V-twin are set in relation to the crankshaft is as follows. Take a piece of paper and, laying it against the side of the crankcase, make a template corresponding with the base of each cylinder. Continue the lines formed by the two cylinder bases until they meet, and then, with a protractor, measure the smaller of the two angles formed. Subtract this angle from 180 degrees to ascertain the angle at which the cylinders are set.

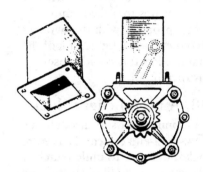

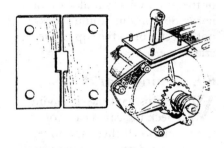

59. Con-rod protection

Crankcase mouth and con-rod of single-cylinder machines can be protected from damage and dust during an overhaul by bolting an inverted cardboard box or a pair of wooden boards to the cylinder base studs.

60. Piston replacement

Most pistons are intended to go into the barrel a particular way round. With a steeply domed piston in an engine with differing valve sizes, mistakes are unlikely. The cut-outs in the piston crown will fit one of the valves – the larger is usually the inlet valve. If the valves are the same size, the piston crown should be marked 'F' for front before removal. Some pistons are marked by the factory, which is another reason for cleaning them carefully.

61. High compression

How far can the compression ratio be raised before the piston hits the head, or the valves the piston? One way to find out is to press slices of plasticine onto the piston crown at points most affected (valve cutaways and the apex of the piston). Replace the head and turn the engine shaft once or twice by hand. Remove the head once more, and measure the indentations in the plasticine.

62. Honing the barrel

Before replacing the cylinder barrel, remove the glaze with fine emery cloth, thoroughly wash away all traces of grit with solvent, and smear the bore with clean engine oil.

63. Lowering the cylinder barrel

On some single-cylinder engines the barrel and head are retained by four long studs which pass through holes in the cylinder fins. To suspend the barrel while refitting the piston rings, insert four thin fillets of wood between the fins halfway up the barrel covering the stud holes. Lower the cylinder over the studs until their tops contact the wooden stops. The barrel is supported while the rings are refitted; then the fillets can be removed and the barrel lowered down to the crankcase mouth.

64. Cylinder replacement – Velocette

This tip was suggested in 1957 for refitting the cylinder barrel onto a Velocette single, but will probably apply to other single-cylinder machines. In order to lower the cylinder into place over the piston without risking damage to the rings, fit the cylinder retaining studs and screw on the nuts. Lower the cylinder over the studs until the first of the full diameter fins is resting on the nuts. Both hands are free to feed the piston rings into the bore. Keeping the piston inside, raise the cylinder just enough for the nuts to be removed from the studs. Remove the cloth you've just stuffed into the crankcase mouth – just in case – then lower the cylinder into position.

65. Piston ring gap

Before fitting new piston rings, check the ring gap in the cylinder bore. Slip each ring into an unworn part of the cylinder – the bottom of the stroke – and use the piston to square them in the bore. The gap should be 0.001 in. for every 5mm of bore diameter – that's 0.016 in. on an 80 mm bore. With a two-stroke the width of the ring peg must be taken into account and due allowance made.

66. Refitting piston rings

Most modern piston rings have a top side inscribed 'top'. They should be fitted accordingly. When feeding the rings back into the bore, ensure

that the gaps are not in line with each other, but an even 120 degrees apart.

67. Mating separate cylinders

On an overhead-valve twin with separate cylinder heads, or a two-stroke twin with separate barrels, fit the induction manifold and lightly tighten its retaining bolts before attempting to tighten the cylinder head or cylinder nuts. This ensures that the manifold mates properly with the two faces. Avoid excessive tightening of the manifold as this could cause distortion.

68. A useful engine lock

A tommy-bar slid through the small-end eye can be used to lock the engine to undo clutch sprockets or the like, but the ends of the tommy-bar should rest on hardwood or aluminium blocks, not directly onto the top of the crankcase.

69. Timing marks

When dismantling an engine check the cam gears for timing marks. If there are none, they can be dotted onto the rim of the gear with a centre punch or a dab of white paint. But this is only recommended if the engine has been running successfully. For new acquisitions bought as non-runners, check the valve timing with a degree disc first.

70. Mainshaft pinion keyways

The object of three or more keyways in the mainshaft pinion is to enable an accurate

valve timing to be obtained, and the one to be used is the one that allows the timing to be the nearest to the setting recommended by the manufacturers. It is not intended that these keyways should be used to alter the timing, and this should certainly not be done when a standard cam is employed.

71. Valve timing

The principle behind valve timing is that when the piston is at top dead centre (TDC), the timing pinions are meshed so that the inlet valve is just about to open and the exhaust valve about to close. (In more modern engines valve timing is advanced so that the inlet valve opens much earlier.) Such a rough guide may be sufficient for some older units; if possible valve timing should be adjusted accurately with a degree disc to the manufacturer's recommended settings.

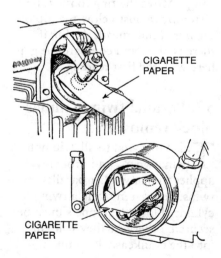

CIGARETTE PAPER

CIGARETTE PAPER

72. Paper thin accuracy

When the exact point of opening of a valve is required for tuning purposes, place a cigarette paper or cellophane between the rocker and the valve stem. Immediately a position of crankshaft rotation is reached when the paper cannot be withdrawn, then the valve is about to open. This method is also useful when setting ignition timing.

73. Accurate valve timing for a single-cylinder

Most engines I have come across have had clear marks on the timing pinions, put there by the factory. However, on one engine the marks were indistinct, and confused by a second group of markings close to the originals. I was advised to set the valve timing in the following manner, and it should apply to most singles:

1. Check the settings in the manual. There will be four figures representing the opening and closing point of both valves. There will also be a setting for the valve clearances on the compression stroke, way in excess of the normal setting. These figures will be for the camshaft originally supplied with that model, so make sure the camshaft is correct.
2. Remove the idler gear.
3. Time the inlet valve first. Set the valve clearances as recommended in the manual.
4. Fix a degree disc to the crankshaft with a pointer, and set the piston at top dead centre (TDC) on the compression stroke. Set the pointer to read zero degrees. Turn the engine backwards until the pointer reads the correct opening for the valve (it will be in degrees before TDC).
5. Turn the camwheel by hand until the slack on the inlet pushrod is taken up.

6. Insert the idler gear. If adjustment is necessary, make the valve open early rather than late.
7. Turn the engine forwards and check the valve is closing at the correct position after bottom dead centre (BDC) on the disc; that is when the pushrod begins to slacken off.
8. Turn the engine forward until the exhaust pushrod tightens up. The disc should read the correct setting before BDC found in the manual.
9. Check that the exhaust valve closes at the correct position after TDC.
10. Finally, reset the valve clearances to the maker's recommended settings for running.

74. Dismantling the timing gear

Before removing the timing cover from the engine, it is as well to make certain that you know the correct setting of the timing. After the securing nuts from the timing cover have been removed, a few light blows with a rawhide mallet around the edge of the cover will free it and enable it to be pulled off. Never insert a screwdriver blade between the faces in order to lever off a cover, as this will ruin the oil-tightness of the casing.

Quite often the cam pinions may pull out of the crankcase with the cam cover, owing to a vacuum set up in the spindle bushes by the film of lubricating oil. Before removing the cover fully, look down through the crack and, with the aid of a knife or clean hacksaw blade, push the camwheels back

into their proper place. When the cover is off, assuming that the pinions have not been disturbed, check that the timing is marked. If it isn't, set the piston at top dead centre on the compression stroke and, with a metal scriber, scratch lines on the teeth that are in engagement.

75. Timing chain wear

On engines with chain-driven timing gear and a slipper tensioner, examine the edges of the chain side plates. Constant rubbing leaves a shiny surface, and this is quite normal. But if the plate edges are noticeably scooped instead of straight, it is time to fit a new chain.

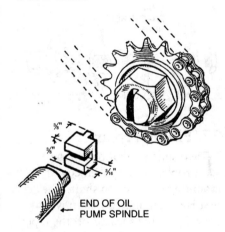

END OF OIL PUMP SPINDLE

76. Oldham oil pump drive

Several magneto chain-drives employed the bottom sprocket to turn the oil pump as well, usually by means of a tongued spindle connecting with a slotted nut. In this case the first few threads of the slotted nut were damaged. The face of the nut was ground off, still leaving plenty of good thread to enable it to be tightened further up the shaft. But the nut's reduced thickness now pushed it too far away to connect with the oil pump's tongue. The gap was filled by an Oldham-type coupling made from a solid square of brass, one side having a slot to accept the tongue and the other side replicating the tongue to fit in the nut. The coupling lasted several years without showing any visible signs of wear.

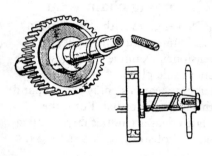

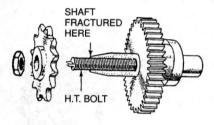

SHAFT FRACTURED HERE

H.T. BOLT

77. Pinion repair

Two similar solutions to the problem of a broken cog mounting on a pinion shaft. The first is on a magneto pinion when over-tightening sheared off the taper for the magneto chain sprocket. The pinion was only case hardened, so the soft core was drilled out and tapped to take a stud. The broken piece of taper was threaded onto the stud, and the sprocket tightened up in the normal way.

The second is a camshaft pinion which again has sheared at the taper, but in this case it took the oil pump drive with it. The shaft was drilled and tapped, and a high tensile bolt screwed home. The bolt head was removed and a tongue cut to engage the oil pump.

78. Primary chain oiler

Pre-war New Imperials had a pressure outlet pipe in the timing box. A good tip was to direct the oil mist emitted from this outlet onto the primary chain by running a thin copper pipe between the crankcase and gearbox. It is worth checking oil pressure outlets on all models to see if they can be converted into chain oilers so neatly and easily.

79. Checking big-end bearings

It is quite in order for the connecting rod to have a small amount of side movement. Ten thousandths of an inch is about the minimum to be allowed between the roller cage (or the big-end eye) and the flywheels, and up to ⅛ in. maximum on an ordinary road machine may be safely ignored providing the con-rod doesn't foul the flywheels. But there must be no trace of up and down play.

80. Cheap big-end cure

If big-end trouble is suspected it is wise just to check first that an exhaust pipe isn't loose in the head. The sound emitted by a loose exhaust is strikingly similar, particularly the push fit pipes fitted to many 60s twins. To effect a cure, bellow out the end of the pipe with a wooden drift lightly tapped.

81. Removal and replacement of bearings in their housing

Without doubt, heat is your best helper. On removal it minimizes the chance of damage to surrounding casings, and on replacement it is the best way to ensure that the bearing seats fully and squarely home. With alloy casings it is surprising how little heat is needed. Heating the area around the bearing housing with a blowtorch is quite acceptable as long as care is taken not to overheat one point and so distort the casing; otherwise put the casing in the oven and heat it to 90°C (194°F), or immerse it in a bowl of very hot water. Always allow the casing to cool down slowly and naturally.

If a drift is being used to replace a cold ball race, always tap in the outer ring of the race – never apply force to the balls or the inner ring.

Once fitted, check that the race is a tight fit in the housing. It is prudent to smear the housing with a modern proprietary bearing glue to ensure that the race won't spin in the housing once the engine is warm.

82. Removing blind bushes

To remove bronze bushes from blind holes, tap a thread over halfway into the bush and insert a bolt. Continuously tightening the bolt after it has reached the end of the tapped section should loosen the bush enough to withdraw it. Alternatively, bushes and bearings can be removed from blind holes in aluminium by heating up the surrounding area enough for them to drop out when the casing is tapped face down on a hardwood surface.

83. Otherwise, try removing blind bushes by filling the hole with oil or grease and tapping in a snug fitting drift with a soft mallet. The hydraulic effect of the oil should push the bush out, but

only if there is room in the housing for the oil to get behind the bush in the first place.

84. Replacing main bearings

This tip was suggested by the Hall Green works specifically for Velocette singles. It is included here because it demonstrates major overhauling with the minimum of work. Think before the spanners begin to fly – there is probably an easier way to do it!

'Mainshaft bearings of M models can be renewed without completely dismantling the engine after it has been removed from the frame. The oil pump, timing gears and steady plate can be left in position. To replace the drive-side bearing, it is necessary only to unbolt and detach the half crankcase from the opposite half, after removing the cylinder. If the timing-side bearing has to be removed, the timing cover and mainshaft nut (left-hand thread) and washer must be taken off. The shaft can then be tapped carefully through the ball race.

'If a roller bearing is fitted, the inner race with cage and rollers will come out of the ring in the crankcase and be detached with the shaft. The timing pinion and pump worm will be left in the case. The timing-side ball bearing on all MOV and earlier MAC models can be replaced by a roller bearing similar to that used on the drive side. Care must be taken when reassembling to engage the timing-shaft key properly in the keyway in the gear, and to thread the shaft through the pump drive worm.'

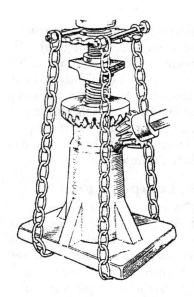

85. Engine sprocket removal

In the workshop section is a list of ingenious home made pullers. However, for the stubbornest of sprockets this method should do the trick. Place two steel bolts behind the sprocket, and link the bolts to the base of a small jack with two lengths of chain. The head of the jack is placed on the sprocket shaft, packed with a protective slip. Screw the jack out to pull the sprocket off.

86. Flywheel jig

This jig was suggested in 1954, but it was designed to hold the flywheel assembly of a Rudge Ulster. The principle can be applied to a number of machines, altering the dimensions to suit.

Two pieces of 1½ in. x ¼ in. mild steel plate were each bent through 90 degrees to L-shape, and the upright arms were drilled with ⅜ in. diameter holes for mainshaft clearance. The horizontal arms were drilled and tapped ⅜ in.; the bench was drilled to accept the two ⅜ in. bolts and, when

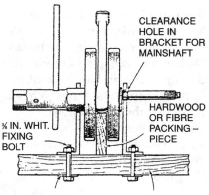

CLEARANCE HOLE IN BRACKET FOR MAINSHAFT

HARDWOOD OR FIBRE PACKING – PIECE

⅜ IN. WHIT. FIXING BOLT

LARGE WASHER TO PREVENT BOLT HEADS SINKING IN UNDER PRESSURE

BENCH TOP

tightening down, the bolts were packed with flat washers to prevent them from digging into the bench top. The plates were slipped over the mainshafts with the vertical arms as close as possible to the flywheels before the jig was fixed to the bench. A block of hardwood was placed between the flywheels under the big-end eye to stop the flywheels from turning while the crankpin nuts were worked on.

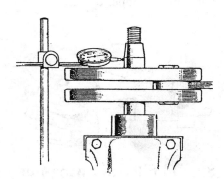

87. Flywheel truing without a jig

This tip was used when converting a 16H Norton into a Big 4, which necessitated fitting new flywheels. First the flywheels were roughly trued with a set-square. Then a piece of bronze was turned and bored to make a bush with a nice running fit for the driving side mainshaft. The bronze bush was placed in a vice, and the driving side mainshaft inserted in it. A dial gauge and stand were set up so that the gauge's pointer contacted the timing side mainshaft. The flywheels could be spun and trued according to the gauge.

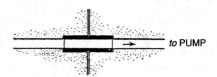

to PUMP

88. Leaking oilway

Oiling systems which rely on drilled passages between mating surfaces are often prone to leak (as long as some bright spark hasn't clogged them up with gasket goo!). One way to overcome this is to expand the diameter of the oilway for a short depth in each surface and tap in a tight-fitting copper dowel.

89. Oil filler cap wing-nut conversion

This suggestion came from the owner of a 1927 ohv BSA, but again is applicable to any number of cases. The oil filler cap in the sump is a hexagon requiring a half-inch spanner. To do away with the need for the spanner, drill a hole in the nut, and fix a wing-

nut to its top with a countersunk screw and nut. The wing-nut will probably need countersinking, but this will ensure oil-tightness. In the original tip, the countersunk screw was burred over on the inside to stop the nut falling in the sump. Brazing wings on the nut would be a better solution.

90. Leakproof joint

To make a sound leakproof joint every scrap of the old gasket must be removed before the new one is put in place. Whatever tool is used to scrape the casing edge, care must be taken not to damage the face of any soft alloy. An old razor or Stanley knife blade might be best for the awkward areas around protruding studs. Another obstacle to a perfectly flat joint face may be where a bolt screws into a tapped hole in one of the joint faces. In time a lip of raised metal could develop around the hole. Remove this by slightly countersinking the hole edge with a rose drill bit.

91. Gasket making

Nowadays it is usually easier to replace unobtainable gaskets with silicon sealant, but this isn't always possible. In many instances the thickness of paper doubled as a spacer to give a narrow clearance, which the compressive nature of modern sealants will fail to provide.

To make a replacement gasket, first select paper of the appropriate thickness. If the old gasket is intact, use it as a template to trace around. If not, some advise covering the surface of the joint with paper and tapping round the edges with a hammer, but usually the risk of

bruising the sharp edge of the soft alloy is too great. A better way is to mark out the joint by pencil and press the paper against screw holes with hand and finger, or run a furniture castor round the edge, and then use a pair of sharp scissors. Alternatively, paint the joint surface with ink and press the gasket paper onto it. The screw holes are best formed by using a hollow punch before the gasket is cut out of the sheet. This will minimize the risk of tearing the edge of the gasket around the hole.

Whether using sealant or gasket, an oiltight joint depends on the condition of the mating surfaces, which must be absolutely true and clean.

92. Double gasket

If a casing, such as a rocker box cover, is secured by only a single central bolt, an oil leak can often be cured by employing two gaskets instead of one. Where a casing is clamped by two or more bolts, extra gasket thickness may distort one face and cause or accentuate a leak. Never overtighten securing nuts or the cover may be warped even when only the standard gasket is used.

93. Oil pump air lock

If the engine is fitted with a plunger-type oil pump which had to be removed, an air lock could be introduced into the system with disastrous consequences. To avoid this, replace the pump, fill the tank and let the oil run out of the open end of the supply line before coupling it to the crankcase union.

94. Revs for speed

Engine revs for a given road speed are obtained from the formula:

$$\frac{336 \times \text{mph} \times \text{gear ratio}}{\text{wheel diameter in inches}}$$

Note that the wheel diameter should be taken inclusive of tyre.

Theoretical road speed at any given rpm can be obtained by the calculation:

$$\frac{\text{rpm} \times \text{wheel diameter}}{336 \times \text{gear ratio}}$$

For example, If an engine is running at 7000 rpm with a top gear ratio of 6:1 and an overall wheel diameter of 24.5 in., the top speed would work out at 85 mph.

95. Horse power rating

Before 1939 motor cycles were often measured in horse power instead of cubic capacity and, as is the way with these things, there were two different systems in operation. The earlier system was an arbitrary rating by which an engine of 250 cc was given an output of 2¼ hp, an engine of 350 cc an output of 2¾ hp, and an engine of 500 cc an output of 3½ hp. Owing to the greater increase in power output, and in an attempt to standardize the arbitrary nature of the system, the Auto Cycle Union introduced its own system in about 1923. Here the assumption was that 100 cc of engine capacity is equivalent to 1 hp. Thus a 350 cc engine has a rating of 3½ hp and a 500 cc engine a rating of 5 hp.

96. Compression ratio

The compression ratio of an engine can quite easily be determined; it is the ratio of the volume of the cylinder when the piston is at bottom dead centre to the volume when it is at top dead centre. In order to find the ratio, fill a measuring flask graduated in cubic centimetres (cc) with oil up to a certain mark. Then, with the piston at top dead centre, pour the oil into the combustion chamber through the spark plug hole. You may have to lean the engine over so that the plug hole is at the top, with no air pocket in the combustion chamber.

When the combustion chamber is full, check the amount of oil poured in. If the cubic capacity of the engine is known, the compression ratio can be found by adding the cc of the engine to the cc of the combustion chamber, and dividing this number by the cc of the combustion chamber. For example, if a capacity of a single-cylinder engine is exactly 500 cc and the combustion space 100 cc, we have (500 plus 100) divided by 100, which equals six. Therefore the compression ratio is 6 to 1.

Do not use petrol to measure the combustion chamber volume. It will run past the piston rings and into the sump, diluting the engine oil, and may even explode the crankcase when the engine fires.

Transmission, clutch and gearbox

97. Rear chain adjustment

Renolds recommended that for rigid machines the correct amount of play on a rear chain was ¾ in. at the tightest point. Swinging arm machines may require more play if recommended by the manufacturer. With a sprung frame the chain tension should be checked when the machine is fully laden, and not on its centre stand. Always check wheel alignment and rear brake adjustment after working on the rear chain.

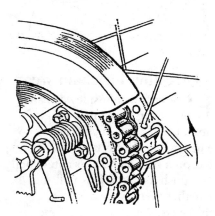

98. The spring clip

The spring clip on a chain must always be fitted the same way; that is on the outside of the chain with the open end of the clip at the rear relative to the direction in which the chain travels.

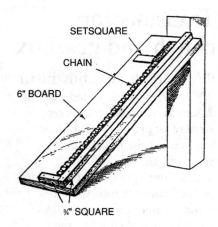

SETSQUARE
CHAIN
6" BOARD
¾" SQUARE

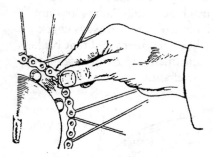

99. Testing for chain wear

Holding a chain sideways and noticing how much it sags is not a proper test of chain wear. The best method is to lay the chain flat on a board and alternately pull and push its ends. This will show whether there is serious wear at the rivets. An ⅛ in. play in one foot of chain is acceptable; but a ¼ in. in one foot is too much, and the chain should be replaced. Alternatively, try lifting the rear chain off its sprocket. If you can see more than half a tooth, the chain is worn out.

100. Replacing a rear chain

When replacing the rear chain, take out the split link and use it to connect one end of the old chain to one end of the new. By this means, as the old chain is drawn off it will feed the new chain over an inaccessible gearbox sprocket.

The same method can be used when removing a chain for cleaning, if an old chain is kept as a spare for this purpose. Place a newspaper under the machine to keep the chain free from grit and dirt.

101. If the chain does disengage from the gearbox sprocket during maintenance, it can be refitted using a length of heavy gauge steel wire bent at right angles half-an-inch from one end. This hook is inserted in the end link of the chain, which can then be easily placed on the teeth of the gearbox sprocket. If a gear is engaged, two or three depressions of the kickstarter will cause the chain to feed over the sprocket.

102. Reconnecting a chain

Chains are most easily reconnected over a sprocket. Have the two ends at 'three o'clock' on the rear wheel sprocket, and they will be at the correct spacing to accept the split link.

103. Chain lubrication

Modern aerosol chainlubes are fine in summer and for trips if applied regularly, but the hot graphite bath is the best way to oil a chain for long life. Many makes are still on the market even if they do need ordering from the retailer, so don't let him fob you off with less!

Clean the chain in petrol or paraffin first, liquefy the graphite grease (I use a camping stove to avoid stinking out the kitchen) and gently lower in the chain on a wire. Leave for a while so that the chain becomes hot, allowing the grease to soak in between all the rollers, then lift the chain out and hang it over the tin to allow the

excess to drain back. For machines used predominantly in the summer this only needs doing once a year in the spring.

104. Primary chain adjustment

In 1956 Renolds recommended that the correct up-and-down movement for primary chains was ⅜ in. at the tightest spot. Taking the engine load off the chain by depressing the kickstarter, check the chain in several places for the tightest position. On some machines it is difficult to judge the free play of the primary chain through the oil filler hole. One suggestion is to paint two white marks the correct distance apart onto the inner chaincase wall.

105. Separate gearbox chain tension

The greatest pull on a separately mounted gearbox is toward the rear, and the effect is to tighten the primary chain. To counteract this, when adjusting the primary drive, first set the chain tension a little tighter than necessary. Now operate the tensioning screw so that the gearbox is pushed forward until the chain tension is correct. Tighten all locknuts, and finally recheck the tension.

106. Refitting a primary chain

It isn't usually possible to reconnect the primary chain over a sprocket, because of the lack of clearance between the back of the sprocket and the rear half of the primary chaincase. However, a spare split link can be fed in from the front temporarily, while the chain ends are over the sprocket. Then, by revolving the chain to a point where there is enough clearance, the real split link can be fed in from the back, simultaneously pushing out the spare link. A crude alternative is to hold the two ends of the chain together with a pair of thin-nosed pliers.

107. Tin primary chaincases

Many find these cases difficult to keep oiltight, particularly the band type, though nowadays there are modern sealing compounds which should help. In the 50s Velocette recommended warming the rubber jointing strip in hot water before reassembly. This makes it more pliable, and so easier to fit, and long enough for the ends to meet without strain.

108. Chaincase seal

This tip for keeping a band type primary chaincase oiltight comes from 1950:

'Repeatedly disturbing the primary chaincase sealing ring while swapping engine sprockets for competition resulted in oil leaks. To cure this I first removed the metal band and the rubber seal and cleaned the joint of the two chaincase halves. I then cut a strip of broad insulating tape the same length as the rubber washer and placed it over the joint of the case all the way round. I sewed the ends of the rubber band together, and stretched it into place on top of the insulating tape. After screwing the metal band in position a perfectly oil-tight joint resulted.'

When removing the case again, it is a simple matter to take off the insulating tape and use a new piece to make a new joint. The rubber band remains in place when fitted, leaving two free hands to deal with the metal band.

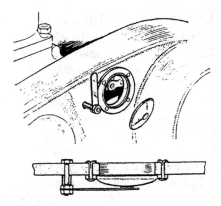

109. Pre-war primary chaincase

Some primary chaincases in the 30s were sealed completely, allowing neither chain inspection nor (in the case of oil bath chaincases) oil drainage. The sketch shows an inspection cover inserted in the primary chaincase of a 1931 Norton, made from a Lucas contact breaker cover. The hole in the chaincase was lined with a ring of heavy-gauge aluminium fixed with brass bifurcated rivets. The cover was held in place by a bolt, spaced out with copper tubing, and locked in place by two nuts. Between the two nuts was a piece of watch spring long enough to reach the centre of the cover.

The oil drainage plug is even more straightforward. This idea was applied to a Velocette KSS MkII. A hole was drilled in the lowest point of the side of the chaincase; the position was checked against a post-war

primary chaincase which had a drain plug. Over the hole a ⁵⁄₁₆ in. nut was welded; a ⁵⁄₁₆ in. bolt, reduced in length, formed the plug.

110. Replacing a chaincase

Many of the tin chaincases of the 40s and 50s were screwed together, and during reassembly it can be difficult to line up the screw holes while keeping the cork or paper gasket in place. To help location, saw the heads off two spare chaincase screws, cut a screwdriver slot in place of the head, and screw them into two holes in the upper half of the chaincase. Place the gasket over the screws and then install the outer chaincase half. Once a number of genuine screws have been replaced, the guide screws can be removed.

The cork gasket can be used again and again if the cases are split carefully. One tip is to cement the gasket to the inner chaincase half only, sealing the outer with grease. When the chaincase is split next, the gasket will remain attached to the inner half.

111. Primary chaincase oil change

On 60s machines fitted with an alternator, merely to top up a primary chaincase with oil is not enough. The sludge accumulated in the bottom of a chaincase can contain metal particles from the chain or sprockets, which will affect the working of the alternator. The metallic content of the sludge, by being magnetically attracted to the coils, can reduce current output. Wash out the chaincase regularly.

112. Engine shaft shock absorbers

These should not be ignored as maintenance-free, even though they lack complicated mechanical components. Mating surfaces should be free from scratches or pitting, and must be kept lubricated (beware the common practice of running primary chaincases almost dry to reduce oil leaks!). Ensure that the shock absorber slides freely on its splines, and on reassembly the spring needs to be tight enough to prevent the unit 'spinning' under load, but not so tight that it can't absorb the shocks.

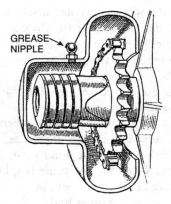

113. Shock absorber lubrication

Although the usual type of engine shaft shock absorber seldom gives trouble, it is essential on machines not fitted with an oil-bath primary chaincase that the splines on which the cam works receive a periodical dose of thin oil. To save having to remove the chainguard each time, drill a hole immediately over the shock absorber, and tap and screw in an ordinary grease nipple. Then, in only a few seconds, oil can be forced through the nipple onto the splines below.

114. Spring compression

Engine shaft shock absorber nuts are sometimes difficult to start because of the strength of the shock absorber spring. One way to compress the spring, provided there is enough clearance, is to locate it between three equally spaced bolts and nuts. Compress by tightening the nuts.

This more usual method was used on a BSA M21. Compress the spring in a vice and hold it compressed with clips made from brazing wire spaced equally around the spring. The nut will start easily, and the clips can be prised off with a screwdriver.

115. Threaded engine sprocket

If a threaded engine sprocket is difficult to shift, a spare length of chain wrapped round the sprocket can be used as a wrench. Alternatively, put the machine in top gear, pull it back against compression, withdraw the clutch and, after wheeling the machine backwards quickly, drop the clutch suddenly.

116. The clutch

The clutch is a much abused component but, if it is kept in correct adjustment, there is no reason why it cannot give long service and smooth operation. Points to remember are that there should always be some free play

(allow ⅛ in. slack in the cable at the handlebar) to avoid the clutch running under a constant load, and the cable should be well oiled. New plates will bed down, so the clutch will need readjusting several times within a relatively short period. This is normal. With multi-plate clutches it is a good idea to free the plates with the kickstarter before setting off in the morning.

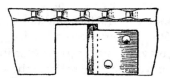

117. Clutch silkiness

The clutch will not disengage smoothly if the tongues are burred or the slots notched. Burrs on the driving plates can be removed carefully with a fine file. Notches in the clutch housing can be more problematical especially, as in this case, they have been worn oversize. Here pieces of steel were riveted in position to reduce the slot to its original size and, at the same time, square it up.

118. Clutch withdrawal tool

Clutches can be difficult to remove from the chaincase for overhaul. Most factories supplied special extractors to take out clutch centres. The following were a few suggestions for when the special tools weren't available. Most clutches will correspond to a similar design, even if the dimensions are different. Whatever is used it is important to avoid burring over any of the splines or tags on a clutch, as this will lead to harsh operation on reassembly.

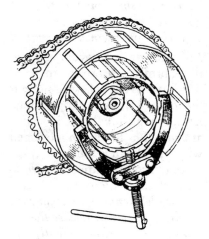

119. Universal clutch centre holder (see also 127)

This method of clutch centre locking uses a sprocket puller whilst the centre nut is slackened.

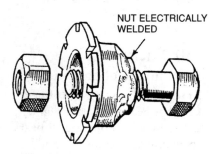

NUT ELECTRICALLY WELDED

120. BSA clutch withdrawal tool

On this withdrawal tool for a BSA clutch, a spare clutch spring retaining ring was reversed and welded to a nut. Another spare spring retaining ring had its hexagon corners reduced to allow it to fit in the other side of the clutch's retaining ring. A bolt was threaded through the tool, and tightened to extract the clutch.

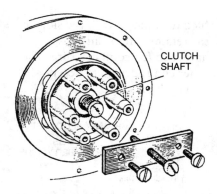

CLUTCH SHAFT

121. Royal Enfield clutch withdrawal tool

Take a length of mild steel strip 1 in. x 5/16 in. x 3 in. long, and drill two ¼ in. holes to coincide with the screws that hold the clutch springs in position. Drill a third central hole and tap it to take a 5/16 in. bolt. To use, screw the two outer bolts into the clutch spring fixings and tighten the middle bolt against the clutch centre. The middle bolt may require a smart tap on its head to jar the centre free. Though designed for a 125 cc Royal Enfield, this idea can be adapted to suit many clutches.

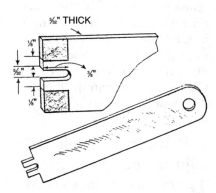

3/32" THICK

1/8"

5/32"

1/8"

3/8"

122. Clutch spring tool

A tool for removing the clutch spring adjusting nuts from a Burman gearbox can be made with a piece of 1 in. x ⅛ in. strip steel 6 in. long. Cut away the shaded

portions indicated in the sketch, then cut a slot about 3 mm wide in the remainder to form two prongs.

123. Clutch relining

If new clutch corks are difficult to fit, don't cut them, but boil them for 10 minutes in water to soften them up. Truing new cork inserts into a clutch plate can present problems. One solution is to construct a jig consisting of a sheet of 16-gauge sheet steel with a hole cut in the middle, large enough to support just the outer rim of the plate and the tangs.

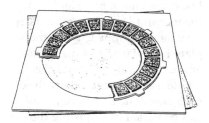

Stick a piece of sandpaper to an absolutely flat surface. Lay the jig on the paper and place the clutch plate, with the corks fitted as accurately as possible by eye, over the hole. Steady the jig with the left hand and rotate the plate to and fro with the right. When the plate lies flush on the upper side of the jig the corks will have a uniform thickness.

124. Clutch cork inserts

Some have recommended reducing the diameter of round corks by rolling them under foot. But if corks are soaked in water for 20 minutes, they will become so rubbery that they can be pressed into clutch plates by finger pressure without any risk of fraying or crumbling the cork.

125. Re-corking clutch plates

When re-corking clutch plates, insert alternate corks in the plate from one side and then reverse it and complete the remainder. This will ease the task of facing up the corks.

126. Clutch renovation

Another way to even up new clutch inserts in a renovated clutch plate is to double over a piece of coarse emery paper (abrasive surface inwards) and slip it between the jaws of a vice. Insert the clutch plate and close the vice until the thinnest cork is very lightly gripped. Work the plate backwards and forwards, gradually rotating it until the whole assembly can be revolved with ease. The degree of thinness can be varied by adjusting the distance between the vice jaws. Wash off all traces of abrasive with petrol.

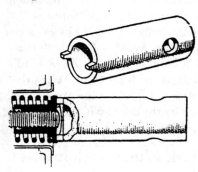

127. Burman clutch tool

This tool is designed to adjust the spring retaining nuts on a Burman clutch, though the same design with different dimensions will fit many multi-plate clutches. The tool is made from a piece of tube with an inside diameter of ⅜ in. On one end two dogs are filed to coincide with the slots in the retaining nuts, and case-hardened for good measure. The other end is drilled to accept a tommy-bar.

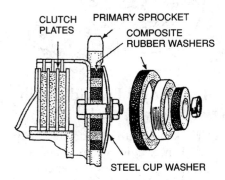

CLUTCH PLATES PRIMARY SPROCKET COMPOSITE RUBBER WASHERS

STEEL CUP WASHER

128. Shock absorber rubbers

Replacement shock absorber rubbers for a Burman clutch can be made from concentric rings of rubber hose. The thicknesses used here ranged from 1½ in. outside diameter and 1¼ in. inside diameter to ½ in. OD and ¼ in. ID. The rings were cut ¼ in. thick and fitted into one another, ending up with the ½ in. OD hose in the centre of each. In this case, where the rubbers had actually been lost, the four steel cup washers were also missing. These were made from stainless steel of 1¼ in. OD, and bored centrally to take a ¼ in. bolt.

129. Burman clutch adjustment

Panther manufacturer's P&M warned about adjusting a Burman clutch entirely with the cable:

'If clutch adjustment on gearboxes with totally enclosed clutch thrust lever operation is made entirely by means of the cable adjuster, a false impression of the degree of thrust rod clearance may arise. A few owners are apt to overlook the thrust rod adjustment, revealed when the small oval plate secured by two studs on the gearbox outer cover is removed.'

AMC elaborated by commenting that Burman gearboxes can develop a strange clicking noise if the internal thrust-rod operating lever, to which the cable is attached, has too much movement when the clutch is used.

'To effect a remedy, screw in the clutch cable adjuster as far as possible. Remove the chaincase clutch cover, and release the thrust-stud locknut. Gently screw in the thrust-stud until contact with the pushrod can be felt. Make sure the stud does not move while retightening the locknut. Replace the clutch cover, and unscrew the cable adjuster until there is ⅛ in.–³⁄₁₆ in. free play.'

130. Sticky Sturmey-Archer

If the clutch rod on a Sturmey-Archer gearbox wears slightly, the screw which operates it bears up against the mainshaft and won't free the clutch properly. To find a piece of metal hard and small enough to intervene between the screw and the rod is not as hard as it sounds. An ordinary ¼ in. ball bearing is a perfect fit.

131. Villiers clutch

When dismantling the clutch of the Villiers 197 cc 9E engine this tool is invaluable. A length of flat mild steel 1 in. x ¼ in. x 18 in. is drilled with two

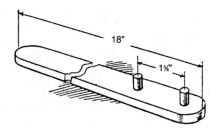

¼ in. diameter holes at 1⅜ in. between centres. Two pegs ¼ in. diameter and ½ in. long are brazed into the holes.

132. Triumph multi-plate clutch

This advice was given by the Triumph factory in 1956, but applies to any multi-plate clutch of that type:

'When assembling a clutch, the plain plates should be checked for distortion on a sheet of plate glass. Then check that the plates slide freely in the housing. If the slots in the housing are worn, they should be cleaned up with a file, or the housing replaced. Before fitting the clutch pressure plate, check that the spring cups are free in their holes; holes in which the cups are tight should receive careful attention with a round file.'

133. Balancing a multi-plate clutch

As a general rule the springs in their retaining cups should be tightened down to begin with until the nuts or screws are flush with the ends of their retaining pins. Fix a pointer to the inner chaincase a set distance from the face of the pressure plate. With the engine in neutral, gently spin the clutch with the kickstarter, and identify when the pressure plate wobbles

towards the pointer. Tighten the appropriate nut, and repeat the procedure until the pressure plate spins evenly.

134. Clutch tool

A tool can be made from an old clutch driven (plain) plate drilled to accommodate a handle as shown. It can be used to hold the clutch centre while the centre nut is tightened or loosened.

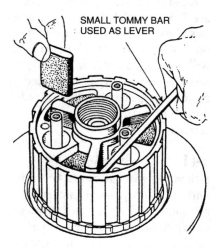

SMALL TOMMY BAR USED AS LEVER

135. Clutch cush drive rubbers

On models with cush drive rubbers in the clutch centre, fit the larger rubbers between the hub and the vanes, and use a small tommy-bar to compress those rubbers against the vanes to ease

the fitting of the smaller rubbers. (This task can be made easier if a little washing-up liquid is applied to the rubbers first.)

136. Velocette clutch reassembly

Though this tip from 1956 is only applicable to Velocette singles, it demonstrates again the use of old parts in the reassembly of a component.

'It is sometimes difficult on single-cylinder models to get the outer clutch plate and the spacing plate beneath it to engage with each other when assembling the various plates prior to refitting the clutch onto the sleeve gear. The job becomes easy if the clutch is mounted first of all on a 'slave' sleeve gear, held splines upward in a vice. A scrap sleeve gear on any single-cylinder Velocette (back to 1922) will serve.

'If, on putting the clutch back on the machine, it is found that the sleeve gear gets pushed through the bearing, it can be drawn out through the clutch back plate by screwing the sleeve gear nut up against it after removal of the spring holder. When the limit of the threads is reached, remove the sleeve gear nut, fit the distance piece, and screw the nut up once more. It is always advisable to engage top gear before refitting the clutch, to prevent the sleeve gear from pushing through.'

137. Gearbox lubrication

It is interesting that *The Motor Cycle* did not regard grease on its own as a suitable gearbox lubricant, even in the mid-30s when several manufacturers recommended it. The reason was that tests had shown that the pinions cut channels in the grease and then ran more or less dry. Their advice was to 'follow the makers' instructions, but if they advise a lubricant which is not fluid, add a little touring engine oil to it.' Incidentally, a quick way to fill a gearbox with grease is to heat the grease until it is a liquid, and pour it in like oil. Take care, though; too much heat may destroy the lubricating qualities of the grease.

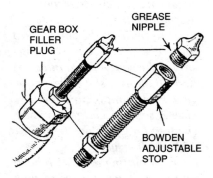

GEAR BOX FILLER PLUG

GREASE NIPPLE

BOWDEN ADJUSTABLE STOP

138. Gearbox filler

Fitting a grease nipple to the gearbox filler cap is an old idea for grease-filled boxes. For awkwardly placed filler caps this extension could be handy. Made from the adjustable stop from a Bowden cable, the hexagon end is tapped to take the grease nipple. The other end is screwed into a tapped hole in the cap. The lock-nut is tightened down to form a grease-tight joint. If the device is fitted into a spare filler cap, an unspoilt cap can be in place for daily use.

139. Calculating gear ratios

The top gear ratio can be determined by multiplying the number of teeth on the clutch sprocket by the number of teeth on the rear wheel sprocket, and dividing the result by the number of teeth on the engine sprocket multiplied by the number of teeth on the gearbox driving sprocket. It is impossible to determine the middle and low ratios accurately unless the reduction effected in the gearbox is known, but if these figures are available it is only necessary to multiply them by the top gear ratio in each case to obtain the lower ratios.

140. A method of determining how the intermediate ratios will be affected by raising or lowering the top gear ratio can be explained by giving this simple example. In a three-speed box, suppose the gears are 5, 8 and 12:1. If the top gear is raised to 4:1, second gear will now be: $\frac{4}{5}$ x 8 = 6.4:1, and bottom gear will be: $\frac{4}{5}$ x 12 = 9.6:1. The formula is: new top gear divided by old top gear multiplied by old middle or bottom gear respectively.

141. A rule-of-thumb guide to estimating gear ratios can be made without mathematical calculations as follows. With the machine on its centre stand, turn the rear wheel until the tyre valve is in line with a convenient mark such as a chain stay. Engage the desired gear and turn the rear wheel, counting the number of revolutions of the engine sprocket, until the tyre valve returns to its original position. If the sprocket goes round six times, then the ratio is 6:1.

142. Gear operating mechanism

A vast difference can often be made to the way a gear control works if a drop of oil is applied to the joints in the control mechanism. Better still, particularly on a handchange system, the little clevis pins should be removed and greased to prevent the ingress of water and grit.

143. Handchange gear selection adjustment

On engines with separate gearboxes and where the primary chain is adjusted by moving the gearbox, the position of a handchange lever may alter in relation to its quadrant when the chain is adjusted. If the gearchange linkage is not re-set, this may cause serious damage to the gearbox. Therefore, increase or decrease the effective length of the gear control rod by means of the adjustment provided until, with the control lever in the neutral position, there is an equal amount of free movement either way before either second or bottom gear is engaged. Finally, check that there is a false neutral exactly halfway between top and middle or third gear (depending on the number of gears in the box). Sometimes a gear gate does not coincide exactly with the gear control so far as the various notches are concerned; in this instance it is necessary to compromise a little.

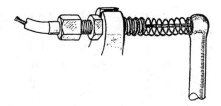

144. Spring-loaded clutch arm

On gearboxes with external operating arms, this tip ensures that the correct amount of free movement in the clutch thrust mechanism is maintained when the clutch is fully home. To keep the required play between the clutch arm and the clutch thrust rod, insert a length of throttle return spring onto the cable between the clutch arm and the cable stop. An added bonus is that the spring stops the arm from rattling, and the coils can be packed with grease to keep the exposed length of inner cable clean and lubricated.

145. Ball bearing adjuster

Certain gearbox designs, such as Albion and some BSA patterns, employ an adjuster screw with a steel ball in the clutch operating arm. It is essential that the ball, which bears against the end of the clutch thrust rod, be kept free running. If neglected the ball will seize in its housing, develop flats, and indent the end of the thrust rod. This is a common cause of heavy clutch operation.

Withdraw the adjuster screw occasionally, grease the ball and, if necessary, grind the end of the thrust rod flat. Some Royal Enfield and BSA adjuster screws are interchangeable, which could be handy in an emergency.

146. Jumping out of gear

When a gear starts jumping out, the fault is generally wear in the change mechanism, or failure to keep the change mechanism properly adjusted. If this is not dealt with promptly there will be a heavy bill for new gear pinions. If the trouble cannot be cured by adjusting the selector, examine the dog-clutches in the gearbox (in certain designs these are inside the pinions). The chances are that they have become rounded off. A cure may be affected by grinding them back to square.

147. Burman gearbox – cover removal

For easy removal of the outer cover of a Burman gearbox, slacken all the fixing screws and nuts by one turn, then operate the clutch lever. This will break the joint.

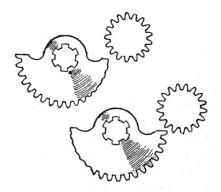

148. Burman kickstart quadrant

Many Burman kickstart quadrants are reversible. So, if several teeth are missing where the quadrant engages the dog, it will just need turning round on its shaft.

149. Burman gearbox selector

It is worth noting when reassembling many heavyweight Burman gearboxes that the gear-operating mechanism has timing marks to align it with the selector. A failure to select a gear (especially top), or a gear jumping out, is simply because of these marks not being properly aligned. Before throwing pinions towards expensive engineers, check the cheapest option first.

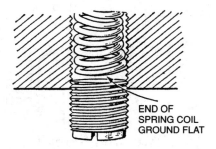

END OF SPRING COIL GROUND FLAT

150. Burman gearbox – selector pawl

Some Burman heavyweight gearboxes have a spring-loaded selector pawl held in place by a grub screw situated on the middle of the underside of the box. To ease the starting of this awkward screw, grind one end of the pawl spring flat. This will give the last half coil a sharp edge which, when pushed up into the box, can be made to catch in a thread pitch. The grub screw can then be started without encountering the downward pressure of the spring.

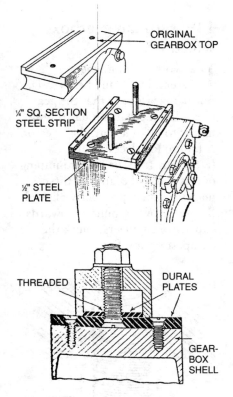

ORIGINAL
GEARBOX TOP

¼" SQ. SECTION
STEEL STRIP

½" STEEL
PLATE

THREADED

DURAL
PLATES

GEAR-
BOX
SHELL

151. Two-stud fixing for four-stud gearbox

When forced to make one good gearbox out of a pile of bits, this adaptation of a four-stud Sturmey-Archer gearbox to a two-stud fixing could be useful. First, remove the four studs and cut a piece of ⅝ in. duralumin plate to fit the top of the box. Drill and countersink four holes in the plate to line up with the tapped holes in the gearbox casting. Marking the centre-line of the gearbox, drill two more holes to line up with the slots in the frame member, and countersink them underneath the plate. Next, cut a piece of ¼ in. duralumin, so that it just fits in the channel of the frame, to act as a guide. Drill and thread two holes in this plate to match up with the frame slots.

Thread two countersunk slotted screws through the thicker

duralumin plate from underneath and through the guide plate, which acts as a nut for both mounting screws keeping them rigid. Ensure the slotted heads are filed flush with the underside of the plate. Attach the gearbox to the ⅝ in. duralumin plate with four more countersunk slotted screws by means of the existing stud holes, and file flush after tightening down. The two channel screws are trapped between plate and gearbox shell, and in this case the frame channel just caught the edge of the four fixing screws as well. It is not important that the gearbox is now ⅝ in. lower than before.

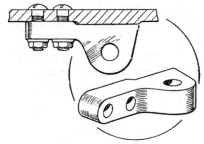

152. Broken pivot lug

This repair copes with a broken pivot lug for the clutch operating arm on a gearbox end cover, without interfering with the footchange mechanism inside the cover. Owing to the small section of the lug and the close proximity of the clutch adjusting sleeve, welding wasn't an option. The broken lug was cut off to within 1/16 in. of the cover face. A piece of 5/16 in. bright steel bar was fashioned as shown in the sketch. A step was left in the steel bar just a shade smaller than the depth of the step in the cover face to ensure that the new lug held securely. Two holes were drilled in the

casing to correspond with two in the lug, the attachment being made by a pair of round-headed slotted screws, washers and nuts. A third hole was drilled in the lug for the clutch arm pivot pin.

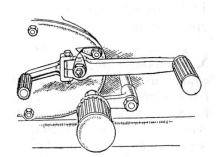

153. Rocking pedal gearchange

Many Italian machines were fitted with a rocking pedal to allow the gear to be changed one way with the heel, the other with the toe. This removed the need to hook the toe under the front pedal, and take up the large amount of associated travel. It was recognized as such a good idea that eventually some British factories even started offering a rocking pedal kit as an extra. This simple conversion comes from 1947 and appears from the sketch to be fitted to a Burman box. The rocking pedal was made from a discarded propstand. The fulcrum part fitted easily over the clamp of the original gear lever. The length was judged by measuring the rider's foot, and bending the stand with heat to an angle of 70 degrees. At this angle the pedal was parallel to the footrest. Then the stand was cut 1½ in. from the bend, and finished off with a short length of rubber tubing. In this way the toe of the new pedal was short enough to clear the leg when the kickstarter was being used.

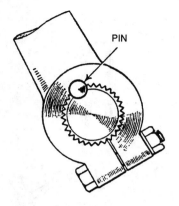

154. Worn kickstart splines

If a kickstart lever is loose on its spline, and replacements are unobtainable, drill a hole biting into both the pin and the shaft, and fit a ¼ in. metal dowel. The pin should be a tight fit in the hole when the clamp bolt is loose. If the end of the shaft needs softening before drilling, heat until red and allow to cool slowly. Keeping the rest of the shaft immersed in water will prevent it suffering damage by the heat.

155. Tougher cotter

The cotter pin which, on some models, secures the kick-starter pedal to its shaft, can give trouble when worn. And standard replacements nowadays are too soft to give any decent length of service. One answer is to replace the pin with a ⅜ in. high tensile steel bolt, with its head cut off and a tapered flat filed on the shank. The nut, larger than that on the standard cotter, enables the new pin to be pulled home really tight.

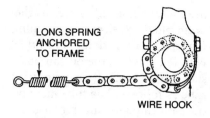

156. Sturmey-Archer kickstart spring

This suggestion for a replacement kickstart return spring in a Sturmey-Archer gearbox comes from 1948, here fitted to a 1926 Royal Enfield. A length of magneto chain is attached to the kickstarter with a wire hook and anchored to the frame by means of a long spring. It may not be pretty, but could come in handy in an emergency, or while waiting to obtain a replacement spring.

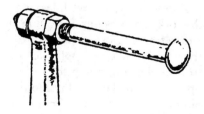

157. Kickstart repair

If the kickstart breaks where the pedal meets the lever, a repair can be made by drilling out the hole and substituting the pedal with a sturdy bolt. The bolt shank should be locked by placing a nut either side of the lever. The bolt head will keep the kickstart rubber in place.

158. Gear indicator

This tip will serve no purpose for most modern users of old machinery, especially those wishing to preserve the originality of their models, but deserves inclusion purely because of its ingenious design and skilful implementation.

Fitted to a BSA B33, the gear indicator is mounted to two of the handlebar clamping screws and is Bowden cable operated from the gearbox. The gearchange pedal shaft passes through the hollow gear selector quadrant shaft. The quadrant shaft projects a short way through the gearbox outer end cover and is provided with two flats externally. An adaptor ring was made to fit these flats, and a short arm was made for attachment to the adaptor ring by three screws. Pivoted to the top of this arm is a yoke which is drilled and slotted to receive a cable nipple. A collar is also provided to prevent the nipple from sliding out of its hole. The stop for the cable outer casing at the gearbox end is attached to an arm clamped behind the footrest hanger.

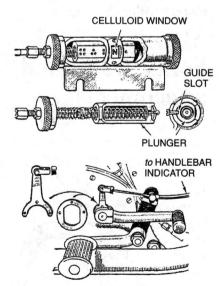

The indicator on the handlebar consists of a spring loaded plunger sliding axially within a cylinder. In the middle of the cylinder is a celluloid window through which the gear engaged is indicated.

Made from brass rod, the plunger was drilled out to contain the spring. The required spring pressure is given by 1½ carburettor springs, which are 'joined' by a brass bush provided with a medial shoulder. The cable is retained by a slotted washer located against an internal shoulder formed at one end of the plunger.

One side of the plunger is filed flat to provide a face on which the gear symbols are imprinted. Bottom gear is represented by one dimple, neutral by the letter N, second gear by two dimples, third by three and top by four. The flat face was painted with cylinder black, and the dimples and the letter N were filled with white paint. Along the opposite face of the plunger a groove is formed. In this groove locates the tip of a setscrew arranged at the back of the cylinder, to prevent the plunger rotating within the cylinder.

Forks, frame and attachments

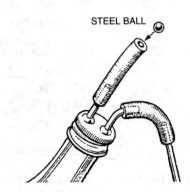

STEEL BALL

159. Telescopic forks – changing oil

To drain the oil out of fork legs the top caps will probably

need to be removed as well as the drain plugs to release the vacuum. On some early fork legs not fitted with drain plugs, the oil can be sucked out with a long copper tube as follows. The tube must be of small enough diameter to get right to the bottom of the fork leg. This means the oil will flow too slowly to use usual syphoning methods. The job can be left to complete itself in an hour if a large bottle is connected to the copper tube, and air sucked out by mouth through a second pipe with a short length of rubber tube connected, causing a vacuum in the bottle. The vacuum is maintained by first pinching the tube and then sealing it with a ball bearing.

160. Draining the fork oil can sometimes be simplified if the drain plugs are removed, leaving the fork top caps in position. Push a drip tray as close as possible to the wall of the tyre, apply the front brake, and pump the forks up and down. This will pump the old oil out in a couple of minutes.

161. Telescopic forks – removing stanchions

It is usually a straightforward job removing stanchions without special tools. This tip was given by BSA for their 1956 range, but the advice will apply to many makes of most ages. With the front wheel and mudguard removed and the pinch bolts in the lower fork yoke slackened off, unscrew the fork top nuts a few threads only. Give a sharp blow on the nuts with a hide mallet to release the stanchions from their tapers in the top yoke, take out the nuts, and withdraw the tubes through the lower yoke.

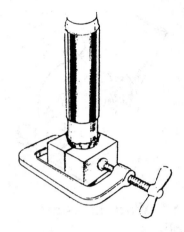

162. Telescopic forks – removing sliders

AMC recommended this tool in 1956 as an effective home-made version of their factory item for unscrewing fork slider extensions. It consists of a wooden block drilled with a 2 in. diameter hole and sawn through longitudinally. Placed round the fork sliders, the clamp can be gripped with a G-clamp or valve spring compressor. They pointed out that earlier fork sliders were fitted with a C-spanner.

163. Telescopic forks – removing oil seal holders

The oil seal holders on most telescopic forks need a special tool for removal. Sometimes a C-spanner will do, but if it won't, this trick from 1960 should help. Bind insulating tape round the seal holder and clamp a worm screw clip over the tape. Use the joint of the clip as a tapping point for a hammer and drift.

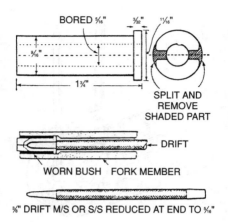

BORED ⁵⁄₁₆" ³⁄₃₂" ¹¹⁄₁₆"

.⁹⁄₁₆"

1¾"

SPLIT AND REMOVE SHADED PART

DRIFT

WORN BUSH   FORK MEMBER

⅜" DRIFT M/S OR S/S REDUCED AT END TO ⁵⁄₁₆"

164. Telescopic forks – removing fork bushes

This tool for removing worn fork bushes from a BSA M20 comes from 1949. The bushes are recessed in the fork and, as there is only about ⅛ in. clear space behind each bush, there is no possibility of driving them out; a special puller must be used. Make up a bush with a collar (to the dimensions shown) preferably from silver steel (mild steel will do if not many bushes need removing). Split the bush and file it until it can be pushed through the bush in the fork (⁹⁄₁₆ in. bore). A ⅜ in. rod, stepped down to ⁵⁄₁₆ in. and tapered for easy entry, is inserted from the far side. This will expand the collar into the recess, and a few good taps will bring out the old bush. Adaptations of this method will work for other early telescopic forks.

165. Telescopic forks – alignment

After replacing the front wheel, do not fully tighten the spindle pinch bolt immediately. First bounce the forks up and down vigorously a few times to allow the legs to align themselves.

166. Gaiter fitting

Many lightweights in the 60s supplied plastic rather than rubber gaiters to fork legs, and owing to the stiff nature of the material these can be difficult to fit. The job is made much easier by immersing an inch or so of the top part in boiling water for 15–20 seconds. The material then becomes quite pliable. Extra care should be taken not to damage the softened plastic when sliding the gaiters into position.

167. Royal Enfield casquette key

To dismantle the front fork of a Royal Enfield equipped with a casquette headlamp mounting it is necessary to use a socket screw key. Did you know that the footrest rod is the correct size hexagon? Don't bend it at right angles, though; use a spanner on the other end!

168. Adjusting steering head bearings

For safe steering it is vital that there is no play in the steering head bearings. At the same time they are correctly adjusted when they are only just tight enough, as overtightening will damage the cups and cones that the ball bearings run in. To check, put the machine on its centre stand so that the front wheel is clear of the ground, and loosen off fully any steering damper. Kneeling in front of the machine and holding both fork legs, try to pull the forks backwards and forwards. If there is any play, the steering column needs tightening. Tighten the steering column a fraction at a

time until just – and only just – all play has been removed.

169. Checking steering head bearings for wear

Again, the front wheel must be off the ground, and the steering damper disconnected. Gently move the handlebars from one lock to the other. The action should be light and smooth. If the action is harsh or the handlebars stick at any point in the arc, the cups and cones may be pitted and need replacing. Do not confuse worn head bearings with stiff action caused by a badly routed wiring loom or Bowden control cables.

170. Steering head removal

When dismantling the steering head, it is usual to place a block or box under the crankcase. The work of dismantling the head, and more particularly replacing it, is greatly simplified if the block is of such a height that the front wheel rests on the ground without bearing any of the weight of the machine. If the block lifts the wheel off the ground, though the machine will be stable, the wheel and forks will be difficult to control single-handedly.

171. Girder fork shock absorber

Girder forks are usually fitted with a shock absorber to damp out the rebound action of the spring. However, if the shock absorber is done up too tightly the spring won't be able to function, transmitting all road shocks to the rider. If not tight enough, the forks will be too lively. Experimentation is the name of the game, as the correct setting will vary not only between different forks, but between different road surfaces and speeds, too.

172. Adjusting girder forks

1. Slacken off the shock absorber completely.
2. Adjusting the spindles one at a time, loosen the nuts and turn the spindle from the squared end until nearly all the play is taken up. Retighten the nuts and check the spacer washers, which should be free to rotate. If too tight, loosen the nuts again and turn the squared end of the spindle clockwise until the correct play can be felt. Retighten the nuts and make a final check.
3. The final adjustment must allow perfect freedom of movement of the fork spindles, with no noticeable side play between any of the faces. A good check of the adjustment is if one spacing washer on each spindle can be turned but has no side play, then that spindle is correctly adjusted.

173. Girder fork support

When testing steering head bearings on machines with a rear stand and girder forks, it is usual to place a block under the crankcase to lift the front wheel clear of the ground. Often the front wheel assembly drops under the action of the fork spring, which can foul the bottom of the steering column.

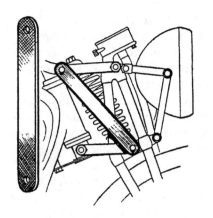

This can be avoided by placing a strip of 1 in. x ⅛ in. mild steel, correctly drilled, over the ends of the top rear and bottom front spindles.

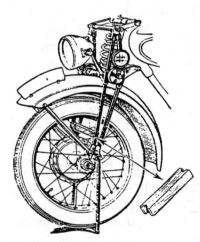

174. When removing the front wheel from girder forks, the fork ends tend to spring together. To ease wheel replacement, the forks can be kept apart by sliding a wooden distance piece through the wheel spokes and between the fork blades. Grooves cut in the ends of the distance piece will enable it to slide up and down the forks, following the movement of the wheel.

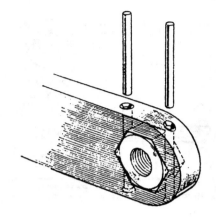

175. Repairing girder fork links

This tip was recommended in 1948 to repair worn threads in girder fork links when complete fork overhaul was not necessary or not possible. Though carried out in a workshop, it should be regarded as a temporary repair until new fork links can be fitted. Place a good quality nut of the same size and thread as the spindle over the worn hole in the fork link, and mark the hexagon onto the link. Drill an ⅛ in. hole in the link at each of the six corners of the hexagon, and file the hole to take the nut as a tight knock-in fit. Drill through the link and nut vertically to take two ⅛ in. steel pins to prevent sideways movement.

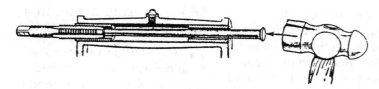

176. Rebushing girder forks

Worn fork bushes are usually very thin, and difficult to drift out in the normal manner. To avoid damage to the surrounding fork components, insert an old taper tap well into the worn bush, and drive out the tap and bush from the other side with a hammer and metal drift.

177. Altering steering lock

Most machines have projections on the forks or the bottom yoke to limit the steering lock. After many years these may wear, causing the fork shrouds to rub the front valances of the petrol tank. This solution from 1959 was intended for use when fitting a fairing, but will apply equally well either way. If the lock stops are drilled and tapped to take a ³⁄₁₆ in. bolt, the screw will prevent the forks fouling the tank with only a negligible reduction in lock.

178. Reversible handlebars

On many pre-war machines, makers' claims of fully adjustable handlebars only applied if the 'bars were unbolted and physically turned round. In this way a standard touring riding position could be converted into a sporting crouch. If you're trying to complete that authentic rebuild and the handlebars look wrong, try turning them round the other way. Some previous owner may have gone for the sporty look and left them in the upside down position. From experience with my own Sunbeam I know how different the two settings can look.

179. Mirror modification

A rear-view mirror can be modified to fit into the handlebar end quite easily. After cutting down a ⅜ in. rod to 10 in. bend it at right angles 4 in. from the handlebar end. Turn a thread onto the shorter portion to match that of a ⅜ in. Rawlbolt (an expanding bolt used by builders), and screw on a washer and lock

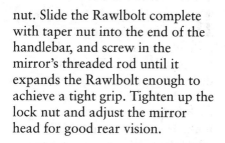

nut. Slide the Rawlbolt complete with taper nut into the end of the handlebar, and screw in the mirror's threaded rod until it expands the Rawlbolt enough to achieve a tight grip. Tighten up the lock nut and adjust the mirror head for good rear vision.

180. Replacing swinging arm bushes

Swinging arm bushes can be replaced by butting the new bush up to the bushed housing on one side, and butting a larger diameter tube on the other side. Slide a threaded rod through the whole assembly, place washers to avoid distortion or burring, and tighten up the nuts. At the same time as fitting itself, the new bush will push the old one out into the tube.

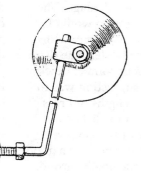

181. Refitting plunger rear suspension

Refitting rear suspension units to a plunger frame is simplified if the units are pre-compressed. Items required are a ¼ in. diameter threaded rod about 15 in. long with two nuts, and two strips of steel (size 4 in. x ½ in. x ¼ in.) drilled to take the threaded rod. Pass the rod through the spring assembly, placing the steel strips top and bottom. Tighten the nuts on the rod until the springs are sufficiently compressed for the steel strips to pass between the lugs of the frame. Unscrew the top nut and remove the rod from below. Tap the spring boxes gently into place, and remove the steel strips with pliers.

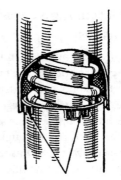

BRASS BEARING SURFACES

182. Rear shock treatment

Girling rear shock absorber units of the late 50s tended to suffer from chrome damage. The chromed lower section would be scored by constant contact with the painted upper slider. The three dimples to prevent contact quickly wore flat. One suggestion was to braze four ½ in. lengths of brass strip at the top of the lower section in place of the dimples, and filing them down to be a good sliding fit with the upper shroud. Girling themselves, acknowledging the problem, approved of this modification on a one-off basis while pointing out it was too expensive for mass production.

183. Oil tank assembly

The central part of a motor cycle is often a complicated compilation of fixtures and fittings, as factories tried to fit all the 'plumbing' accessories in a neat space without detracting from the machine's overall appearance. If left alone they cause no comment, but once one component has to be removed, every nut and bolt seems to relate to the next, all equally inaccessible.

For example, the oil tank, air filter and battery box on a mid-50s Triumph Tiger Cub are assembled as one unit, which is supported by two bolts passing through lugs brazed to the saddle tube. If the tank has to be removed for flushing out, or the air filter element for cleaning, it is necessary to remove the complete assembly; and reassembly calls for skill in juggling with distance pieces, washers, nuts and bolts.

With a bit of thought it is possible to simplify reassembly in a way not open to the factory for cost reasons. In the Tiger Cub's case, replace the two bolts with threaded studs, passed through the frame lugs. Assemble the distance pieces and retain with washers and thin nuts. The oil tank can be positioned at one side and the battery box at the other, each secured by nuts and washers. By removing the appropriate nut it will be possible to remove either tank or battery box independently.

184. Tank buffers

Refitting fuel tank bolts where the tank is mounted on rubber buffers at each corner can be an exasperating task. The main difficulty is usually to get the hole in the buffer to line up with those in the supporting bracket and tank. The task is simplified if, when the tank is off, the rubbers are stuck to it in the correct position with a latex-based adhesive. They will then be found to guide the bolts home.

185. Locating a leak in a petrol tank

Pressure testing a petrol tank under water can be carried out as follows. Cut an old inner tube either side of the valve, leaving 3 in. one side and 6 in. the other. Tie off the longer end of the tube with string, and stretch the other end over the mouth of the tank, binding it with tape. Use the valve to pump in enough air for the pressure test.

Alternatively, tape over the breather hole in the filler cap, close the petrol taps, and submerge the empty tank in a bath of hot water. The air inside the tank will expand, and a stream of bubbles will indicate the leak.

186.

This method of finding a leak in a petrol tank eliminates the need for a large receptacle of water, and the risk of fire from a tank containing only compressed air and petrol vapour. Make a blanking plate for the filler hole with a T-bolt, steel disc and fibre or leather washer. Fill the tank with water. Insert the head of the T-bolt so that it bridges the orifice, slip on the washer and steel disc, and tighten down with a nut to make the filler hole completely watertight. Adapt the connections so that a bicycle pump can be fitted to the petrol tap, and with a few strokes of the pump, pressurize the tank. The leak will immediately reveal itself as a fierce jet of water. Even if above the waterline, the leak can be pinpointed by a loud hissing sound. When the hole is found and marked, the tank can be drained and welded in the normal way.

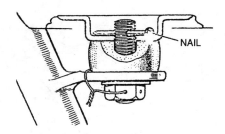

187. Tank lug repair

In cases where there is not enough room to tap out a hole, this sketch shows a neat repair to a stripped thread in a tank mounting lug. Cut the head off the correct sized bolt, and drill a hole to take a split pin. (The sketch shows a nail, but a split pin would make a better job.) Offer up the bolt, and insert and bend back the split pin. With the usual mounting rubbers and washers in place, screw up the nut and drill and wire it for extra security.

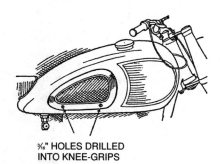

3/16" HOLES DRILLED INTO KNEE-GRIPS

188. Draining knee grips

Bulky rubber knee grips, common on petrol tanks in the 30s and 40s, can have a habit of collecting water, which in time will rust the back plates. An easy cure is to drill two 3/16 in. drainage holes along the base of the grips.

189. Hinged filler caps

Hinged filler caps will leak if the hinge eye on the cap is misaligned. Remove the split pin on which the cap hinges, and tighten down the cap fully. Try to pass the hinge pin through the assembly, setting the eye as necessary to ensure that the pin is a free fit.

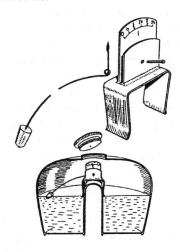

190. Simple petrol gauge

The sketch shows a simple petrol gauge fitted in the tank of a BSA, but it would suit most saddle tanks. The clip and the needle carrier were made from 20-gauge hard brass sheet, and the carrier was soldered to the clip. A long hat pin, flattened at one end for a pointer, was used for the needle and float wire. An ordinary wine cork was fixed to the other end for a float. A split pin formed the pivot, allowing the needle to ride quite freely between the plates. The scale was graduated in half gallons by filling the tank from zero by measure, marking each half gallon off on the scale and punching in the numbers afterwards. The gauge clips firmly onto the tank partition just forward of the filler cap aperture, so that it can be seen at a glance when the cap is removed.

191. Tank instrument panels

When replacing the instrument panel into the recess in the petrol tank, it is difficult to start the union nut for the oil pressure gauge. To prevent the nut slipping down out of reach, twist a rubber band or piece of insulating tape round the pipe an inch or so below the union.

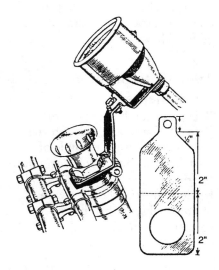

192. Speedometer mounting

This speedo bracket was made to fit a Model 9 Sunbeam. A piece of mild sheet steel 3/32 in. thick was cut into the shape shown in the sketch. The large hole fits over the top of the steering head below the damper, while the small one is for attaching the secondary bracket. This is a U-shaped steel strip fixed between the speedo cable nut and the fixing screw underneath the speedo head. The advantages of this arrangement are that the line of the speedo cable is almost dead straight, the speedo is easy to read, and the handlebars are left uncluttered.

193. Removing a chrome rim

Removing smooth chrome rims, such as round the top of a speedometer head, without damaging the chrome or the rim is a tricky task. One way is to cut a rubber band from an old inner tube, and stretch it over the rim. Sufficient grip should be given to allow the rim to be unscrewed. If not, the rubber sleeve will provide adequate protection from adjustable wrench jaws.

194. Waterproof instruments

Water can be kept out of ammeter and speedometer glasses by painting a couple of coats of clear nail varnish around the rim. Any grease or oil should be cleaned from the joint with methylated spirit before the varnish is applied.

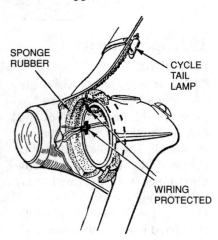

SPONGE RUBBER

CYCLE TAIL LAMP

WIRING PROTECTED

195. Fairing fit

Fitting a proprietary fairing, such as an Avon, to an unfaired machine can lead to an untidy mess unless a bit of care is taken. Here, the gap between the inside of the fairing and the top of the headlamp nacelle was filled by fixing a strip of sponge rubber to the fairing with adhesive. Improved instrument illumination was obtained by mounting a small stop lamp on the middle bolt connecting the screen to the fairing. Arranged to shine downward onto the instruments, it was fitted with an aluminium shield to prevent glare. The lamp was wired into the speedo lamp circuit. Extra care was taken that the extended cables into the fairing weren't allowed to chafe against the edge of the original headlamp mounting.

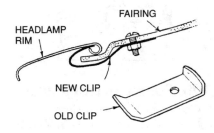

HEADLAMP RIM

FAIRING

NEW CLIP

OLD CLIP

196. Lamp rim retention

Many people have found that the standard headlamp rim clips are inadequate for holding the rim into a handlebar fairing. This idea from 1960 does away with the old clip in place of a surer design. Unlike the standard clip with its short 45 degree flange, the new clip has one end bent through 180 degrees to form a hook which locates under the rolled edge of the headlamp rim. With the rim pressed firmly into position the hole in the clip registers with that through the fairing, enabling the retaining screw to be inserted. The thread for the screw to engage is provided by the nut soldered onto the under-side of the clip.

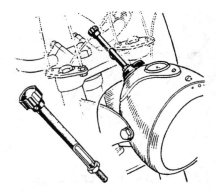

197. Switch accessibility

Operating a headlight switch once a handlebar screen has been fitted can be difficult at best and dangerous at worst. To overcome the problem, remove the switch knob securing screw and substitute it for a length of 2BA threaded rod, locked to the knob by a nut. The rod should be long enough to pass through a convenient slot cut in the screen. Protect it with a length of rubber tubing, and finish it off with a knurled knob for easy manipulation.

198. Leg shields

We all know that the gearing should be altered for sidecar use. But what about the effects of wind resistance on a solo? This advice came from BSA in 1956.

'Leg shields can have a much greater effect on performance than many riders realize, and can reduce the top speed of a model A10 by as much as 6 mph. This can be improved by fitting an engine sprocket with one tooth less than the original to reduce the gear ratios.'

199. Radiator repair

It sometimes happens that after long usage a radiator on a water-cooled machine springs a leak somewhere in the middle of one of the honeycombs. Even if the hole is accessible, the copper may be so weakened by gallons of hard water passing through it that the mending of one little leak may start another. The best thing is to get some copper tubing which will just push through the comb. Then saw off a length sufficient to reach from front to back of the radiator. Tin it over with solder until it is just a push fit and, having scraped the honeycomb until it is clean, push the tube through and apply a little solder at each end. The honeycomb will now be watertight, and the air will pass through almost as freely as before.

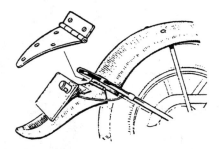

200. Hinged rear mudguards

Many pre-war machines had a hinged rear mudguard tail section to aid rear wheel removal. Certain gate hinges may be suitable as replacements for worn mudguard hinges, particularly as the long shank of the hinge will give the tail section extra support.

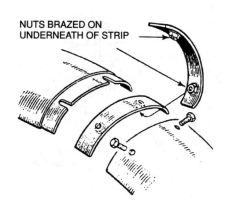

NUTS BRAZED ON UNDERNEATH OF STRIP

201. Bolted rear mudguard sections

The rear section of some rear mudguards (Norton and Velocette) unbolt, instead of hinge, to aid wheel removal – a system which has several disadvantages. The nuts underneath are awkward to get at because of the lack of clearance between wheel and mudguard. The bolt holes in the mudguard become elongated because of the stress on the fixing by vibration and countersunk because of the subsequent overtightening of the bolts. The fixing area also becomes distorted through repeated overtightening on the thin mudguard metal. This can be reduced by cutting a piece of mild steel strip and shaping it to fit across the underside of the joint between the two mudguard sections. Drill holes in the strip to coincide with the holes in the mudguard and weld nuts underneath. Cut away the holes in the main mudguard section to form slots. Loosely assemble the strip to the rear mudguard piece, slide into position with the main mudguard and tighten the bolts. The bolts only need to be slackened off from above to remove this section in future.

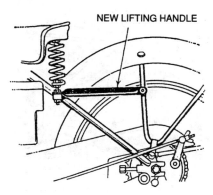

NEW LIFTING HANDLE

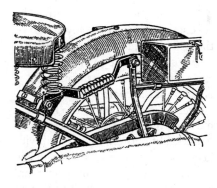

202. Side lifting handle

Many rigid machines with rear stands have a lifting handle formed by an extension of one of the stays across the rear mudguard. This idea of a side lifting handle allows the motor cycle to be pulled onto its stand while holding the handlebars, thus avoiding the risk of over-balancing. It was made from a piece of steel tubing to match the mudguard stays. Both ends were flattened at 90 degrees to each other; one end could then be bolted to the saddle spring bolt, the other to the vertical mudguard stay with the help of a clamp.

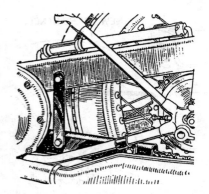

203. Lower chainguard

Few machines are fitted with a chainguard over the lower run of the rear chain, mainly because the chainguard is more to protect the rider and pillion from the moving chain than the chain from the elements. Tucked below the frame member, the lower chain presents no danger. But a lower chainguard will keep road dirt off the chain, and can be made easily from thin sheet metal and fitted unobtrusively. The sketch shows the front fitting attached to the upper chainguard. A preferable fixing point would be the frame lug, behind and above, to which the upper chainguard is attached.

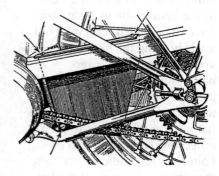

204. Lower chain shield

Alternatively, if your sheet metalwork is not up to a full chainguard, this flat shield fixed to the upper chainguard and the lower frame member is a reasonable compromise.

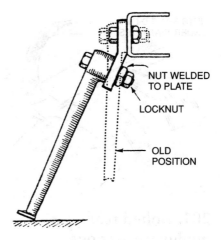

NUT WELDED TO PLATE

LOCKNUT

OLD POSITION

205. Prop stand improvement

This tip is to improve the propstand on a pre-war Francis-Barnett, but it will apply to many 30s machines fitted with short propstands. By bolting a small plate to the frame the pivot point was lowered below the frame, and the leg given more cant. The original ovalled fixing point was drilled out to accept a bigger bolt, and a nut was welded to the back of the plate in the new fixing position. The original stand and return spring were reused.

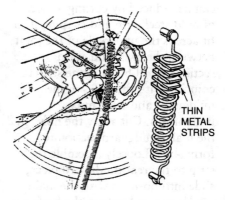

THIN METAL STRIPS

206. Removing a centre stand spring

To remove a spring under tension, such as a centre stand

spring, fill the spans between the coils with packing washers or coins when the spring is extended to full stretch.

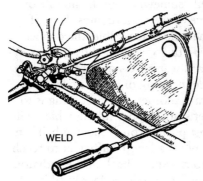

WELD

Tensioning the spring with the aid of a screwdriver and string loop also works, but pad the screwdriver point with rag to preserve paintwork, and mind your fingers.

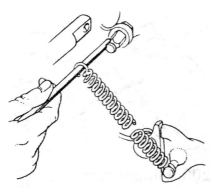

207. Refitting a centre stand spring

This tip for fitting springs on Ariel centre stands comes courtesy of the Selly Oak factory, but applies to almost any marque. A special tool was made from an 8 in. length of mild steel rod $\frac{5}{16}$ in. in diameter. A $\frac{1}{2}$ in. flat was filed at one end. At $\frac{3}{16}$ in. from the end, an indent was formed with a centre dot and drill a $\frac{1}{4}$ in., just deep enough to catch the tip of the stand spring peg. The rod can be pushed through the eye of the spring and the indent placed over the tip of the peg. On levering the spring open, the eye runs up the rod and lands on the peg. A similar tool can be made up for prop stands, but it may need a deeper indent.

208. A clanking centre stand

On a particular 1955 125 cc two-stroke, the centre stand, when raised, used to hit the bottom of the frame tube which went up to the seat pillar. The cure was to stuff a cork up the bottom of the tube, thus protecting the stand and the frame, and stopping an annoying noise. This is a problem common to many machines, if manifested in slightly different ways, and the cure is usually as simple. I prevented the centre stand from fouling the non-standard exhaust system on my Triumph Trident by sliding a spare kickstart rubber over the extended foot.

209. Footrest rubbers

To ease replacement of footrest or handlebar rubbers, moisten with a dab of petrol. Oil, grease and soap will help the rubber on, but also help it off again. Petrol will quickly evaporate once the rubber is in place.

SELF-TAPPING SCREWS INTO MUDGUARD

210. Footboard extension

Some LE Velocette owners found that the footboards were too short for their pillion passengers, who suffered from water run off from the front of the rear mudguard. A simple but workmanlike extension could be made from channel section aluminium shaped to fit over the original footboard, and light alloy sheeting between the footboard and the mudguard. The alloy sheet was riveted to the footboard and fastened to the mudguard with self-tapping screws.

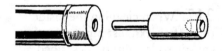

211. Tyre inflater

Finding a tyre inflater to complete a restoration is hard enough, but will it fit when you do find it? This idea from 1948 suggests the problem isn't new. Make up a distance piece from a short length of mild steel rod. Turn one end down on a lathe to form a socket capable of sliding into the bottom of the pump. Countersink a recess in the other end to clip onto the frame fixing.

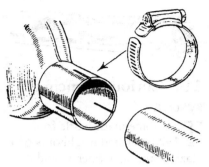

212. Exhaust sealing

Sealing motor cycle exhausts is a perennial problem, as many of the proprietary sealers available to the car world are excluded from motor cycling on grounds of appearance. Bolts distorted by heat may need replacing each time they are disturbed. Brass shim is invaluable as a packing aid, and can be reused time and again, but only if the tolerance between parts isn't too great. Here, the sloppy fit between exhaust pipe and silencer has been taken up by cutting three slots in the silencer stub, and tightening up with a worm screw clip.

However, one of the wide range of chromed exhaust clamps now on the market would improve on the appearance of the clip.

213. Silencer baffle

New baffles can be made for silencers from a piece of sheet steel. Cut a piece about 9 in. x 7 in., and punch 3/16 in. holes at regular intervals all over it. Roll the steel into a tube and feed it just into the end of the exhaust pipe. Slide the silencer over the lot, and tighten up in the normal way. Noise reduction will be even greater if the other end of the baffle is clamped shut before the silencer is replaced.

214. Curious silencing system

This home-made baffle from 1924 placated neighbours of a Hazlewood-Jap owner. Could it help early machines through future noise regulations? It consists of a long length of 1⅝ in. copper pipe fitted over the machine's exhaust pipe, and into this are knocked several lengths of electrician's conduit piping, which is about ½ in. diameter. The lengths of the pieces of conduit vary from 8 in. to 12 in.

215. Cleaning exhaust pipes

Many chroming plants are reluctant to rechrome exhaust systems because of the risk of deposits fouling their chrome bath. Here is a selection of ideas which may reduce their fears.

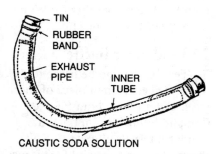

216. Enclose the exhaust pipe in an old inner tube which has had the valve cut out and one end sealed by a tin held in place with a rubber band. Fill the tube with a solution of 3 lb caustic soda to one gallon of water, and seal the other end likewise. Leave for half an hour, and wash off in clean water.

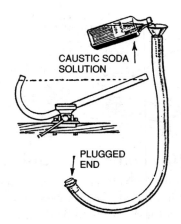

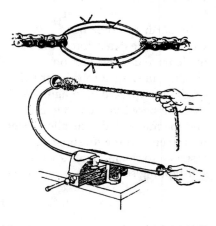

217. When cleaning the inside only of an exhaust pipe using the caustic soda solution described above, the pipe can be plugged at one end with a potato, or it can be held at an angle in the soft jaws of a vice as shown on the sketch, before being filled with the solution.

To loosen the carbon beforehand, connect two lengths of old drive chain with a ball of wire, and pull it backwards and forwards through the length of the pipe.

218. Removing burnt oil

Burnt oil can be removed from the outside of exhaust systems by applying petrol or methylated spirits with a cloth or stiff brush. To avoid damaging the chrome, do not use a wire brush (a plastic scrubbing pad may not scratch the chrome, but check it gently first). Buff up with chrome polish.

219. Protecting exhaust chrome

A blued exhaust pipe can sometimes be avoided if three or four strands of thin copper wire are wound tightly around the pipe as close to the exhaust port as possible; the wire efficiently dissipates heat.

220. Two-stroke exhaust cleaning

Carbon deposits in the exhaust will quickly affect the performance of a two-stroke. The Norman factory recommended cleaning the carbon out of the expansion chamber with a mixture of 3 lb caustic soda to one gallon of water, left to soak overnight. Rinse thoroughly with tap water before refitting.

221. Two-stroke silencer cleaning

In the 50s manufacturers recommended decoking two-stroke silencers by filling them with a hot caustic soda solution. This wasn't easy on models fitted with fishtails which were not detachable. The solution? 'I have found that after pushing the fishtail into a large potato, the silencer can be filled with hot caustic solution and left to stand – overnight if need be –without leakage.'

222. Burnt out

One drastic idea for removing stubborn carbon deposits from a two-stroke exhaust system was to pour about half-a-pint of paraffin into the pipe, and shake vigorously to ensure that the carbon becomes thoroughly soaked. The surplus paraffin is poured away, the pipe is propped against something fireproof, and a lighted twist of paper is dropped in to start the burning. After the pipe has cooled (it doesn't get hot enough to damage the plating) a few taps with a piece of wood leaves the interior beautifully clean.

Wheels, brakes and tyres

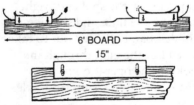

SLOTS FOR ADJUSTMENT

223. Checking wheel alignment

Over the 50 years of 'Hints and Tips' there were many suggestions for checking wheel alignment after adjusting the rear chain. Most followed the same theme of some sort of straight edge using a slotted board or taut string. The following method is the best for its combined simplicity and accuracy:

Select a long board with a straight edge, and cut any necessary notches for centre stands or other obstructions. Then select two pieces of hardwood (size 15 in. x 3 in.) with good straight edges, and cut two slots in each. Loosely attach the hardwood strips to the board in such a position as to line up with the wheels, and line them up using a taut string. Tighten the screws. Now check the wheel alignment by butting the hardwood strips up to the wheel rims. The advantages? Because the alignment is checked against the rims, the check will still be accurate if the machine is fitted with different size tyres. It doesn't matter if the board warps a bit during storage, the hardwood strips can be readjusted in their slots next time.

On the road, wheel alignment may be judged by straightening the handlebars, squatting down behind the rear wheel, and sighting through the two wheel rims. A centre-punch dot on one face of each chain adjuster nut hexagon will ease accurate adjustment.

224. Wheel balancing

When new tyres are being fitted, correct balance is essential to avoid dangerous handling and rapid tyre wear. Remove the brake linkages and chain, and use the frame/forks as a jig. Mount the wheel so that it can be spun freely, and ensure that neither bearings nor brakes are interfering with its movement. When an unbalanced wheel is spun, as soon as it loses momentum it will oscillate backwards and forwards until the heaviest part comes to rest at the

bottom. A perfectly balanced wheel will come to rest at a random position after spinning, and remain absolutely stationary without any movement in the reverse direction. If you cannot buy proprietary balancing weights for spoked wheels, balancing can be achieved by winding lead wire round a pair of adjacent spokes opposite the heaviest part. Do not use cored solder as the flux may corrode the spoke.

225. Spindle clamp

A simple way to loosen front wheel brake plate nuts is to use the front fork as a vice. Take out the wheel completely, place it alongside the fork and clamp the spindle end (opposite the brake plate) to the base of the fork leg.

226. Rear wheel removal

It not usually considered advisable to tilt motor cycles over on the centre stand too much while trying to remove the rear wheel, because of the risk of bending a footrest, scratching a silencer or spilling various nasty liquids. However, Ariel were happy to recommend tilting their 50s models over onto the nearside foot of the centre stand in order to take out the rear wheel without removing the tail section of the rear mudguard. This advice follows for many machines, particularly more recently when rear mudguards tended to be in one piece.

227. Rear wheel nuts

Many factories fitted the rear wheel to the hub by three or four large nuts. In the normal course of events these should be removed by a box or socket spanner. AMC, at least, approved of the idea of making a saw-cut across the top of each nut so that it could be screwed home without the bulky spanner. This could be useful on the road. However, AMC stressed the fact that the nuts must be finally tightened fully by means of a good fitting spanner.

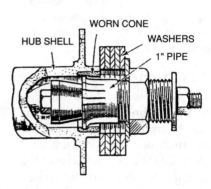

HUB SHELL · WORN CONE · WASHERS · 1" PIPE

228. Removing wheel bearings

This tip is to remove cones of front wheel hub bearings from a Francis-Barnett. A similar tool could be made up for other models. Select a piece of pipe about 2 in. long which will slide easily into the worn cone. Thread one end; burr the other end over with a hammer to form a flange which will only just go into the cone. The flange end is then cut with a hacksaw down its length to a depth of ½ in. eight times to form 16 segments, which should then be case hardened. A rod of steel ¾ in. long is drilled down its centre to take a ⅜ in. bolt, and tapered on a grindstone to fit into the 16 segments.

Loosely assemble the tool by pushing the tapered rod into the segments, and finger-tightening its ⅜ in. bolt. Place the segments flange into the cone, and tighten this bolt up fully so that the

segments open out and grip the worn ring of the cone. Place a spacer over the threaded pipe large enough to accommodate the cone (large washers will do) and tighten up the pipe nut and its washer. Continuing to tighten this nut will draw the damaged cone out.

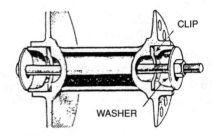

CLIP · WASHER

229. Pressing in wheel bearings

A threaded rod, two nuts and two stout washers can be used to press in bearings, such as the front wheel cups shown in the sketch. This will ensure even seating and no risk of damage from mallet blows, but the washers must be robust enough to avoid concaving.

230. Adjusting front wheel bearings

When adjusting taper roller front wheel bearings, the hubs are correctly adjusted when there is just a trace of side play at the wheel rim – approximately 1⁄64 in. is correct.

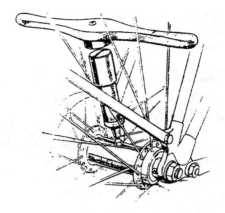

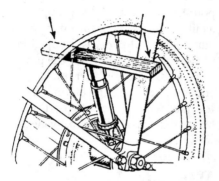

231. Greasing wheel hubs

Wheel hubs can be greased by placing the gun on the nipple inside the spokes at right angles to the hub, and slipping a wooden bar, hollowed out to take the end of the gun, through the spokes. The operation of the grease gun is now simpler and less messy.

232. Smear the fork ends with grease before refitting the rear wheel. It helps it in, and keeps the wheel spindle and chain adjuster threads in good condition.

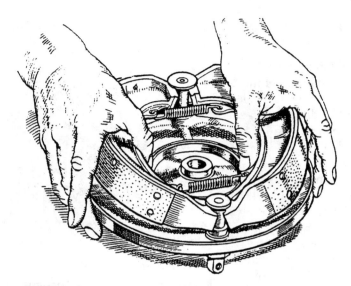

233. Brake shoe assembly

This method of refitting brake shoes is recommended in most factory manuals of the 60s onwards, but doesn't seem to have been suggested much before then. One earlier tip involved fiddling about with bits of string to extend the springs – not very practical considering the depth of hook on brake shoe springs.

Hook the return springs in position on the shoes, then hold the shoes at an angle to form a V over the brake plate. Lower the V so that the shoe ends take up a position on each side of the cam and fulcrum, then press down firmly with both hands. The shoes should snap into place.

234. Brake drum alignment

After assembling the brake shoes onto the back plate, they should be centralized in the drum. Slacken off the pivot nut, apply the brake hard with the handlebar lever, and retighten the nut.

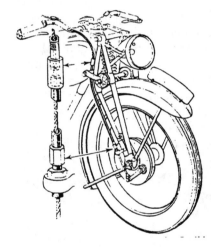

235. Front brake efficiency

Front brake efficiency can be enhanced by replacing as much of the flexible outer cable as possible with rigid small bore steel tubing, as it avoids the contraction in length which takes place when the brake is applied. The sketch shows an arrangement fitted to a Model 18 Norton, where the length of flexible outer cable was reduced to 18 in. The detail is of one of the adaptors necessary when linking the tube to the remaining outer cable.

236. Twin front brakes

Royal Enfield gave this advice for the front brakes on their 1956 models, but it applies to balancing most twin front brakes. When adjusting cables of the dual front brake, watch carefully to see that both sets of shoes come into operation simultaneously. If, for example, when applying the brake by means of the handlebar lever, the cam lever on the right side of the hub continues to move after the lever on the left side has reached the end of its travel, the cable adjustment should be tightened until both cam lever settings are in unison.

237. Twin rear brakes

To check both rear brakes are operating effectively (such as on a Vincent), tighten the wing-nuts fully home and then slacken them both an equal number of turns until the wheel is just free to rotate. This setting will ensure that both brakes operate together.

238. Scored drum

If a brake drum is badly scored it is useless merely to fit new linings. The drum, too, should be renewed or skimmed. If skimmed, the new brake linings should be thicker than standard to compensate for the extra depth.

239. Brake linings

Brake linings should be checked for wear periodically, and replaced before they get anywhere near the rivets. Otherwise the drum itself will be damaged. Some firms now bond new linings onto the shoes with glue, and they will be able to quote a pile of scientific proof that suggests not only is this as good as riveting, it is probably better. However, the number of instances I know first-hand of bonded linings coming off the shoe prevents me from ever trusting or recommending it. Brake lining material can become glazed before the linings need replacing. The glaze can be removed carefully with fine emery cloth.

240. Cleaning brake linings

Boiling linings in a strong solution of household detergent will remove grease unaffected by petrol. The same tip can be used for clutch plates. Make sure all detergent is washed off, and dry thoroughly before re-using the brakes. If petrol has been used as a cleaning agent, do not remove it by setting it alight as this may fuse the wire bonding.

241. Harsh brakes

Grabbing brakes may be cured by chamfering the leading edges of the shoe linings with a coarse file.
WARNING: brake linings contain asbestos, so do this outside, wear a face mask, and clean up filings with a damp cloth.
Another reason for the harshness could be that the brake drum has become worn or warped, which would require having it skimmed on a lathe or replaced. However, the trouble may simply be due to dirt or grit in the brake drum, in which case a thorough clean would cure the problem. Before reassembly, the cam faces, cam spindle and bearing should be smeared sparingly with high melting point grease.

242. Fitting new brake linings

Remove the old linings with a small chisel by cutting off the ends of the rivets on the under-side of the shoes, and by driving out the rivets with a punch. Wrap a new lining round one of the shoes, and mark on the lining the position of two rivets near one end by means of a pencil or bradawl, the point of which is passed through the holes. At the positions marked, drill holes of the correct size for the rivets, and countersink them so that the rivet heads bed down well below the surface of the lining. The depth of the countersink should be half the thickness of the lining. Push the rivets through the lining and shoe, and cut them off so that they protrude an ⅛ in. Rivet them carefully in position. Remember that brake linings contain asbestos, so do not breathe in the dust.

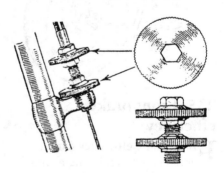

243. Front brake

This tip is to make early Bowden cable adjusters adjustable by hand. Brass discs of about 1 in. in diameter (depending on available clearance) and ³⁄₁₆ in. thick were drilled with an ⅛ in. bit, then the hole was filed into a hexagon to slide over the Bowden adjuster. The disc was then soldered to the adjuster nut, and

the edge milled with a hacksaw for extra grip.

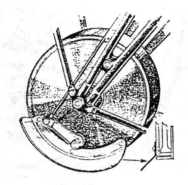

244. Rain deflector

Early front drum brake designs did not exclude water, nor were the brakes fitted with water deflectors. Straightforward water deflectors can be cut from the rim of a frying pan of the correct circumference and bolted or riveted to the brake plate. If cut neatly and properly finished it need not look out of place.

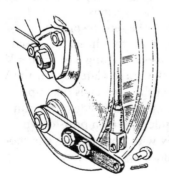

245. Extra leverage

Extra leverage can be obtained on a front brake if the operating arm is lengthened by an extension piece. This can be made to look neat, and will exert no extra strain on the control cable or nipples.

246. Reversed cam lever

It is possible for the cam lever on a brake to travel past the right-angle position before the linings need replacing. If the cam lever is removed, reversed and replaced, the cable will be too short. To save making up a new cable, a spare chain connecting link can be used to extend the existing cable to the cam lever.

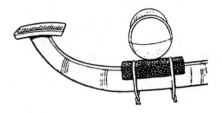

247. Brake pedal setting

Some earlier machines do not have adjusters for the rear brake pedal position. They can be lowered by fixing a pad between the pedal and the footrest. This will also protect the pedal from damage where it hits the footrest.

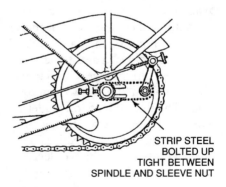

STRIP STEEL
BOLTED UP
TIGHT BETWEEN
SPINDLE AND SLEEVE NUT

248. Better braking

If the brake cam spindle nut is replaced by a sleeve nut, and a piece of mild steel strip (1 x ⅛ in.) is drilled and fitted as shown in the sketch, a useful outrigger support is provided and side pull

on the brake cam bearing reduced. This support, fitted as standard by some factories such as Velocette, will also prevent any tendency for the shoe plate to flex when the brake is applied.

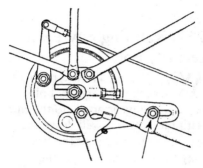

249. Rear brake anchorage

When setting back the rear wheel, don't forget to take a glance at the method of rear brake anchorage. On later machines the old slotted arrangement gave way to rigid bolting. Unless the bolt is slackened off before the chain adjusters are rotated, there is a risk that the anchor plate will be bent. On rod operated brakes, adjust the brake after moving the wheel backwards or forwards.

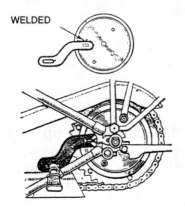

WELDED

250. Worn rear brake plate

This solution for correcting a worn brake plate locating stud

is intended for a 1936 Ariel, but a similar arrangement could be adapted to fit many models with this problem. Cut the stud away from the frame. Drill and cut a piece of mild steel to the shape shown in the sketch, and weld it to the brake plate. Secure the slotted end of the plate to the frame by means of the pillion footrest bolt.

251. When pins holding brake rods or gear linkages become worn in their housings, they can be bushed out by using the hollow rollers from an old drive chain.

252. Coupled brakes

For the best results with coupled brakes, the front wheel brake should come into operation slightly before the rear wheel brake. There are two reasons for this: first, that there is a certain amount of spring in the cable used for operating the front brake. Second, as the brakes are applied the weight of the machine is thrown forward, thus improving the adhesion of the front tyre and detracting from that of the rear tyre. Always check the adjustment of both brakes after resetting the tension of the rear chain.

253. Removing a tyre

When removing a tyre, insert a lever three or four inches from the valve and, maintaining pressure on this lever, push the wall of the tyre into the well of the rim all the way round. Then insert a second lever on the other side of the valve. Pushing the wall well into the rim will negate the need for a third lever; the cover should come away with the use of only fingers.

254. Refitting a tyre

When refitting, start by pushing the edge of the cover over the rim at the point farthest away from the valve; leave the valve portion to the last. Smear the wall of the tyre with soap to help it slide into place. Slight air pressure in the tube will ensure it is not twisted. It may be easier to pump up the tube to untwist it and then let out the air again before proceeding. This will minimize the risk of pinching the tube with a lever. Once the tyre is on, check that the moulding line on the cover is equidistant from the rim all the way round; otherwise the wheel will not run true and rapid tyre wear and imbalance will result. If it is not true, either bounce the wheel up and down on the floor, or overinflate the tyre for a short time. Both methods should push the tyre into position.

255. Last on, first off

To help remember whether the valve should be tackled first or last, famous trials rider Roy Peplow used to think of stowing his bike on the Isle of Man steamer. If he was last on, he would be first off. In other words, if you're putting a tyre on a rim, deal with the valve area last; if you're taking one off, tackle it first.

256. Puncture location

A good aid to puncture location is, when fitting a new tyre, to position it on the rim so that a certain point (such as the 'X' in the size, or the first letter of the maker's name) is adjacent to the valve hole. If on removing the tyre a nail is embedded in the tyre wall or the tread a quarter circle from the 'X', the puncture should be in a corresponding position in the tube. And, in reverse, if the puncture is located in the tube, you can judge which particular cut or hole in the cover is responsible, even if the offending nail has worked itself out.

257. Refitting a tyre with security bolts

When fitting a new tyre to a wheel with security bolts, leave the bolts attached to the rim with the nuts run well down the stem. The first edge of the tyre may be fitted without paying attention to the security bolts, as they will easily fit in the correct position between tyre and rim. Once the second edge is fitted, insert two tyre levers under it either side of the security bolt, close enough to lift the tyre edge with one hand. This will give room for the other hand to seat the security bolt in its proper place inside the cover.

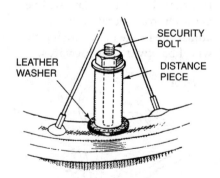

258. Security bolt tip

One way of saving precious seconds when a tyre has to be removed in a hurry is to fit a distance piece to the security bolt, thereby greatly reducing the length of thread over which the nut has to be screwed. The distance piece should be a length of light alloy tube separated from the rim by a fibre washer, and from the nut by a flat steel washer. If the nut, washer and tube are brazed into one unit, they are less likely to get lost on the grass verge.

259. Rim tape security

New rim tapes usually have no provision for security bolts. Any attempt to cut a hole for the bolt with a sharp knife is likely to cause a jagged tear when the tape is stretched in position. To avoid this, punch the hole with the correct diameter bolt, preferably with a convex end. Incidentally, security bolts shouldn't be overtightened.

260.
Never use plastic insulating tape instead of a proper rim tape. When the tyre is inflated, the plastic tape will be pressed into knife edges that will cut through the tube.

261. Tinned tyre levers

To protect enamelled or chromed wheel rims when using tyre levers, the levers can be tinned. The best way is to clean the levers with petrol, melt a bar of plumbers' solder in a suitable container, dip the levers in flux and then in solder, and allow them to cool. The thin film of soft solder effectively prevents scratching.

An easier, but less effective, method is to cover the tyre levers with a layer of insulating tape.

262. Tyre pressures

Tyre pressures vary between make of machine and tyre; there is no simple rule to follow, as the required pressure is related to what the machine is being used for and what weight it is likely to carry. For example, a hard tyre is preferable for speed work in warm conditions, a soft tyre for trials work. With older machines it is often difficult to find factory recommended pressures, but it is worth asking the advice of the tyre supplier. Add a few pounds to the rear tyre when carrying a pillion or heavy luggage.

263. Tyre pressure points

A tyre which wears faster in the middle of the tread than at the sides indicates that too high a pressure is being used. Conversely if the sides wear faster, the pressure is too low. Though it is possible if the machine is being used for long distance touring on motorways that the centre of the tyre will wear quicker at the correct pressure, because of the constant fast speeds, heavy load, and lack of cornering.

A rough guide to carrying heavy loads is to add 2 psi to the front tyre and 8 psi to the rear for a pillion, though if possible the correct pressures for each machine should be checked with the manufacturer's handbook.

A tyre tread which wears at one side more than the other suggests that either the rear wheel is incorrectly aligned, or that the frame or forks are bent.

264. Care of tyres

Rub well into the tyre a mixture of equal parts of glycerine and water, and dust over with French chalk. This mixture makes the rubber soft and pliable, and if applied once a month will prevent cracking or splitting of the rubber. (Could this tip be used to rejuvenate old, hardened tyres?)

265. Inflation tips

Before topping up the tyre with air, depress the valve core momentarily to blow out any grit which may be lodged in the valve body; if this is not done the grit will be blown into the tube and may get under the core seating. Always give a few sharp strokes of the pump to force any grit clear before screwing the connector onto the valve. And remember to replace the valve cap.

266. Tube fitting

Especially with a narrow section rim, a method of persuading the valve through its hole in the rim is to insert a lever under both edges of the tyre. Using the far edge of the rim as a pivot, heave both tyre walls clear of the rim well. The valve can now be slipped through its hole and be kept in place by the collar wound on a few turns. On releasing the lever the remainder of the tube can be tucked in.

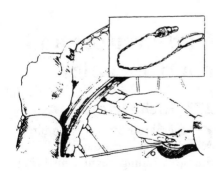

267. Tube fitting tool

One of the most difficult aspects of fitting a new tyre is persuading the valve stem on the tube to go through its hole in the rim. This special tool could help in a well-equipped workshop. Remove the plunger from an old

valve core and solder a wire to the threaded portion. Screw this core into the valve of the tube. By feeding the cable through the hole in the rim, the valve can be pulled into position.

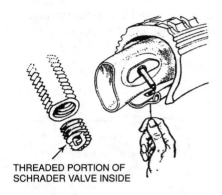

THREADED PORTION OF SCHRADER VALVE INSIDE

268. Drill a hole in the top of a spare tyre valve, screw this into the tube, and feed a length of wire through the rim hole. A bit of wiggling will soon persuade the valve to emerge through the rim.

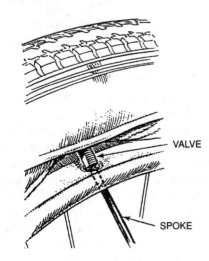

VALVE

SPOKE

269. Another solution is to use a spoke. Some heavy-gauge spokes have the same diameter and thread as a Schrader valve. With the valve core removed, manoeuvre the tube roughly into position, push the spoke through the hole in the rim and thread it into the valve. With a bit of manipulation the valve can be pulled through the rim.

270. Perhaps the simplest method of fetching the valve through the hole in the rim is to push the pump connector backwards up through the hole, screw the pump end into the valve, and use it to feed through the valve.

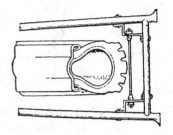

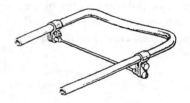

271. Nail catcher

There were several makes of proprietary nail catchers on the market 50 years ago. This tip proves that they were quite easy to make at home. For the rear wheel, two brackets of thin strip steel are welded or attached by screws to the rear stand. Each bracket has a slot wide enough to admit a spoke head, and long enough to accommodate the wheel movement resulting from adjusting the chain. The catcher is made from a wheel spoke cut to the right length, threaded both ends, and attached to the bracket with two spoke nipples.

For the front wheel two lengths of strip steel are bent to form clips to fit round the front wheel stand or mudguard stay. They are drilled twice to take fixing bolts and spoke nipples. The clips are adjusted on the stay to give an ⅛ in. clearance from the tyre, tightened up, and the catcher spoke fixed in position.

272. Tubes punctured from inside

The discovery of a puncture on the rim side (as opposed to the tread side) of an inner tube implies one of the following causes:
1. Tube pinched in fitting.
2. Tube chafed through on spoke heads, owing to the absence of rim tape or proud-fitting spoke head.
3. Tube chafed through a twist in fitting.
4. Tube has been run under-inflated, and has nipped between rim and cover.

Carburettors and control cables

273. Rich mixture?

General indications of an ultra-rich mixture are heavy, thumpy running, regular misfiring (eight stroking in the case of a four-stroke engine), black smoke at the exhaust, and soot on the plug. A weak mixture is apparent by spitting back through the carburettor, a tendency for the engine to knock readily, and by the plug showing signs of heat.

274. Choke check

Before altering carburettor settings, verify the correctness of the fuel feed, stop air leaks, check over ignition and valve operation and timing. Then, if at a particular throttle opening the choke is partially closed and the engine goes better, weakness is indicated; if the running is worse richness is indicated. It is not correct to cure a rich mixture at half throttle by fitting a smaller main jet because the main jet may be correct for power at full throttle; the proper thing to do is to lower the needle.

275. Low speed richness

Too rich a mixture at low engine speeds can point to a loose pilot jet (this is a taper fit onto its seat). Any slackness will permit fuel to pass in addition to that governed by the actual jet. Don't force it though; the jet should be tight, but no more than that.

276. Heavy fuel consumption

The last thing to suspect is the main jet because, if the correct jet was fitted initially, no amount of petrol flow will wear it larger. A gradual rise in consumption during average running would indicate a worn needle jet, enlarged by a sloppy throttle needle clip. The throttle needle is unlikely to wear, though it may be bent. So, when replacing a needle jet change the needle clip at the same time, and check the needle for straightness by rolling it on a sheet of glass.

277. Slow tick-over

When adjusting the slow-running mixture remember to finish the job by resetting the throttle stop. Although the setting for slow-running affects the mixture strength only at low speeds, so much mileage is covered in towns that unnecessary pilot jet richness makes a big contribution to heavy fuel consumption.

278. Heady mixture

At high altitudes an engine will show signs of rich mixture, and the rarified air will result in loss of power. For normal mountain pass storming there is no need to make carburettor adjustments, and the power drop will not be enough to worry about, but these figures will be of interest to Alpine and Himalayan travellers.

At 3000 ft the mixture should be about 5 per cent weaker than at sea level; at 6000 ft, about 9 per cent; and at 9000 ft, about 13 per cent.

Power loss is about 10 per cent at 3000 ft; 20 per cent at 6000 ft; and 30 per cent at 9000ft.

For Triumph TRW owners planning that lifetime trip to China, Her Majesty's User's Handbook gives a 22 per cent power loss at 5000 ft and 40 per cent at 10,000 ft. Hard luck!

279. Rule-of-thumb mixture guide

Heavy lumpy running with, usually, black smoke (not the blue of too much oil) from the exhaust, indicates richness. When the mixture is weak the running is erratic, and may be accompanied by spitting back through the carburettor. Another indication is firing in the silencer with the throttle closed and the engine on the over-run.

280. Spark plug test

When testing for mixture strengths at high speeds by judging the spark plug colour, don't come to a standstill with the engine running slowly or allow it to tick over. It is best to kill the engine on the ignition cut-out, get into neutral, and coast in.

281. Twin mixture

Plug reading should only be treated as a rough guide as it can be misleading. For instance, by examining the plugs of a parallel twin it might appear that the right hand cylinder is running slightly richer than the left. On a twin-carb engine this may be so – but there is another factor to be considered. On most twins the main oil feed to the crankshaft is from the timing side and, consequently, that cylinder is likely to get a shade more oil than the other. Therefore, the plug deposit is possibly the dark carbon of burnt oil rather than the soot of richness.

282. Amal carburettors

Amal carburettors are straightforward, workmanlike instruments which can be readily adjusted to obtain fuel economy.

Instructions for tuning the Type 276 also apply to the later Monobloc and Concentric. The basic difference between these three designs is the position of the float chamber. In normal circumstances it will be found that the best all round settings for performance are those recommended by the manufacturers of a machine, with the idling individually adjusted to suit a particular engine by means of the pilot air screw and the throttle stop screw.

283. Amal Type 276 carburettor

The Amal Type 276 was a pre-war design with a separate float chamber. The main jet screws into the bottom of the needle jet. It is calibrated to indicate the number of cubic centimetres of petrol that will

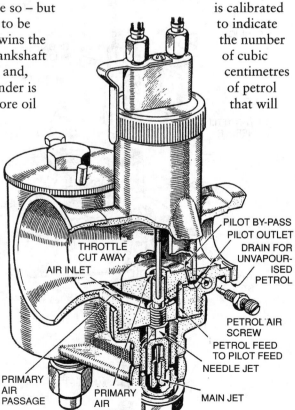

THROTTLE CUT AWAY
AIR INLET
PRIMARY AIR PASSAGE
PRIMARY AIR CHOKE
PILOT BY-PASS
PILOT OUTLET
DRAIN FOR UNVAPOURISED PETROL
PETROL AIR SCREW
PETROL FEED TO PILOT FEED
NEEDLE JET
MAIN JET

flow through the orifice under given conditions in one minute. A jet stamped with the number 140 will pass 140 cc, and it follows that the smaller the number the smaller the jet and vice versa.

284. Remote floats on Amal carburettors

Remote float Amal carburettors could be supplied with one of three thicknesses of mixing chamber union nuts. They were usually supplied with the middle one. The thinner one would have the effect of raising the level of the float chamber, providing a greater

reserve of fuel for snap throttle openings or for hilly work, such as in trials. Finer adjustments can be obtained by using varying thicknesses of fibre washer inside the nut.

285. Stuck lids

Stubborn remote float chamber lids can be removed by using a leather strap and a pair of pincers as a makeshift gentle pipe-wrench.

286. Amal Monobloc carburettor

This exploded diagram of the Monobloc, introduced in 1955, clearly indicates its constructional features. The float chamber is now part of the main body of the carburettor, instead of being separate. The main and needle jets screw into the ends of the jet holder. The pilot jet is detachable, and the throttle slide is guided internally on the jet block.

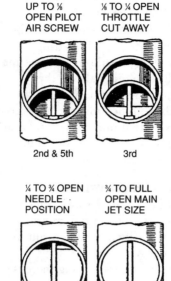

SEQUENCE OF TUNING

UP TO ⅛ OPEN PILOT AIR SCREW — 2nd & 5th

⅛ TO ¼ OPEN THROTTLE CUT AWAY — 3rd

¼ TO ¾ OPEN NEEDLE POSITION — 4th

¾ TO FULL OPEN MAIN JET SIZE — 1st

287. Amal mixture strength

It is important to remember the influence that each variable has on the mixture. If one has constantly in mind that (a) the pilot air screw controls the mixture up to ⅛ throttle opening, (b) the throttle cutaway from ⅛ to ¼, (c) the throttle needle from ¼ to ¾, and (d) the main jet from ¾ to full throttle, the effect of changes from standard settings can be anticipated fairly accurately. Further, it is a simple matter to decide where to start in altering carburettor settings.

To take an extreme case, it is a waste of time fitting a smaller main jet if economy at 30 mph is required. At that speed the throttle is less than a quarter open and the major influence on mixture strength comes from the throttle cutaway. It should not be inferred from the Amal instructions that

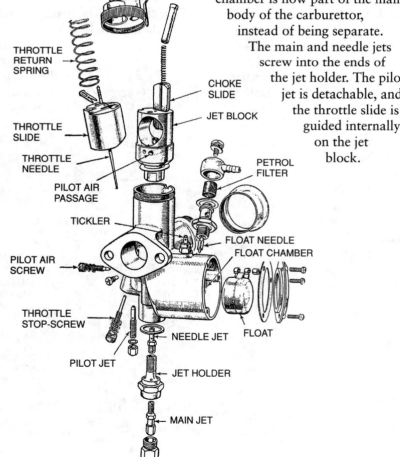

THROTTLE RETURN SPRING

THROTTLE SLIDE

THROTTLE NEEDLE

PILOT AIR PASSAGE

TICKLER

PILOT AIR SCREW

THROTTLE STOP-SCREW

PILOT JET

CHOKE SLIDE

JET BLOCK

PETROL FILTER

FLOAT NEEDLE
FLOAT CHAMBER

NEEDLE JET

FLOAT

JET HOLDER

MAIN JET

mixture control by pilot air screw, throttle valve cutaway, throttle needle position and main jet takes place in clear-cut stages. It does not. There is a certain amount of overlap, and it will be found, for instance, that an over-rich pilot air screw setting will cause a measure of heavy fuel consumption, though the machine may be driven for long periods on half throttle. However, these stages of mixture control are the key to the methods used in tuning.

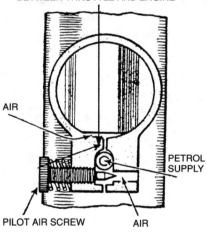

PILOT MIXTURE SUPPLY HOLE
BETWEEN THROTTLE AND ENGINE

AIR

PETROL
SUPPLY

PILOT AIR SCREW   AIR

288. Satisfactory idling on an Amal

At its business end the pilot air screw is tapered. Turning the screw clockwise brings the taper closer into the air orifice and gives a richer slow-running mixture; turning the screw in the other direction weakens the mixture. When making this adjustment the best results are achieved by co-ordinating the throttle stop setting. The only point to watch is that there is enough slack in the cable to allow the throttle valve to seat on the head of the stop screw.

Further, it must be remembered that satisfactory idling will never be obtained if there are air leaks between the carburettor and the combustion chamber, or if there are ignition faults. Once the desired tickover has been obtained, the slack in the cable can be taken up by means of the adjuster in the outer casing or at the top of the carburettor.

289. Amal throttle valve markings

Throttle valves are identified by markings such as ⅚, ⅝ and so on. The first figure identifies the type of valve with its type of carburettor. The second figure gives the depth of the cutaway in $\frac{1}{16}$ths of an inch. Thus, a ⅚ valve has a $\frac{5}{16}$ in. cutaway, and a ¾ valve has a ¼ in. cutaway. The deeper the cutaway the weaker will be the mixture.

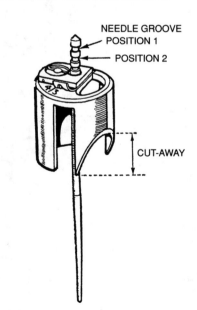

NEEDLE GROOVE
POSITION 1

POSITION 2

CUT-AWAY

290. Amal – weaker or richer?

The final adjustment in the sequence is that of the throttle needle position. Needles are

tapered and have five notches at the top end. The needle operates in the needle jet through which the fuel passes up into the mixing chamber. A spring clip located in the notch selected attaches the needle to the throttle valve, and the needle thus moves up and down with the throttle. Putting the clip in a notch nearer the top of the needle lowers the needle relative to the throttle and results in a weaker mixture. Raising the needle has the reverse effect.

291. Tuning twin engines with twin carburettors – setting the valves:

First of all, slacken the throttle stop screw valves and put the twistgrip in the shut-off position to allow the throttle to shut off. There should be a slight backlash in the cables which can be obtained by screwing in the cable adjusting screws on top of the carburettor. Then, with the handlebars in the normal position, and with the throttles closed, adjust the cable adjusting screws so that on the slightest opening of the twistgrip, both throttle valves begin to open simultaneously.

To make an exact check on the simultaneous throttle opening, wait until all other adjustments have been made. Then, shut the twistgrip back so that the throttles are resting on the throttle stop screws. Insert the fingers into the air intakes and press them on the throttles; with the other hand gently open the twistgrip and feel that the throttles lift off their stops at the same time.

292. Tuning twin engines with twin carburettors – running adjustments

Main jet sizes are selected by checking the effect of the mixture on the spark plugs after taking a run at full throttle over a straight piece of road, preferably under load. You don't need to be in top gear. The smallest pair of jets that give the best maximum speed is usually correct, provided that the plugs do not show any signs of excessive heat. It might be that for really critical tuning one carburettor will require a slightly different jet size from the other.

293. Slow running

For slow running, set the twistgrip to make the engine run slowly but just faster than at tickover. Then gently screw in the throttle stops to just hold the valves in that position, and return the twistgrip into the shut position, leaving the engine running on the throttle stops. The next thing to do is to set each carburettor to obtain the idling by screwing down the throttle stop screws and adjusting the pilot air screws accordingly.

294. Pilot jet

Regarding the setting of the pilot jets, a fairly satisfactory method is to detach one spark plug lead, and set the pilot air adjusting screw on the other cylinder as a single unit, reversing the process for the other cylinder. It may be found that when both leads are connected to the spark plugs, the engine runs slightly quicker than desirable, in which case a slight readjustment of the throttle stop screws will put this right. It is important that the speed

of idling on both cylinders is approximately the same, as this will either make or mar the smoothness of the get-away on the initial opening of the throttle.

295. Regarding the lower end of the throttle range, which is always the more difficult to set, one can only take excessive pains to make quite sure that the control cables are perfectly adjusted, without any excessive backlash or difference in the amount of backlash between one carburettor and another. Otherwise one throttle slide will be out of phase with the other, resulting in lumpy running. It is essential with twin carburettors

that the throttle slides are a good fit in the bodies, and also that there is no suspicion of air leaks at either of the flange attachments to the cylinder.

296. Amal concentric

The sketch shows the Amal Mk 1 Concentric carburettor which is ideal for a twin set-up. Earlier Monoblocs had their float chambers mounted on one side, which either made them awkward to adjust when paired, or more costly to manufacture when handed. The Concentric overcame these problems by positioning the float chamber underneath the body of the carburettor.

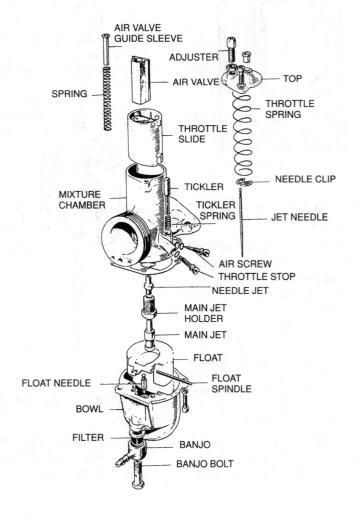

297. Twin carb tuning – the Douglas way

A Douglas owner found this method quite satisfactory for setting up his machine's twin carburettors in 1951:

'The Douglas is put on the centre stand with the rear wheel clear of the ground. The engine is started and allowed to warm up for a few minutes. One of the gears is then engaged (usually second), the throttle opened a certain amount, and a note made of the speedometer reading with one plug disconnected. Without altering the throttle position, I replace the disconnected plug cap and remove the other one; the speedometer reading should be the same. If not, the required adjustments are made. This process can be repeated for various throttle settings except for very slow running. A good tickover can be adjusted with both pots firing.'

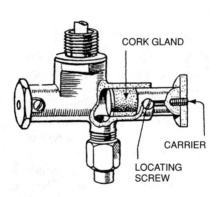

298. Leaking petrol tap – early type

The Ewarts reserve tap is common to many machines, and it relies on cork glands to prevent petrol leakage along the plungers. Each plunger is screwed into a carrier for the cork gland. The carrier is tightened to shorten the length of the gland and thus expand its diameter and make it a tighter fit in the tap body. Usually, a turn or so of the carrier (when the plunger is withdrawn by slackening off the locating screw) will remedy a leak, but there is a limit to the range of adjustment. If necessary new cork glands can be obtained.

299. Leaking petrol tap – later type

Later Ewarts taps are a single unit and more awkward to renovate. Before embarking on needless expense it is worth boiling the tap to see if the cork swells. And before buying just a new plunger check that the body hasn't worn oval. If it has, this idea from 1960 might do the trick:

'Take a clutch cork for flawlessness, and drill it carefully to fit the plunger. Use a smear of petroleum jelly to ease it into the barrel if necessary. The extra thickness of this type of cork should cancel out the tap's ovality, and be flexible enough not to be too stiff to operate.'

300. Villiers carburettors

Villiers carburettors resemble Amal instruments in that they embody a throttle slide and variable needle jet and operate on a multiphase principle. However,

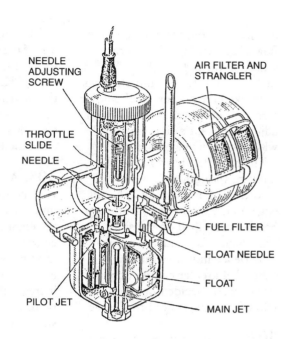

Villiers employed an annular float surrounding the centre-piece or jet holder. The Junior carburettor fitted to 98 cc engines is of simpler design than the larger types. Its main jet is simply a hole in the wall of the centre-piece and so cannot be varied, whereas on the remaining models it is separate and, except in the case of the S22, screws into the centre-piece. The S22 – fitted to the 249 cc twin and the 173 cc 2L – has its jet in the bottom of the float bowl. Different main jets are available for the larger carburettors, but nothing will be gained by fitting a smaller size unless the mixture is appreciably rich above three-quarters throttle – indicated by a tendency to four-stroking.

301. Villiers junior

On the Junior and on all pre-1954 carburettors there is no separate pilot system; the slow-running supply is drawn from the needle jet. S19, 22 and 25 models have a pilot jet which projects downward from the body into the float chamber. The air metering screw, on the right of the carburettor, is turned anti-clockwise to weaken the mixture; it should be screwed out ⅛ turn at a time when adjusting, as far as is compatible with good starting and idling.

The throttle slide governs the mixture strength from ⅛ to ¼ throttle and has a cutaway lower edge on the intake side. Cutaway height is stamped on the slide, the units being sixteenths of an inch. Experience indicates that, in general, a greater cutaway than standard, as decided by the manufacturers, is not practicable.

302. On all carburettors except the S22, the taper needle (which controls the mixture from ¼ to ¾ throttle) is held up by a light spring against an adjusting screw in the throttle slide. Clockwise rotation of the screw lowers the needle and so weakens the mixture. The thread has 32 tpi, so that one turn moves the needle ¹⁄₃₂ in. Weakening can be taken as far as is possible without a marked adverse effect on performance, but a quarter-turn at a time is the maximum recommended.

303. A five-groove needle with wire clip location is a feature of the S22 carburettor; the usual setting has the clip in the fourth groove from the top. Because of the intervals between the grooves it is unlikely that a weaker setting than normal will be found practicable.

304. Some earlier carburettors are of the two-lever pattern on which the needle is raised by a second handlebar control to richen the mixture for starting. This scheme was superseded by an air slide or a shutter-type strangler embodied in the air filter.

305. A final word of warning: with petroil lubrication, a weaker mixture means less oil drawn into the engine. It is unlikely that the engine will run satisfactorily on a mixture lean enough to affect lubrication but, if in doubt, increase the oil content in the petroil mixture slightly – from the standard 1 in 20 to, say, 1 in 16.

306. Pre-war Villiers carburettors

After long service the taper needle which controls the size of the jet on Villiers carburettors will show signs of wear. The resulting rich mixture will be apparent by excessive fuel consumption and a tendency to four-stroke. A worn taper needle should be suspected if the machine will run with the mixture control lever on the 'full weak' setting.

The needles were sold in various degrees of taper ranging from 1½ per cent to 7 per cent, and it is important that the right taper goes into a particular engine. If the engine has been interfered with, or a handbook is not available, it would be wise to try a range of needles to obtain smooth running at a reasonable mixture setting.

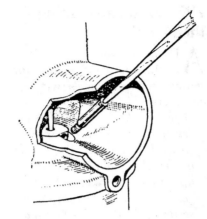

307. Toothpick technique

The Villiers midget carburettor of the type employed on the 125 cc engines has a small pipe (compensating tube), slotted at one end, which screws at an awkward angle into the top of the jet. It is impossible to balance it on a screwdriver – it just falls off – but a thin slip of wood, such as a matchstick tapered to a point or a toothpick or cocktail stick, can be pushed into the top to grip. This will start the tube in the thread, so that it can be nipped up tight with the screwdriver.

308. Two-stroke fuel

Once run in, two-strokes will often run quite happily on rather less oil than the maker recommends. If the engine accumulates carbon more quickly than it should, the oil content of the mixture is probably too generous. For the average engine a 32:1 petrol/oil ratio should be fine. That is ¼ pint of oil to each gallon of petrol. For the timid, 24:1, or ½ pint of oil to 1½ gallons should be completely safe.

309. Petroil mixing

It is essential with two-strokes lubricated by petroil to ensure that the petrol and oil are properly mixed. It is advisable to shake up the mixture in the tank regularly, in addition to mixing thoroughly when refuelling. Otherwise the oil will separate from the petrol and the engine will not be lubricated. Because of this separation, it is advisable to switch off the engine a few hundred yards before reaching home at night. This will empty the carburettor and prevent the oil separating in the float chamber overnight and fouling the engine the next morning.

310. Exposed air intake on a two-stroke

Many pre-war two-strokes had the carburettor mounted to the side. To protect the air intake from the rider's clothing, solder two pieces of wire across the bell mouth. If preferred thin gauze can then be soldered to the wire, but this may necessitate lowering the jet needle or reducing the jet size, as the gauze will richen the mixture.

311. Straight-through pipe

Removing the silencer or running with a racing silencer requires a richer setting and a larger main jet.

312. Starting from cold

Prime the carburettor by depressing the tickler sharply three or four times, and close the air valve: set the ignition at about half retarded. Then shut the throttle and open it a little (about ⅛ open) and kickstart. If it is open too much, starting will be difficult.

313. Starting – engine hot

Do not flood the carburettor but close the air lever. Set the ignition and close the throttle, then open the throttle about ⅛ travel and kickstart. If the carburettor has been flooded and won't start because the mixture is too rich – open the throttle and air lever wide and give the engine several turns to clear the richness, then start again with the throttle ⅛ open, and the air lever wide open. Generally speaking it is not advisable to flood at all when an engine is hot.

314. Starting – general

By experiment, find out if and when it is necessary to flood, and also note the best position for the air lever and the throttle for the easiest starting. Some carburettors have the throttle stop fitted with a starting position onto which the throttle must be shut down.

315. Starting – single lever carburettors

Open the throttle very slightly from the idling position and flood the carburettor more or less according to the engine being cold or hot.

316. Cable controls

See that there is a minimum of backlash when the controls are set back and that any movement of the handlebar does not cause the throttle to open: this is done by the adjusters on the top of the carburettor. See that the throttle shuts down freely.

317. Petrol feed, verification

Detach the petrol pipe union at the float chamber end; turn on the petrol tap momentarily and see that the fuel gushes out. Avoid petrol pipes with vertical loops as they cause air locks. Flooding may be because of a worn or bent needle or a leaky float, but nearly all flooding with newly restored machines is because of impurities in the tank – so clean out the float chamber periodically until the trouble ceases. If the trouble persists, the tank may be sealed with a chemical sealer. Note that if a carburettor, either vertical or horizontal, is flooding with the engine stopped, the overflow from the main jet will not run into the engine but out of the carburettor through a hole at the base of the mixing chamber.

318. Fixing air leaks

Erratic slow running is often caused by air leaks, so verify there is none between the carburettor and the cylinder head or inlet pipe – check by squirting oil onto the suspect joint. If the engine smooths out, eliminate the air leak by new washers and the even tightening up of the flange nuts. In old machines look out for air leaks caused by a worn throttle slide and carburettor body, or worn inlet valve guides.

319. Banging in the exhaust

This may be caused by too weak a pilot mixture when the throttle is closed – or by too rich a pilot mixture and an air leak in the exhaust system. The reason in either case is that the mixture has not fired in the cylinder and has fired in the hot silencer. Violent explosions in the silencer during the descent of hills may be because of the throttle not closing properly. If the banging happens when the throttle is fairly wide open the trouble will be ignition – not carburation.

320. Bad petrol consumption

Bad petrol consumption may be because of flooding caused by impurities from the petrol tank lodging on the float needle seat and so preventing its valve from closing. If the machine has had several years of use, flooding may be caused by a worn float needle valve.

Bad petrol consumption will also be apparent if the throttle needle jet has worn; it may be improved by lowering the needle in the throttle, but if it cannot be – then the only remedy is to get a new needle jet.

321. Air filters

These may affect the jet setting, so if one is subsequently fitted to the carburettor the main jet may have to be smaller. If a carburettor is set with an air filter and the engine is run without it, take care not to overheat the engine through too weak a mixture; testing with the air valve will indicate if a larger main jet and higher needle position are required.

322. Air filter care

Air filters should be cleaned or replaced periodically to ensure the correct flow of air into the mixture. Many older machines are not fitted with air filters, allowing grit and water entry to the engine

via the inlet tract. If originality is a key requisite, it is advisable to fit a bath plug into the exposed carburettor bell mouth while the machine is parked. If not, there are several foam filters on the market which will clamp neatly onto the back of the carburettor. Check and adjust the carburation after fitting, as the new filter will probably richen the mixture.

323. Spitting back

The explanation for an engine spitting back through the carburettor when the mixture is weak is that the weak mixture produces a slow-burning charge which leaves a certain amount of flame in the cylinder, even until the subsequent induction stroke. This flame ignites the incoming mixture, and thus causes the spitting back. Very occasionally spitting back will set the carburettor alight. Instantly turn off the petrol, and if the engine is running, open the throttle wide; this will suck the flames into the engine and all will be well. If the engine is not running beat out the flames or smother them. Never use water on a petrol fire; it only spreads the flames.

324. Carburettor care

Never poke pieces of wire through the drillways or jets of a carburettor. Instead blow through them in the reverse direction of petrol flow with an airline if possible (a bicycle pump may do); any grit which has floated in with the petrol will only lodge more firmly if you blow the wrong way.

325. Carburettor repair

The stripping of the thread at the top of old carburettor bodies is a common problem. This tip was suggested as a temporary money-saver in 1954, but with today's shortage of spares it could be adapted for more permanent use. With the ring-nut in place, drill a hole right through the ring nut and the top of the carburettor, and slide a split pin through the hole.

326. An alternative, which might be more useful on the road, is to cut the ring with a hacksaw and clamp it in place with a worm screw clip.

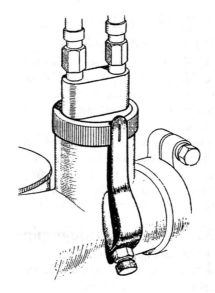

327. The ring nut at the top of most post-war carburettors is kept in place by an L-shaped spring clip screwed into the top. Many earlier carburettors can be fitted with a blade held in place by the throttle stop screw and extending to the ring nut.

328. Carburettor flange washers

Carburettor flange washers for making a joint at the induction face should not be thicker than 0.015 in. Thicker washers may result in distortion of the flange when the nuts are tightened. Whatever the joint seal, whether washer or O-ring, always avoid overtightening the flange nuts, as this is the easiest way to distort the flange.

329. Fuel economy

Fibre washers in carburettors should be replaced periodically whether they leak or not. The thickness of the washers at the base of the mixing chamber and at the top of the banjo union is critical, because of their influence on float chamber height (and hence petrol level at the jet). After a while the washers compress, the petrol level is raised and the mixture becomes rich, with a consequent tendency to provoke rough running on restricted throttle openings. When tuning for economy it is a good plan to replace the banjo union top washer with one which is 0.020 in. thicker than standard.

330. Stopping leaks

Petrol will harden carburettor gaskets and fibre washers. To avoid leaks it is best to replace these once they have been disturbed.

331. Modified throttle stop

Some Amal carburettors, such as fitted to the Velocette Mk.II KSS, had a simple cold start lever on the throttle stop screw. Such a device is easy to make at home.

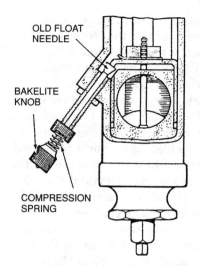

OLD FLOAT NEEDLE

BAKELITE KNOB

COMPRESSION SPRING

Drill the throttle stop axially and insert a spare (but straight) float needle, with the lower part spring-loaded against a plastic knob fitted on the end. Push up the knob to richen the mixture when starting, leaving the spring to keep it in the correct running position afterwards.

332. Adjusting the jet needle

On many single-cylinder models it is difficult to adjust the jet needle without first removing the petrol tank or the carburettor or both. To avoid extra work, unscrew the knurled ring at the top of the carburettor and lift the carburettor top piece as high as possible. Then slowly turn the twist-grip until the top of the throttle slide appears above the carburettor body. Insert a pair of tweezers through the bell mouth and grip the stem of the throttle needle; with the other hand remove the needle clip. The needle can then be moved to the required position by means of the tweezers, and the clip replaced. This method of adjustment carried factory

approval providing care was taken not to damage the needle with the tweezers.

333. Throttle slide removal

On some machines there isn't sufficient clearance between the top of the carburettor and the frame tube to allow the throttle slide to be extracted easily. A way round the problem is to replace one of the carburettor mounting studs by a setscrew. Then, to remove, slacken the remaining stud nut, take out the setscrew, and the carburettor body can pivot round enough for the slide to be lifted out.

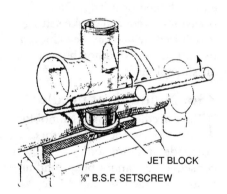

JET BLOCK

⅛" B.S.F. SETSCREW

334. Jet block removal

If the carburettor jet block is corroded into position, screw a bolt into the main jet thread and hold the carburettor body in the vice by this bolt. Place a wooden block behind the mixing chamber (a hammer handle was used in the sketch, but the bottom surface ought to be flat), and use two steel bars to lever up the carburettor body. The levers should be padded with rags to prevent indentations in the soft alloy of the carburettor.

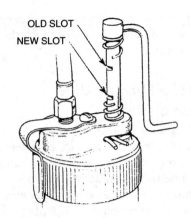

OLD SLOT
NEW SLOT

335. Early Monobloc chokes

Amal Monobloc carburettors fitted with the lever choke, rather than cable-operated, have no half measures; the engine is either choked or it isn't. On occasions a reduced choke setting is required, which can be achieved by cutting a second notch in the air slide plunger.

336. Nylon float needle

Float needles in Amal Monobloc and Concentric carburettors are made of nylon, and consequently cannot be ground in to improve their seating. If the seating is poor, change the needle after checking the profile of the seat on the needle holder.

Because they sit at an angle, nylon needles in Monobloc carburettors can stick in the slot, which either means an empty float chamber or petrol pouring out of the tickler. Again this is best cured with a different needle, though the three bearing edges on the needle shank can be carefully eased with a fine file in an emergency.

For those who forgot to check before they pulled out the float, the needle should be put back pointy end up.

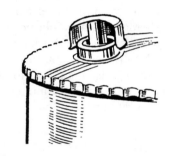

337. Waterproof tickler

Extended ticklers can be bought for Amal Monobloc and Concentric carburettors. This suggestion from 1931 is for converting the tickler on a remote float. First solder a small brass collar to the float chamber lid surrounding the hole from which the tickler emerges. Then solder a brass cap to the top of the tickler. The cap must be a little larger in diameter than the collar to allow it to be depressed to the float chamber lid.

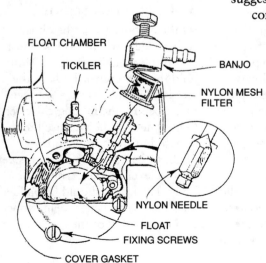

FLOAT CHAMBER
TICKLER
BANJO
NYLON MESH FILTER
NYLON NEEDLE
FLOAT
FIXING SCREWS
COVER GASKET

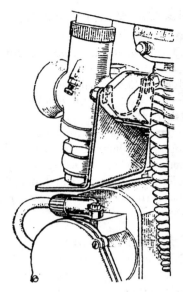

338. Carburettor drip shield

BSA fitted a drip shield between the carburettor and magneto pick-up to some of their 50s models. This tip comes from November 1947, was fitted to an ex-WD machine, and was made out of tin sheet cut to about 6 in. x 3 in. The corners were rounded, and one end was profiled and slotted to fit round the carburettor and coincide with the carburettor studs, and the metal was then bent to clear the top of the magneto.

339. Transparent petrol pipe

If a transparent petrol pipe is being fitted to the carburettor, make it long enough to form a loop lower than the bottom of the float chamber. Any water or sediment in the fuel will fall to this point and be visible. It is only necessary to disconnect the pipe at the float chamber and run the fuel for a moment to clear it.

340. Petrol pipe leakage

Leakage at the petrol pipe unions is often caused by incorrect assembly. The olives must sit squarely in their seats before the union nut is tightened up. If a rigid copper supply pipe cannot be bent to align properly, it is wise to cut it and insert a short length of rubber tubing. This will not only ensure alignment, but also prevent pipe fracture.

341. Copper fuel pipes

Rigid fuel pipes made from copper can fracture through vibration. One way to avoid this problem, such as Velocette did, is to cut out a short section of the copper and replace it with a flexible rubber link piece.

342. Petrol pipe fracture

Pipe fracture on machines fitted with all copper supply pipes can be avoided by winding it into several horizontal coils along its length. These will be capable of absorbing the stresses.

343. Petrol stains

Petrol stains can be removed from carburettor bodies with either acetone, methylated spirits or cellulose thinners.

344. Cable routeing

Routeing of Bowden control cables is important for the smooth operation of the control, and to avoid chafing of the outer cable on a sharp protrusion such as a tank flange. Route the cables without sharp bends, and test them by operating the levers and twisting the handlebars before final fixing.

345. Cable chafe

One common area of risk from chafing on many 50s singles is the proximity of the clutch cable to one of the battery leads. Unless carefully routed and tied back, in time the constant movement of the clutch cable will chafe through the lead, and short the battery.

346. Cable free play

Clutch and valve lifter cables should have an ⅛ in. free play. The other cables should have none.

347. Cable oiling

The best oil for cables is a thin motor oil such as cycle or fork oil. But one suggestion from 1955 was to use undiluted soluble machine cutting oil as the lubricating agent. Any water which works into the cable mixes with the cutting oil rather than displacing it.

348. Oiling a magneto cable

Take care not to over-oil the magneto advance and retard cable. You don't want oil on the contact breaker points!

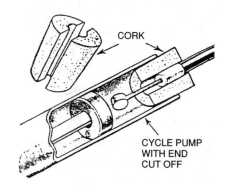

CORK

CYCLE PUMP
WITH END
CUT OFF

349. Home-made cable oiler

Cut the end off an old bicycle pump. Drill a hole the diameter of the cable down the centre of a wine bottle cork, then cut it in half down its length. Fill the pump with oil, push the cork-encased cable into the open end, and pump. A collection of differently drilled corks will fit all your cables to the same pump.

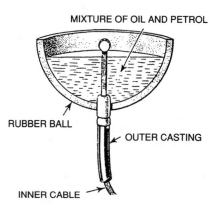

MIXTURE OF OIL AND PETROL

RUBBER BALL

OUTER CASTING

INNER CABLE

350. Cut in half a hollow rubber ball of about 2 in. in diameter. Punch a hole in the bottom smaller than the diameter of the cable, so that it is a tight push fit. Fill the ball with thin oil, and let it drip through until a smear emerges from the other end. If the cable is detached from the machine, pin the rim of the ball to a shelf edge. If still attached to the machine, undo the control lever end, lean a board against the handlebars, and pin the ball to that.

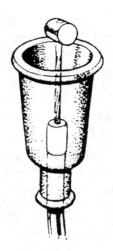

351. One suggestion from 1956 was to use the rubber waterproofer from an HT lead; ideal if it's a tight enough fit on the cable.

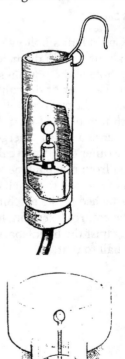

352. These two alternatives using a split cork are both neat. The

bottle idea appeals to me more, but the metal tube will be easier to hook up out of the way.

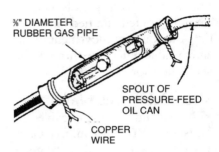

⅜" DIAMETER RUBBER GAS PIPE

SPOUT OF PRESSURE-FEED OIL CAN

COPPER WIRE

353. This idea from 1954 suggested it was pressure fed, and therefore quick. A boring job; I prefer to let it sort itself out.

354. Don't forget the small lengths of exposed control cable around the levers, or the joints of the levers themselves. And the moving parts on a tank-mounted hand gearchange. They can make all the difference to smooth operation.

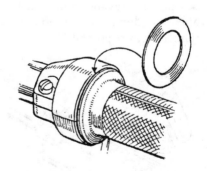

355. Smooth twistgrip

Sometimes the reason a twistgrip sticks or works in a jerky fashion is because the glove protector flange on the rubber grip is binding on the side of the twistgrip drum. The best cure for this is to fit a washer made from light gauge plastic sheet between the rubber and the drum.

356. Cable cutting

Never cut a Bowden wire without first soldering the strands together, otherwise they are sure to unravel. If the ends are unravelled and need to be fed into a nipple, this can be done by forming a piece of thin tin sheet into a cone and pushing the frayed ends through the top. The small hole will hold the ends together to allow the nipple to slide on.

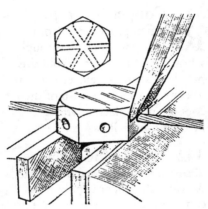

357. Alternatively, to avoid any risk of fraying while cutting Bowden cables, drill a cable-sized hole through the head of a nut. Hold the nut in a vice by its shank, slide the cable through up to the cutting point and cut with a sharp chisel. If the bolthead is drilled three ways, it will be able to accommodate three different cable thicknesses.

358. Cable cutting tool

A pair of pliers can be adapted to cut Bowden cables neatly as follows. Open the jaws of a large pair of pliers and drill a ³⁄₃₂ in. hole through both bosses of the fulcrum rivet. To cut a cable, tin it in the normal way to prevent spreading of the strands, open the pliers, thread the cable through the hole and close the jaws sharply.

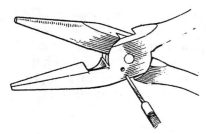

The cable is cut with an easy shearing action.

359. Shortening cables

If the correct length cable is not available, and the inner cable is too short, the outer cable can be shortened to redress the balance. First ease the ferrule from the casing end and slip it up the wire out of harm's way. Cut away an appropriate amount of the casing cover to expose the metal coils. Slip the knife blade between the outermost pair of coils, twist the blade to separate them, then run the cover round and round between the fingers so that the unwanted coils peel away. When enough coils are peeled, snip them off with wire cutters, and slide back the ferrule.

360. Outer cable protection

To avoid outer cables from burning on hot engine parts, such as cylinder barrel or exhaust pipe, wind a coil of copper wire round the section of cable at risk. The copper dissipates the heat while keeping the actual cover from making contact with the hot surface.

361. Soldering nipples

It is important that all components are clean. Remove traces of oil from the cable end, and if an old nipple is being reused

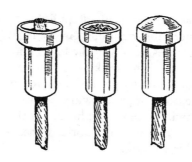

run out the old solder with the soldering iron. Tin the cable, run solder into the nipple, and push the nipple just beyond the end of the cable. Splay the exposed cable ends with a penknife, and fill the nipple recess with more solder, pulling the cable fully home at the same time.

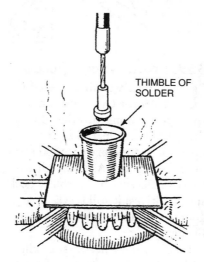

THIMBLE OF SOLDER

362. Alternative nipple soldering

It is possible to solder a nipple on a cable using a solder bath instead of an iron. Prepare the cable end, making sure it is quite clean, and slip the nipple over the cable leaving about ⅛ in. protruding. (The cable end should already be tinned to prevent the strands unravelling.) Separate and bend back the strands so that they lay in the well of the nipple. Place

a thimble-sized container full of solder over a flame and, when it is molten, flux the nipple and completely submerge it in the molten solder. Allow the solder to permeate the cable and nipple thoroughly, and remove to cool. File off any excess solder before refitting the nipple into its housing.

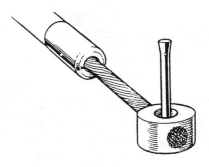

363. Resoldering large cable nipples

Some larger cable nipples do not have a countersunk end for splaying the cable before soldering. A substitute is a panel pin driven through the centre of the nipple, and cut off flush either side. Solder afterwards in the normal way.

364. Bath solder

Mass-produced control cables are usually fitted with nipples which have been immersed in a solder bath. As a result the nipple gets a coating of solder on the outside. Unless this is eased off before fitting the cable to its socket the nipple may not work freely, and could lead to premature cable breakage.

365. Clutch cable nipples

Nipples for the gearbox end of clutch cables can be made from bicycle spoke nipples. Countersink the head, and run a fine drill down the hole to clean it and remove the thread. Solder in the cable in the usual way.

366. Cable holder lifter

An old spoke with nipple still attached can be bent to form a useful tool for lifting recessed cable holders, such as found on Velocette gearboxes and Panther rocker boxes.

367. Broken cable adjuster

This tip from 1960 enabled a broken clutch cable adjuster to be removed without dismantling the gearbox, even though the adjuster had broken off flush with the casing.

Disconnect the cable at both ends and pull hard on the nipple at the handlebar end, turning it anti-clockwise at the same time. The resultant pressure and rotation at the gearbox end should cause the broken piece of adjuster to unscrew enough to get a grip with a pair of pliers.

368. Speedo cable lubrication

Properly fitted and lubricated, a speedo cable should last for years, but often lubrication is neglected. From time to time disconnect the drive from the speedometer head and pull the inner cable right out. Grease it lightly especially at the lower end where it is most likely to rust up. Don't grease right up to the top of the cable or grease will work its way into the speedo head. For the same reason don't lubricate the cable with oil.

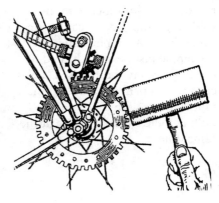

369. Front wheel speedo

This advice was first offered by *The Motor Cycle* when new speed restrictions introduced by the government in 1935 led to a flurry of proprietary speedometers onto the market. As many girder-forked machines have front wheel speedo drives, it still serves as a good lesson in the correct way to fit them.

Take out the wheel first of all, and fit the driving pinion of the speedometer to the spokes. Do not, however, tighten the fixing screws more than is necessary to hold the pinion in position. Refit the wheel and mount the cable and driven pinion so that the teeth of both pinions mesh to about half their depth. Now you will find, on spinning the wheel, that the teeth mesh more deeply in some places than in others. Lightly tap the driving pinion in the appropriate places until the teeth mesh evenly

through a whole revolution. Then the screws should be tightened equally, and the driven pinion adjusted until it meshes with the driving pinion and leaves approximately ¹⁄₃₂ in. gap at the teeth.

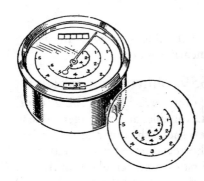

370. Engine rev indicator

Fifties Triumphs were fitted with a speedo superimposed with recommended revs for each gear at a given speed. To make such a device is quite straightforward, if not as neat as the original. Take out the glass cover of the speedo and replace with a dial of perspex, suitably scribed, ³⁄₃₂ in. thick. The sketch shows the type of markings necessary. The inner line is for second gear use, the middle line for third gear, and the outer for top. The numbers on the speedo dial will still show through the perspex as they did the original glass.

371. Non-slip handlebars

The handlebar must be firm in its clamps and the levers tight on the bar. One way to get a good grip is to roughen up the chromium plating on the sections of handlebar underneath the clamps. If the clamps are a slack fit, use emery cloth packing pieces.

372. Securing levers

A way of securing loose levers without damaging the

handlebar is as follows. File a number of shallow V-shaped grooves inside the lever's clamp parallel with the handlebar. Take a length of small diameter control inner cable, and solder a short piece into each V, trimming off the ends with sharp wire cutters. When the lever is refitted to the handlebar the hard strands of the control cable will bite into the handlebar and stop any further slip.

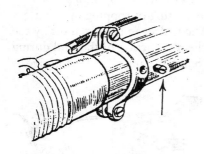

373. Loose control levers

Loose control levers are dangerous. How often are the pattern handlebars just a mite too thin for those beautiful original levers? If handlebar levers won't quite tighten up firmly, it may be possible to pack out the clamps with some brass shim. Alternatively, if it is the levers that are patterns, drill and tap an ⅛ in. hole in the centre of the back piece of the clamp, and fit a small grub screw.

374. Screw tip

Should a machine be dropped there is a possibility of snapping one of the handlebar lever clamp screws. A screw broken flush with the clamp can be awkward to extract. If a saw-cut is made across the threaded end of each screw before you fall off, any broken pieces can be removed with a screwdriver.

Electrical equipment and ignition systems

375. The battery

The battery is one of the few components on a motor cycle which can deteriorate swiftly either when used or left idle. In use, the polarity of the earthing must be correct before the battery is connected to the charging circuit, and the level of voltage supplied to it must be controlled. When idle, the battery's voltage must be checked every six weeks or so, and recharged if necessary.

Excessive charge and vibration are the battery's main enemies. Excessive charging will cause gassing of the electrolyte and subsequent loss of acid through the vent holes.

376. Electrolyte

The electrolyte in a battery should consist roughly of five parts water to one part sulphuric acid. Only distilled water should be used when making the electrolyte. The acid must be added to the water very slowly; never add water to acid. Do not use electrolyte to top up a battery. Only the water evaporates, so adding more electrolyte will increase the amount of acid.

377. Acid level – regulated system

The acid level in the battery should always cover the tops of the plates by ¼ in. to allow for the acid washing about. It shouldn't be any higher or there

won't be sufficient space for the hydrogen gas produced when the battery receives a charge. However, over-filling the battery is unlikely to cause serious damage (the worst is the risk of spillage ruining smart paintwork). A drastic remedy is to empty out the cells completely and refill with solution of the correct specific gravity: this should be 1.25 to 1.28 when the battery is fully charged, or 1.15 to 1.18 when fully discharged. Though it should be quite satisfactory to leave the battery over-filled; in time the water will evaporate and the level and specific gravity will revert to normal.

378. Acid level – rectified system

Never overfill the battery of rectified lighting systems or the acid will 'boil' and result in spillage and damage to the battery. The correct level is when the electrolyte comes just above the top of the separators.

379. Acid level measurement

To determine accurately the acid level above the plates in a black rubber battery, insert the end of a length of ¼ in. diameter glass or clear plastic tubing through the vent plug hole until it rests gently on top of the plates. Place a finger on the top end of the tube to seal it, and lift out. The column of acid picked up in the bottom of the tube gives the height above the plates. On removing the finger from the end of the tube, the acid will fall out.

380. Distilled water

Everyone knows that batteries should be topped up with distilled water. But did you know that the water accumulated from a defrosted refrigerator is, though not chemically pure, good enough for use in a battery?

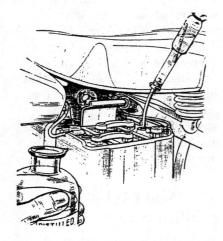

381. Hydrometer top-up

One of the easiest ways to feed distilled water into a battery is with the hydrometer. There is no chance of the water being spilled around the terminal posts, and each cell will receive the correct amount, and no more.

382. Positive and negative poles

It is possible to distinguish between positive and negative poles in a battery from the fact that the positive plates are dark brown in colour, and the negative plates are grey. In addition, every cell contains one negative plate in excess of the number of positive plates. To distinguish in batteries with black casings, place two leads from the terminals in a vessel containing a weak sulphuric acid solution (acetic acid, or vinegar

will do). Bubbles will appear at the negative wire.

383. Modern batteries

Many 50s machines are designed to accommodate a large upright black six-volt battery, usually strapped to the machine instead of enclosed in tinware, making alternative arrangements awkward or unsightly. New batteries of this type can still be bought, but they are relatively expensive and only as reliable as their predecessors. Once one of these batteries is no longer serviceable, strip out the insides, just leaving the black rubber casing. This is easily large enough to accept a modern six-volt battery.

384. Battery tool box

If a modern battery system is employed, perhaps with the unit concealed out of sight, the old Exide-type six-volt battery can be hollowed out and used as a toolbox. It can even be fixed by the original battery straps.

385. Modern battery breathers

If a modern battery is fitted, it will have a nozzle for a breather tube on one side at the top of the battery. A tube should be fitted to the nozzle and routed through the machine so that its end is well below the bottom frame member. This will avoid acid vapours damaging alloys or paintwork. A tube will be supplied with the battery, but I have yet to find one that was long enough.

386. Battery protection

Battery terminals and connections can be protected from the corrosive effects of acid if they are brushed with melted paraffin wax or liquid candle grease. The wax sets into a hard film, but can be removed easily if required.

387. Battery cell

Never bring a naked light close to the cell openings when inspecting or topping up a battery. The hydrogen gas given off by the chemical action of the acid during charge is dangerously explosive.

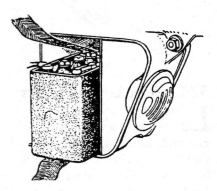

388. Battery carrier

On some machines the battery is held tightly in an enclosed compartment. To ease removal, wrap a length of upholsterer's webbing vertically round the battery before replacement.

389. Fitting a new loom

This tip from 1948 is intended to help trace connections when rewiring, without the need to strip individual wires from the loom or constantly consult a wiring diagram. Theoretically it is brilliant in its simplicity, but in practice we know how few old machines now have the correct colour-coded wiring. For those that do, follow this advice. When taking out the old loom, don't disconnect any of the cables, but cut them off short of the various electrical fittings. When you come to fit the new loom, the colour-coded tags still attached to the connections will aid accurate rewiring.

390. Rewiring aid

Often wires are a tight fit through grommets, either because an extra wire is now needed or because the new wires are thicker. To slide two wires through a small hole, push a twist drill bit through the grommet's hole and feed the wires along the spiral grooves of the drill. Unscrew the drill to remove it, leaving the wires in place.

391. Horn wiring

Most electrical items are wired via the ammeter, but not the horn or the stoplight. This is because they require a heavier current, and may strain the delicate meter by throwing the needle beyond the marked limit. Therefore, a discharge caused by a fault with the horn or the stoplight will not be registered by the ammeter.

392. Horn adjustment

Usually a small grub screw will be found on the back of an electric horn. By carefully turning this screw in the required direction the tone of the horn can be altered. If this adjustment does not have any effect, it is possible that the diaphragm (through age or neglect) is not able to flex. Dismantling, cleaning, and reassembling may be the cure.

393. Louder horn

Where dry battery operated horns are fitted to lightweight machines, the power of the horn can be increased by using camera flash gun batteries in place of the standard. Photoflash cells have a high discharge rate for a short period and recover quickly when not in use.

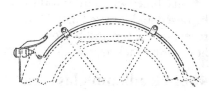

394. Rear light wiring

The original routeing for cables to rear lights on rigid machines was usually haphazard. If originality isn't so important the cables can be neatly and effectively protected by a length of thin copper tube fixed to the curve of the underside of the rear mudguard. The mounting brackets shown in the sketch coincide with the mudguard stay bolts, so no additional drilling was required. The wires should be shrouded with rubber at both ends of the tube to avoid chafing.

395. Headlight switch removal

The Bakelite switch knobs on most early headlights can be easily broken if levered off with a screwdriver. A suggestion from 1960 to avoid damage is to slide a piece of cloth under the knob, and cross both ends. When the cloth is pulled, an equal pressure is applied round the knob's circumference.

396. Headlight clips

Though they don't know it, garden centres stock clips for holding headlight reflectors into the rim. They are used today for clipping glass into aluminium greenhouse frames.

397. Headlight signalling

It is easy to adapt an earlier lighting circuit to accommodate a headlamp flashing switch, which will work regardless of whether the headlamp switch is set at off, pilot or high. All that is required is a horn button of the type that has two wires which does not earth against its mounting. One wire is attached to the main beam terminal of the dip switch. The other wire is taken to that terminal of the headlamp switch which is connected to one side of the

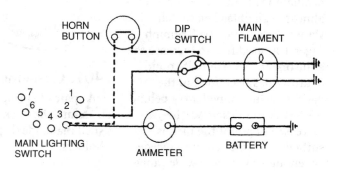

ammeter. The existing wiring need not be disturbed in any way. The wiring diagram shown is for a dynamo, not alternator, system, but the principle is the same. Two harmless side-effects are that when the headlamp switch is at high, flashing can be by means of the dip switch. And if the button is operated when the dip filament is in use, the main filament will also light.

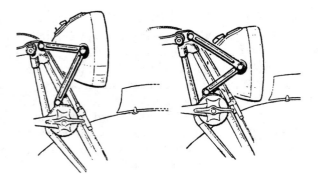

The headlamp position on many machines with girder forks can be raised and lowered merely by reversing the top and bottom headlamp brackets.

400. Headlamp glass seal

Old headlight glasses were protected from vibration damage by a cork seal cushioning them from the rim. If this seal is missing, a good replacement can be made from small bore rubber tubing split longitudinally and pushed over the edge of the glass.

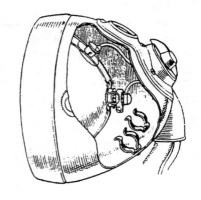

401. Carrying spare bulbs

A pair of spring clips riveted into the back of the headlamp shell make ideal spare bulb holders.

402. Single and twin filament bulbs

When a lighting set is wired for double filament bulbs, the system of wiring precludes the use of single filament bulbs unless considerable alterations are made. But in an emergency this tip will enable a single filament bulb to be used without disturbing the wiring. All that is necessary is to join one of the contact studs of the bulb to the brass outer casing. The lamp-holder contact stud should not, however, be allowed to touch this pip, which can be avoided by the use of tinfoil or copper wire and insulating tape. And the bulb must be fitted the right way round.

A more permanent adaptation is to take a small brass washer and solder it to the central spot of solder of the centre contact bulb. Both 'full' and 'dip' plungers in the lamp-holder will bear on the washer, giving the 'full' light no matter what may be the position of the dipswitch.

403. Stoplight trouble

January 1959 saw a spate of differing opinion on stoplight protection. First, drill a hole in the bottom of the switch to let out any water. Then pack the switch with Vaseline as well as drilling a hole. Lastly, don't let water in in the first place. Keep the water out by

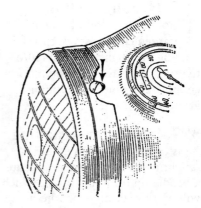

398. Headlamp adjustment

The beam adjustment range of a nacelle-enclosed headlamp is often severely restricted because the rim securing screw is fitted too close to the front edge of the nacelle. Possible elevation of the beam, obtained by swivelling the headlamp rim and reflector, is thus almost negligible. The sketch shows the nacelle of a Triumph Tiger 100 modified to increase the adjustment. A small half-round cutaway has been filed in the nacelle casing immediately behind the shank of the screw. The increased depth of the nick is sufficient for the screw to recede far enough to allow a wide range of beam adjustment.

399. Lower headlamp

sliding a section of old inner tube over the outside of the switch. No doubt everyone thinks their own idea is the best solution.

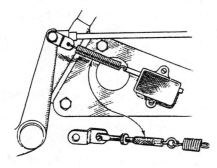

404. Stop light tensioner

Some machines are fitted with brake light switches just behind the brake pedal and operated by a metal tab attached to the clevis pin joining the pedal to the brake rod. To make these adjustable it is possible to replace the standard spring with the adjuster from the control of a Sturmey-Archer bicycle hub gear. Remove the externally threaded portion from the gear-operating chain and rivet it to the anchor tab. Insert a short length of bicycle spoke cut about an inch from the head in the tubular internally threaded part of the adjuster to protrude through the end. Bend the exposed part of the spoke into a loop, and attach a shortened spring to the loop at one end and the switch at the other. Connect the two parts together, set for the correct tension, and use a locknut for security.

405. Twistgrip dipper

An old twistgrip can be adapted to operate a dipswitch as follows. Cut a radial slot in the cable drum of the twistgrip and engage the toggle arm of the

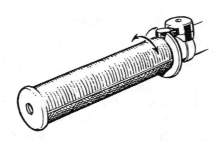

switch. A short circumferential slot is cut in the metal sleeve of the grip, which is mounted on the bar minus the drum housing that normally clamps the grip in place. Drill and tap the handlebar to receive a grub screw to locate in the circumferential slot. Hence the grip is held axially and is limited in rotation by the length of the slot. The grub screw is long enough to screw into the tapped hole on the opposite side of the handlebar tube. It is held from unscrewing by the rubber covering of the grip sleeve.

406. Blowing bulbs

A blown bulb that has burnt out will go black, whereas one that turns milky or yellow indicates the entry of air through a loose bayonet cap or broken glass. If the filament is broken, vibration may be the problem. If the filament has melted, suspect voltage surge.

   If bulbs blow regularly and often, there is a fault in the system. Provided that the bulb is of the right type, check the following:
1. Excessive high voltage. Check the charging system.
2. Worn or damaged battery leads.
3. Faulty earth connection of the lamp shell, or the charging system, or the battery.

Lack of illuminating power from a bulb may not be because of a run down battery, but to vibration causing the filament of the bulb to sag out of centre with the reflector.

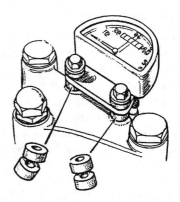

407. Filament breakages

Many complaints about short-lived bulbs – particularly in stop lights – can be traced to vibration combined with rigid mounting points. One cure is to rubber-mount the light unit using ordinary tap washers with the centre drilled out to take the larger diameter bolt. The sketch shows another vulnerable item – the speedo bulb.

408. Earthing

Electricity won't earth through paint; a washer-sized divot will have to be carved out of that beautiful new paintwork to earth the battery to the frame. Many components earth through their fixings, dynamos through their outer casing to the holding strap, rear lights through the mudguard. A paint layer separating any of these could prevent efficient earthing.

409. Bad earth

Many electrical failures are because of insufficient earthing. One story going round the clubrooms is of someone who returned a 'defective' sidecar light which he had earthed to a fibreglass mudguard.

410. Rectifiers

It is tempting to tuck rectifiers out of the way to avoid damage by wet weather. However, manufacturers deliberately positioned them where they would have a constant flow of cool air. If rectifiers are placed in toolboxes, holes should be drilled to provide an airflow.

411. Villiers direct lighting

In the event of total failure of a Villiers lighting set, check for the following faults:

1. Tail lamp not having a proper earth.
2. Failure of either bulb.
3. Broken connection in circuit.
4. Loose plug connection in armature plate.
5. Short circuit to earth anywhere between headlamp bulb and magneto.

412. Two-stroke stoplight

UK legislation requires a stoplight to be fitted to all machines manufactured after 1938, even though many post-1938 motor cycles were not originally supplied with stoplights; this applies to most early 50s two-strokes with direct lighting. The problem can be overcome by connecting one end of a length of cable to the main lead between generator and headlamp, and taking the other end of the cable to a stoplight switch mounted in the conventional position. Run a lead from the switch to the stoplight. Use of the stoplight shouldn't affect the intensity of the headlamp beam.

413. Direct lighting stoplight – the BSA alternative

This suggestion came from a reader in 1957, and is quoted in full, followed by the BSA factory's comment. 'Although my Bantam is equipped with direct lighting, I have successfully fitted a stoplight with twin bulbs. From pin No. 4 of the Wico-Pacy ignition generator I led a length of plastic-covered cable up inside the covering of the HT cable and then to the stoplight switch; 12-volt bulbs are used in the lamp. The lights work only when the engine is running, so do not interfere with the battery parking equipment.' BSA replied:

The method described can be used only on certain Bantam models and not all, depending on the type of generator fitted. The modification is certainly possible on pre-1956 models with ignition generator type 1130, using a third lighting coil. From August 1955 onward a type 1452 generator was fitted; this has only two coils and the modification cannot be made. It shouldn't be necessary to use 12v bulbs, provided 6v bulbs of at least 1.5 amps are fitted.'

414. Direct battery charging

Some mid-50s two-stroke lighting systems were equipped with a half-wave rectifier for battery charging. In many cases it is possible to connect the rectifier to a transformer so that the battery can be charged from an ordinary domestic power point. It is best to use a small mains transformer, such as for a door bell, designed to give an output of eight volts at one amp. To avoid the generator demagnetizing when charging from the mains, fit a snap connector in the lead between the rectifier and generator. When charging from the mains, disconnect the generator, connect the input side of the transformer to the power point, and leads from the transformer output terminals to an earthing point on the frame and to the snap connector on the rectifier/generator lead. The rate of charge is about half an amp.

415. Charging systems – the alternator

Little can be said about repair and maintenance of an alternator, since should repairs be possible they will need to be carried out by a specialist. As for maintenance: if it works, leave it alone. However, care must be taken in fitting an alternator. The rotor must be tightened up fully (Triumph recommended a torque wrench setting of 30 lb/ft), and the tab washer should always be replaced. The stator is more delicate; it should be eased onto its three fixings carefully, avoiding catching the plates on the stud threads. The nuts should have the correct thick washers behind them, and should be tightened evenly.

416. Lucas AC generators – extra charge

Additional charge can be got from Lucas AC generators, as fitted to late 50s Triumphs, by altering the wiring as follows. Remove the link connecting terminals 5 and 6 in the lighting switch; this will bring an extra coil into the circuit. To bring four of the six coils into the circuit reverse the position of the dark green and mid-green (later green/yellow) leads at the junction of the generator main lead and the machine's cable harness. This is particularly useful if the machine is not being run enough to generate charge, as in winter or limited summer use in gloomy conditions. But before making any changes, check that the wiring on the particular machine still corresponds to the original Lucas diagram.

417. Dynamo maintenance

Two points to remember about dynamos are (a) they have a rooted aversion to petrol and oil, and (b) the live battery lead should be removed before the dynamo is touched.

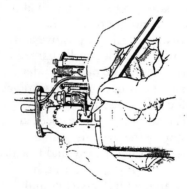

Before removing the brushes check which way round they fit in their slots, and mark them to ensure correct replacement. Many brushes may look the same, but be of a different hardness of material. If too hard, they will quickly wear away the commutator.

The brushes should slide freely in their holders, and should be held squarely against the commutator by the spring clip. Unevenness can be removed by

using fine glasspaper wrapped round a pencil. According to Lucas, brushes should be replaced when the top end of the brush is halfway down the slot in the side of the brush box, for then the spring pressure has started to weaken.

418. Dynamo brush bedding

After fitting new carbon brushes to a dynamo, and before replacing the dynamo end cover, start the engine and allow it to tick over. Press down very lightly on the brushes for a few moments. This will ensure a good contact with the commutator.

419. The third brush

Badly fitting brushes or a dirty commutator have the affect of making the dynamo charge irregularly. If your dynamo relies on a third brush for the control of its output and this sticks or doesn't bed down properly, the output may be so high as to cause the windings to overheat and burn out. On some larger machines this brush is adjustable; it can be raised and lowered depending on the level of output required, thus protecting the battery, for example, from overcharging on a sunny day when no lights are in use.

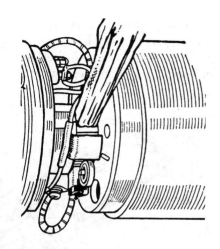

420. The commutator

The commutator should be kept clean and free from oil. Initially this is done by removing a brush from its holder, inserting a rag soaked in methylated spirits (petrol if you must, but meths is better), and spinning the commutator until it gleams.

If this is not sufficient, the commutator can be cleaned with fine glasspaper once the armature has been removed.

If carbon deposits clog the commutator grooves they must be scraped clean with a sharp point, taking great care not to damage the soft copper of the commutator itself by drawing the point away from the commutator. When undercutting the insulation it is important to cut the correct profile; use a broken hacksaw blade to ensure a flat cut over the full width of each mica segment.

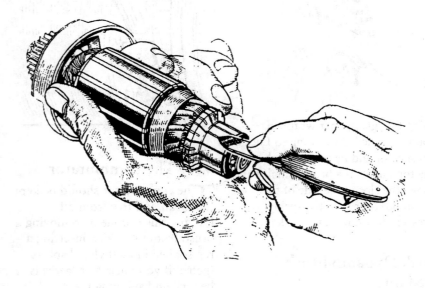

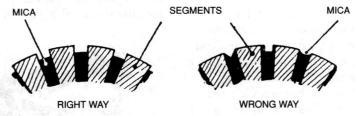

MICA   SEGMENTS   MICA

RIGHT WAY   WRONG WAY

421. Armature removal

Two or three long screws hold the driving side end-plate in place. After tightening, these will have been burred over, either at

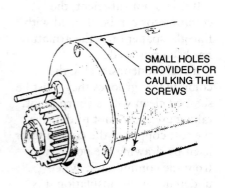

SMALL HOLES PROVIDED FOR CAULKING THE SCREWS

the screw head or through a small hole ⅛ in. from the end-plate. A good twist with a snug fitting screwdriver will usually remove the screws but, if not, the burrings may need to be drilled out before the screws are undone. Take care not to damage the screws in the process.

422. Dynamo reassembly

When reassembling the dynamo after routine maintenance, make sure that the armature bearing has enough, but not too much, grease. Tighten up

the long screws and burr them over again. At the business end of the dynamo there are a lot of leads in a compact space; ensure that all connections are correct and tight, and that when the steel cover is slid into place, one will not be able to touch another. If the wires are a loose fit through the rubber grommet, keep water out with a light smear of grease or silicon sealant. If the dynamo is belt driven, as on many Velocette machines, the belt should be tensioned so that if the dynamo pulley is rotated by hand the belt will turn the engine pulley against compression.

423. Dynamo fault finding

The field windings can be tested by earthing the dynamo, and connecting a voltmeter in series between the live terminal of a six-volt battery and the F terminal on the dynamo. If no voltmeter is available, touch the positive and negative leads of a well-charged battery simultaneously on adjacent commutator bars. Sound windings will produce a spark.

The armature can be checked by motoring the dynamo with a battery. Connect the F and D leads on the dynamo with a length of wire and, with the battery and dynamo body earthed, touch the battery live lead across the shorted terminals. The armature should show an inclination to spin.

To test if there is contact between one or more of the windings and the armature, bridge the commutator segments one by one with the armature spindle. There should be no passage of current, and therefore no spark, if the insulation of the armature windings is intact.

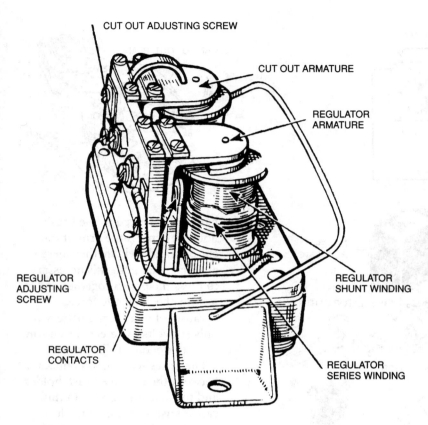

CUT OUT ADJUSTING SCREW

CUT OUT ARMATURE

REGULATOR ARMATURE

REGULATOR ADJUSTING SCREW

REGULATOR CONTACTS

REGULATOR SHUNT WINDING

REGULATOR SERIES WINDING

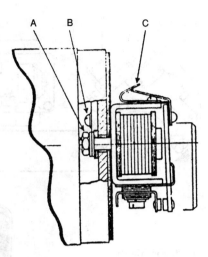

A B C

424. Lucas voltage regulator and cut-out

Lucas compensated voltage control units contain two windings; one is the dynamo cut-out and the other the voltage regulator. First check that it is wired correctly. All responsible manuals advise meddlers to leave CVC boxes well alone. However, they can be adjusted by the grub screws on the back of the windings. In the case of the cut-out, anti-clockwise rotation of the grub screw lessens the spring loading on the cut-out blade, causing the points to close earlier and open later. Rotating the screw clockwise has the opposite effect. For regulator adjustment, turning the grub screw clockwise increases output and vice versa. Loosen and retighten the locknut before and after adjustment. When checking a dynamo's output against an ammeter, before fiddling with the control unit remember that a dynamo charges at a higher rate when cold than it does after it has been in operation for a minute or two.

425. Lucas voltage control

Lucas didn't alter their control units that much over the years, but it is worth recognizing a couple of outward changes. The factory recommended that the model RB107 could be used to replace the earlier MCR unit. However, the order of connection had changed from the notorious F-A-D-E of the MCR to F-A-E-D on the RB107, where F = Field, A = Ammeter, D = Dynamo and E = Earth.

426. Miller dynamo cut-out

In the case of the Miller units the cut-out is bolted to the commutator end bracket, although it works on the same principle as the Lucas unit. To test the Miller cut-out, disconnect the three outside dynamo leads, clip the positive side of a voltmeter to the B+ dynamo terminal and earth the negative side. If there is no reading on the voltmeter with the engine running, clip the positive side of the voltmeter to the D+ connection. This by-passes the cut-out, so if there is now a reading it indicates that the dynamo is charging, but the cut-out is faulty. The sketch shows a cross-section of the cut-out with A the fixing nut, B the earth connection, and C the tension spring.

427. Miller voltage regulator

The Miller regulator is a separate unit fixed to the top of the dynamo. It can be tested by disconnecting the battery live lead, and putting a voltmeter across the positive and negative base

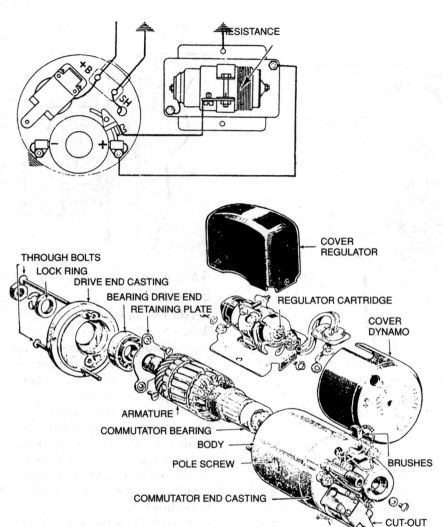

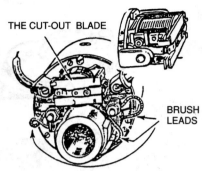

terminals of the regulator unit. With the engine running at 1000 rpm the voltmeter should record 7.5-7.9v. Below 7.5v suggests over-regulation, and adjustment can be made by screwing out the negative contact screw (visible at the conical end of the unit) two complete turns. Under-regulation is adjusted by slackening the screw at the other end of the unit a quarter of a turn. The exploded sketch and accompanying wiring diagram show how the voltage regulator relates to the DVR dynamo.

428. Lucas voltage cut-out

Early Lucas dynamos mounted the cut-out with the commutator. In the cut-out there are two windings – shunt and series. The shunt winding is straight across the main brushes of the dynamo. Therefore, to test, lift the brushes and apply the leads from the battery to the brush holders. There should be a small spark which, since the current is only about 0.2 amp, is difficult to detect unless one looks closely. A surer way of testing is to leave the battery connected to the brush holders, depress the arm of the cut-out, and feel whether there is any magnetic pull. It is necessary to press the points together and feel for the magnetic force because, of course, the battery is only six volts, whereas the cut-out is set to operate at 7.5 volts.

The series winding is connected between the positive brush holder and the insulated point. In this case a flash test can be made – quickly and not too often, because otherwise you may burn out the winding and damage the battery. Flash between the positive brush holder and the fixed point – that is, the insulated one.

When the end cover of the dynamo is replaced, care must be taken that none of the cables fouls the cut-out blade. This may cause late cutting in; so, too, may loose or dirty connections in the field circuit, though generally dirty connections will prevent cutting in.

429. Lucas dynamos

The Lucas E3H type dynamo was fitted to a large number of machines during the Second World War and immediately afterwards. The drawing shows the component parts and the comparatively simple order of dismantling this instrument.

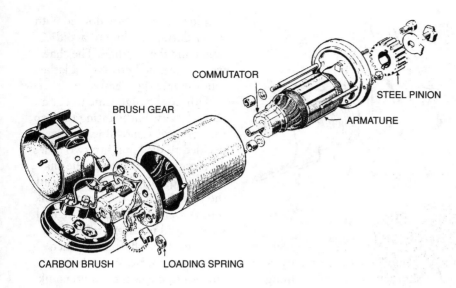

COMMUTATOR
BRUSH GEAR
STEEL PINION
ARMATURE
CARBON BRUSH   LOADING SPRING

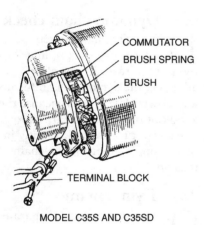

COMMUTATOR
BRUSH SPRING
BRUSH
TERMINAL BLOCK

MODEL C35S AND C35SD

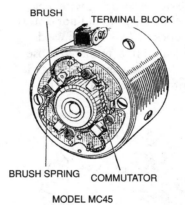

BRUSH   TERMINAL BLOCK
BRUSH SPRING   COMMUTATOR

MODEL MC45

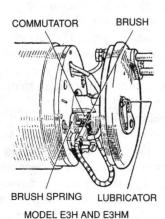

COMMUTATOR   BRUSH
BRUSH SPRING   LUBRICATOR
MODEL E3H AND E3HM

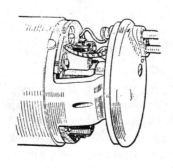

MODEL E3LM

Other Lucas dynamos are structurally similar, as can be seen from the comparison of four different Lucas dynamo end-brackets.

430. Dynamo cut-out – points to watch

Violent arcing at the cut-out points signifies a short-circuit between the battery cables, a live battery cable worn through and touching the frame of the machine, or a loose cut-out fixing.

The most probable cause of the cut-out spring overheating and losing its tension is poor electrical contact at the hinge of the cut-out armature, because of wear. This causes the current, when the contacts are closed to flow through the spring to the cut-out frame, instead of through the armature. The spring, being of fairly high resistance, gets red hot when a current flows through it. The trouble may be cured by connecting a flexible lead across the cut-out hinge, soldering one end to the armature and the other end to the cut-out frame.

Avoid bending the blade of the cut-out, and watch out that when the cover is refitted no wires foul the blade.

431. Ammeters

An ammeter should be put in the positive dynamo lead if it is of the type showing the charge current only. It should be put in the positive battery lead if it is of the centre zero type showing both charge and discharge.

432. Reversed polarity

If a dynamo should reverse its polarity (usually denoted by a discharge ammeter reading when the dynamo is on charge), the trouble is either because of the battery connections being crossed over or a bad earth return circuit between the body of the headlamp shell and the dynamo. If the battery has been wrongly connected, reverse the leads. If the earth is bad, clean to bare metal and protect with petroleum jelly, or run a spare lead between the headlight shell and earth. Then start up the engine and run it at a tick-over to open the voltage regulator cut-out points. Now hold the points together for a second, which will reverse the dynamo polarity.

433. Dynamo overheating

While there is nothing abnormal in the dynamo getting warm after a long run, excessive overheating may be because of one of the following:

1. Dirty or oily commutator.
2. Worn armature bearings, which may cause fouling of the pole shoes.
3. A short-circuited armature, which would cause the dynamo to give a reduced and intermittent output.

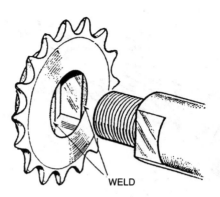

WELD

434. Dynamo – stripped keyway

A stripped keyway on a dynamo shaft can be cured by filing two flats on the worn shaft. Then fill two sides of the hole in the centre of the sprocket with weld; electric welding should not distort the sprocket. Tidy up the welds, and file two flats to match those formed on the worn shaft so that the sprocket is a tight push fit.

435. Dynamo – sheared keyway

When a Woodruff key shears it's likely to damage the shaft as well. In this case the dynamo armature key sheared taking about an ⅛ in. of metal from the shaft with it. Once the armature was withdrawn from the housing, the shaft was built up with weld,

keeping the armature doused with water during welding to avoid damaging the winding. The shaft was then turned down on a lathe to refit the sprocket centre.

With not enough time to cut a new keyway, but wanting to keep the sprocket removable, it was decided to drill and tap two holes on a centre-line through the shaft, cutting equally into the shaft and the pinion. Once the countersunk screws were in place, the original washer and nut were refitted on the end of the shaft. For added security the washer was big enough to cover the countersunk screw heads.

436. Dynamo chain check

Engines with chain driven dynamos, like the pre-unit BSA twins, require a recheck after adjusting the dynamo chain for up and down play. This is because the action of tightening the dynamo clamp can turn the unit slightly in its housing – upsetting the chain tension.

437. Twin dynamo

On some twins with a separate dynamo, such as the Triumph, withdrawal of the dynamo is hindered by the left-hand exhaust pipe. The factory recommended that it was best – and easiest – to remove the exhaust pipe. But sealing exhaust systems neatly is one of the bugbears of motor cycling, and disturbing a good joint seems a pity if there's an alternative. The dynamo can be made to clear the pipe if the band cover is removed, and the moulded commutator end cover displaced sideways after taking out the retaining screw.

438. Ignition systems

As with charging circuits, the more mechanical the component the more maintenance is required; on the other hand, the higher the chance of a successful repair. Hence the most modern electronic system requires no maintenance whatsoever, even when it malfunctions – because then it has to be chucked in the bin. Coil ignition with contact breakers tolerates a certain amount of fiddling; and with a magneto the possibilities are endless, as long as you can remember how it all came apart. Friends with degrees in electronics have regularly assured me over the years of the simplicity of magneto repair. I have yet to watch one of these wizards convert his words into deeds, and until I do the magneto will be sent away to the professional, despite the usual equation of price divided by efficiency equals a long wait. However, not all magneto problems are beyond the capabilities of the amateur.

439. Ignition timing

The details of ignition timing vary from machine to machine, but the principle is as true on a 1909 Minerva as a 1994 Honda FireBlade. The piston must be in the correct position when the spark plug ignites the charge in the combustion chamber. To time a magneto fired post-war single, proceed as follows:

1. Disconnect the magneto from the engine by removing the magneto pinion or sprocket from its shaft.
2. Select top gear, and revolve the engine until the piston is at top dead centre (TDC) on the compression stroke, when both valves will be closed.
3. Attach a degree disc to the end of the crankshaft and a wire pointer to a convenient fixing, ensuring that with the piston at TDC the pointer registers zero degrees on the disc.
4. The maker's manual will give the correct setting in degrees before TDC (say 40 degrees). Turn the engine backwards beyond the 40 degree setting on the disc, and bring it back up to the exact mark. It is more accurate to go beyond the mark and bring the engine back up to it, to take up any play in the engine.
5. Check that the points gap is correct when fully open – most makes recommend 12 thou. Then, with the ignition fully advanced, revolve the contact breaker unit until the points are just opening. This is best measured by placing a thin material, such as cellophane or a cigarette paper, between the points, and gently tugging on it until it is released. At this point the timing is correct.
6. Refit the magneto pinion or sprocket and chain, and tighten up taking great care not to disturb the setting. After tightening, recheck the settings.

440. Twin-cylinder timing

Once one cylinder has been timed, the points for the other cylinder should be correct automatically. But always check. Minor discrepancies can be remedied by adjusting the points gap. Large differences will probably be caused by worn components.

441. Timing a V-twin

Though this tip comes from 1923, it should be useful for later engines where no manual is available.

'Sometimes when a V-twin engine is to be timed, trouble arises because the cams of the magneto contact breaker are not stamped '1' and '2'. If they are, No.1 refers to the back cylinder. If not, their identity can be established by a simple process of reasoning. Because the cylinders of a V-twin do not fire at even intervals, there must be a greater gap between the firing points of No.1 than of No.2. If the contact breaker cams are inspected, it will be seen that they will not be exactly opposite. In the direction of the magneto's rotation, the smaller gap is between the end of No.2 cylinder's cam and the beginning of No.1. The reason for this is that when No.1 cylinder is firing, No.2 piston is only half way up the exhaust stroke. No.2's firing point, therefore, is more than a complete revolution of the engine behind No.1's. Hence the greater gap between the cams.'

442. Electric ignition timing

For those not happy with cigarette paper, this system was suggested as a more accurate method of establishing exactly when the contact breaker points are opening. Not trusting the idea of checking or adjusting the timing without the central bolt in place, I will only offer it as an alternative.

First remove the central bolt of

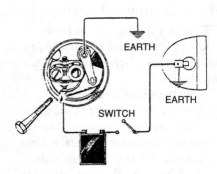

the contact breaker, taking care that the latter doesn't work loose on its taper. Disconnect the battery earth return of the lighting system and connect the negative pole by means of an insulated wire to the stationary, or insulated, part of the contact breaker. Ensure that no contact be made with any other part. Now switch on the lights and check that they go on and off with the closing and opening of the points. If they do, the exact instant of opening is given by the lights dimming visibly, and going out with the slightest further movement of the contact breaker.

443. Timing tip

An accurate way to establish ignition timing on a coil ignition system without special tools is to use the ammeter. Set the piston at the correct position before top dead centre, switch on the ignition and rotate the cam until the points are closed. A slight discharge will register on the ammeter. Rotate the cam in the correct direction, at the same time watching the ammeter. The moment the points separate, the needle will flick back to zero. The clamping bolt can then be tightened.

444. Manual ignition timing control

With manual advance and retard, retard the hand ignition control for starting, but advance as soon as the engine is running at speed. For normal running, the control should be kept in the advance position, and should be retarded only when the engine is labouring on full throttle. Any slackness in the cable can be taken up by sliding the waterproofing rubber shroud at the magneto end up the cable and turning the exposed hexagon adjuster. After adjusting, return the rubber shroud to its original position.

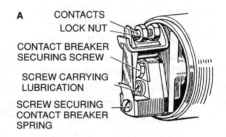

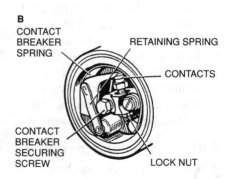

445. Rotating armature magnetos

These magnetos have the magnet cast in the body, and the armature and contact breaker rotate within the casting. Two designs of contact breaker are in common use. Single-cylinder

magnetos usually employ the Face Cam Type (sketch A), while magnetos for twin-cylinder engines have the Ring Cam Type (sketch B).

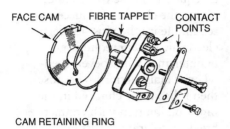

446. Lubrication – every 3000 miles. Face Cam Type

The cam is lubricated from a wick contained in the contact breaker base. To reach the wick, take out the screw which secures the spring arm carrying the moving contact, and lift off the backing spring and spring arm. The screw carrying the wick can then be withdrawn. At the same time, unscrew the contact breaker securing screw, take the tappet which operates the contact spring from its housing and lightly smear with thin machine oil. Extract the spring circlip and remove the face cam. Lightly smear both sides of the cam with light grease. When refitting, take care that the stop peg in the housing and the plunger of the timing control engage with their respective slots. A recess is provided for the eye of the circlip. When refitting the spring arm, see that the backing spring is fitted on top with its bent portion facing outwards.

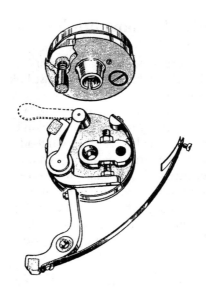

447. Lubrication – every 3000 miles. Ring Cam Type

The cam is supplied with lubricant from a felt pad contained in a pocket in the contact breaker housing. A small hole in the cam, fitted with a wick, enables the oil to find its way to the surface of the cam. Remove the contact breaker cover, turn the engine over until the hole in the cam can be clearly seen, and then carefully add a few drops of thin machine oil. Do not allow any oil to get on or near the contact points. If the cam ring is removed, the wick should be taken out and soaked in thin machine oil. Before replacing, wipe the wick to remove surplus oil.

448. Contact breaker rocking arm lubrication

The contact breaker rocking arm pivot also requires lubrication, and the complete contact breaker must be removed for this purpose. Take out the hexagon-headed screw from the centre of the

contact breaker and carefully lever the contact breaker off the tapered shaft on which it fits. Push aside the rocker arm retaining spring, lift off the rocker arm and lightly smear the pivot with light grease. Remove the cam ring, which is a sliding fit in the housing, and lightly smear inside and outside surfaces with light grease.

449. Removing and refitting the contact breaker cam

Removal and refitting of the cam can be made easier if the handlebar control lever is half retarded, thus taking the cam away from its stop pin. Apply one or two drops of thin machine oil to the felt cam lubricator in the housing. Refit the cam, taking care that the stop peg in the housing and the timing control plunger engage with their respective slots. If an earthing brush is fitted at the back of the contact breaker base, see that it is clean and can move freely in its holder, before refitting the contact breaker.

450. Refitting the contact breaker

When refitting the contact breaker, see that the projecting key on the tapered portion of the contact breaker base engages with the keyway cut in the magneto spindle, otherwise

the timing of the magneto will be affected. Replace the contact breaker securing screw and tighten with care.

451. Cleaning contacts

Every 6000 miles take off the contact breaker cover and examine the contact breaker. Dirty or pitted contacts can be cleaned with a fine carborundum stone or, if this is not available, very fine emery cloth. Wipe away any dirt or metal dust with a cloth moistened with petrol. Contact breaker springs should be examined and any rust removed. The contacts can be removed for cleaning. After cleaning, check the contact breaker setting, which should be between 10 and 12 thou.

452. Armature and condenser test

Armature windings and the condenser of the magneto or Magdyno can be tested by temporarily replacing the contact breaker screw in the threaded end of the shaft and running a wire from it to the positive terminal of a test battery, with an ammeter in series. Another wire should be run from the negative side of the battery to the armature earthing track. A reading of some 4 amp should be shown if the primary winding is sound. To test the secondary circuit leave the battery positive connection as it is; twist a piece of bare wire around the slip ring and lead it to within ¼ in. of the armature body. The lead from the negative side of the battery, flicked against the opposite end of the armature shaft, should produce a healthy spark. If none is forthcoming, then condenser trouble is possible: alternatively there may be a fault in the HT windings.

Withdrawing the armature impairs the quality of the permanent magnet and it is desirable to place a keeper, a bar of soft iron or a spanner will do, across the pole pieces. Nifal, an alloy containing nickel, iron and aluminium, has been used for magneto magnets since the mid-30s and is less susceptible to this trouble than was the previously-used cobalt steel which, if a keeper was not put in position at once, deteriorated considerably.

Before reassembling the magneto, check that the pick-up segment in the slip-ring is flush; a sharp edge will result in a rapidly worn carbon brush and a harmful coating of dust on the pick-up and earthing contact points. The armature, reassembled in the magneto body and, if necessary properly shimmed, should spin freely on its two bearings.

453. Condenser fault finding

The condenser, sometimes called a capacitor, absorbs current which might otherwise arc across the contact breaker points at the moment of separation. Such an occurrence would not only impair induction, but quickly burn away the hard contact points. Slight, spasmodic sparking can sometimes be detected, particularly if, as a test, the contact breaker cover is removed with the engine running at night. It does not usually indicate a condenser fault, however. If, on the other hand, the flash-over is constant, taking the

form of a flame rather than a spark, and starting and slow running are noticeably poor, then condenser trouble may well be suspected. An open-circuited condenser is betrayed by a white deposit of tungsten around the contact breaker points, as well as by arcing. A short-circuited condenser cuts out the contact breaker and stops the engine altogether.

454. Magneto overheating

If a magneto runs hot – so hot that the shellac varnish round the windings starts to melt – the usual cause is that the armature bearings have worn to such an extent that the armature fouls the pole shoes.

455. Earthing brush

Check the condition of the earthing brush. If it is not doing its job, i.e. that of a last link contact in the earthed return route of the HT ignition circuit, either the spark at the plug points will be bad, or earthed current will tend to find a return path through the bearings. That means pitted races – a problem which can occur in the event of the paper bearing cups having been faultily assembled, or having deteriorated over a period.

456. Lucas and BTH magnetos

The Lucas K2F magneto is fitted to a large number of vertical twin-cylinder engines. In working on this instrument, important items to note are the insulating paper cup and bearing assembly, and the use of the shims to give armature end clearance.

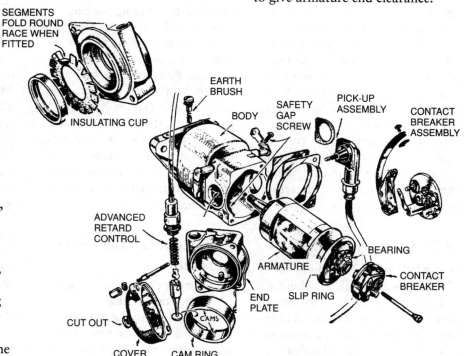

LUCAS K2F MAGNETO

SEGMENTS FOLD ROUND RACE WHEN FITTED

INSULATING CUP

EARTH BRUSH

BODY

SAFETY GAP SCREW

PICK-UP ASSEMBLY

CONTACT BREAKER ASSEMBLY

ADVANCED RETARD CONTROL

ARMATURE

BEARING

CONTACT BREAKER

CUT OUT

END PLATE

SLIP RING

COVER

CAM RING

CAMS

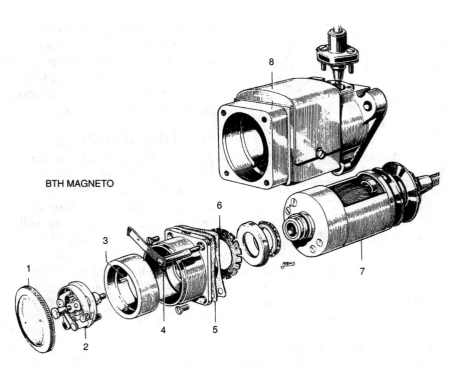

BTH MAGNETO

The main parts of a BTH magneto are as indicated on the sketch:
1. The contact breaker cover.
2. The contact breaker assembly.
3. The cam ring.
4. The contact breaker housing; note the eccentric peg on the left-hand side.
5. Shims to adjust the armature end float.
6. The fibre washer which insulates the ball race.
7. The armature.
8. The magneto body, pick-up brush and holder.

457. Twin-cylinder magnetos

Check that the two contact breaker cams have not worn to an unequal height, otherwise it won't be possible to adjust the points gaps accurately. One way to counter wear is to remove the cams from the timing ring and pack them with paper shims.

458. Non-stop engine

If operation of the cut-out button on a twin fails to stop the engine (and it is not just the case of the engine tending to run on after prolonged hard riding), the likely cause of the trouble is failure of the spring-loaded brush in the magneto to make proper contact with the armature. Often merely cleaning the brush and spring will affect a cure.

459. Twin-cylinder magneto on a single

There are two ways of using a twin magneto on a single:
1. Earth one of the HT leads by attaching it to the frame of the magneto or the machine, thus allowing the HT current to escape without damaging the windings.
2. Extend one of the existing cams about half way round the cam ring, so that during half a revolution of the armature the points are held apart. Therefore,

no current will flow in the primary circuit, and the redundant HT brush can be removed.

460. High tension pick-up

About every 6000 miles remove the high tension pick-up, secured by means of a clip or two screws. Wipe the moulding with a clean dry cloth. Check that the carbon brush moves freely in its holder, but take care not to stretch the brush spring unduly. If the brush is dirty, clean it with a cloth moistened with petrol. If the brush is worn to within ⅛ in. of the shoulder it must be renewed. Before refitting the high tension pick-up, clean the slip-ring track and flanges by pressing a soft dry cloth on the ring with a suitably shaped piece of wood, while the engine is slowly turned.

461. Renewing high tension cables

When high tension cables show signs of cracking or perishing they should be replaced using 7 mm neoprene-covered rubber ignition cable. To replace a high tension cable on a Lucas Magdyno, proceed as follows. Remove the metal washer and moulded terminal from the defective cable. Thread the new cable through the moulded terminal and cut back the insulation for about ¼ in. Pass the exposed strands through the metal washer and bend them back radially. Screw the terminal into the pick-up moulding. Do not solder the washer to the cable.

462. Intermittent misfiring

Intermittent misfiring on magneto contact breaker points may be caused by dampness in the bush of the rocking arm, or even swelling of the fibre pad at its end. This will prevent the points from closing completely, and can be checked by sliding a piece of white paper behind the points and examining them squarely with a strong light.

463. Slipped magneto timing

On many engines with chain driven magnetos, the sprockets are not keyed onto the magneto shaft but held by means of a taper and locknut. Unless this locknut is kept dead tight, the sprocket may slip because of the power put through the chain drive, upsetting the timing. Excessive stretching of the magneto chain will have a similar effect. An easy check is to retard the ignition control a touch while fully under way. If the engine slows dramatically, the ignition needs advancing because, correctly adjusted, slightly retarding the ignition should not affect the running of the engine.

464. Magneto chain adjustment

The minimum slack in a magneto chain, as recommended by Renolds, should not exceed ¼ in. One way of adjusting a slack magneto chain is to insert packers under one side of the magneto body. Indeed, this was recommended practice on pre-war AJS machines. An alternative would be to elongate the magneto fixing holes into the more usual

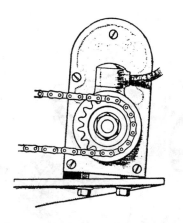

slots. In this original tip of 1921, it was suggested as a way of extending chain life beyond the natural length of the slots in the magneto platform. A replacement chain would be preferable.

465. Socket head pick-up

On many models it is awkward to undo the screws of the magneto pick-up because of lack of space for a screwdriver. If they are replaced by socket head screws, there is usually enough room for an Allen key.

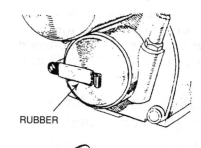

RUBBER

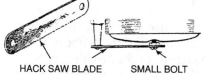

HACK SAW BLADE   SMALL BOLT

466. Magneto spring clip

Loose spring clips on magneto covers can be packed out with a short piece of rubber tubing. Broken clips can be replaced by a

short length of hacksaw blade, cleaned up and drilled at either end. One end is riveted to the existing stub, the other fitted with a tiny nut and screw to locate into the indentation in the cover.

467. Fibre pinions

If the teeth strip off fibre pinions from, say, a Magdyno, clean thoroughly the teeth from the adjacent pinion before fitting a new one. Otherwise that, too, will soon be ruined. A toothbrush dipped in petrol and inserted through the hole for the dynamo pinion will enable the old grease and fibre dust to be cleaned from the driving pinion.

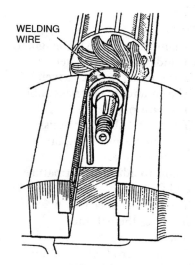

WELDING WIRE

468. Armature bearing removal

To remove tight armature bearings, bend into a U-shape a piece of ³⁄₃₂ in. welding rod, put it round the ball track and grip the rod (and, through it, the track) in a vice. Then, with a hammer, drive the shaft out of the bearing using a soft copper drift, making sure that the body of the armature is supported at all times.

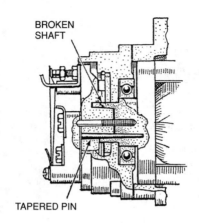

BROKEN SHAFT

TAPERED PIN

469. Magneto repairs

This tip from 1954 describes how to repair a damaged magneto:

'Some time ago the contact breaker cover on my machine worked loose, jammed between the primary chaincase and the contact breaker and sheared the semi-circular driving segment from the end of the magneto shaft. Faced with the prospect of buying a new and expensive armature and shaft, I carried out a home repair. After removing the magneto from the machine, I completely dismantled the contact breaker mechanism before refitting the base block to the shaft and tightening the securing screw as far as possible. Then, at a point midway between the securing screw and the lubricating wick, I drilled an 1/8 in. hole to a depth of about 3/4 in., sighting the drill so that on penetrating the base block it took a path between the central core of the casting and the counterbore of the shaft, thus forming a semi-circular keyway in each. After removing all swarf, a taper pin was tapped home in the keyway and the contact breaker reassembled.

'While repairing the magneto armature and shaft, I broke the pick-up brush, and made a replacement from the carbon of an old torch battery. An inch long piece of the carbon was gripped in a drill chuck and, by careful manipulation of a smooth file, one end was turned down to the required diameter. The carbon was reversed in the chuck and further reduced by about 1/8 in. to fit into the pick-up brush spring, after which I trimmed it to the required length and refitted the pick-up.'

Alternatively, send your magneto to an expert.

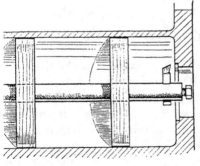

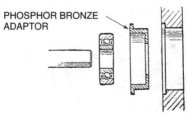

PHOSPHOR BRONZE ADAPTOR

470. Loose magneto bearing

First a jig has to be constructed to drill out the housing to take a phosphor bronze bush for the bearing. Drill a 5/8 in. hole in the centre of two pieces of hardwood, trued up in the lathe to fit tightly into the body of the magneto. Next, drill a suitable length of 5/8 in. mild steel to receive a cutting tool made of 5/16 in. silver steel and held in place with a 5/16 in. screw. Set the tool up in the lathe to cut the enlarged housing. Turn the phosphor bronze housing so that it is a good fit for the bearing and a shrink fit in the magneto body.

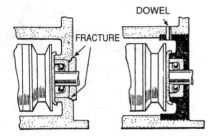

DOWEL

FRACTURE

471. Renewing a magneto bearing housing

Magneto housings have been known to fracture about the pinion bearing. Two obvious cures are to acquire a new magneto body or find a friend who can weld alloy; neither might be possible. This tip replaces the end of the magneto housing without the need for welding, but requiring some pretty nifty lathe work. First the whole of the end around the fracture was machined out, and the magneto shell screw-cut. A new bearing housing was made from duralumin on the lathe, and threaded to screw into the magneto shell. Finally a dowel was fitted to lock the two threads.

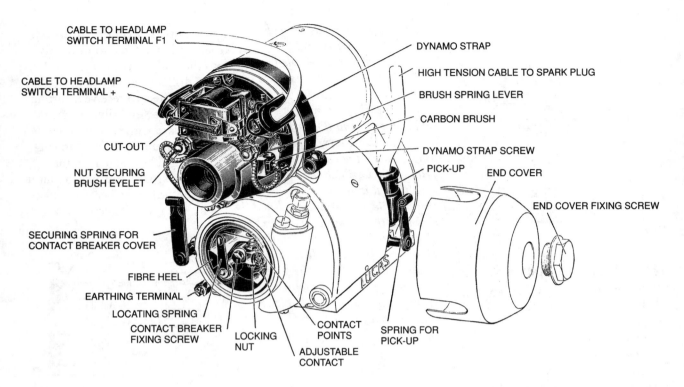

CABLE TO HEADLAMP
SWITCH TERMINAL F1

CABLE TO HEADLAMP
SWITCH TERMINAL +

CUT-OUT

NUT SECURING
BRUSH EYELET

SECURING SPRING FOR
CONTACT BREAKER COVER

FIBRE HEEL

EARTHING TERMINAL

LOCATING SPRING

CONTACT BREAKER
FIXING SCREW

LOCKING
NUT

CONTACT
POINTS

ADJUSTABLE
CONTACT

SPRING FOR
PICK-UP

DYNAMO STRAP

HIGH TENSION CABLE TO SPARK PLUG

BRUSH SPRING LEVER

CARBON BRUSH

DYNAMO STRAP SCREW

PICK-UP

END COVER

END COVER FIXING SCREW

472. Lucas Magdyno

The Lucas Magdyno shown in the sketch is arranged for driving in an anti-clockwise direction. With a clockwise machine the positions of the terminals marked + and F1 are interchanged, and the control brush box is situated on the opposite side of the contact breaker housing.

473. Dismantling the Magdyno clutch

When dismantling the slipping clutch on the Lucas Magdyno a U-shaped tool will prove invaluable. Made from ¼ in. mild steel rod, the U-shaped tabs are of a length to suit the depth of the locating holes, and the distance between their centres is 3³⁄₁₆ in.

474. Magdyno care

Avoid constant blipping of the throttle on Magdyno machines when the engine is in neutral. The dynamo portion of the instrument has considerable inertia, and rapid changes in engine revs will destroy the teeth on the fibre pinion. Later Magdynos are fitted with a dynamo-driven clutch to prevent this. When reassembling, the central locknut should be tightened to 10 ft/lbs to avoid clutch slip.

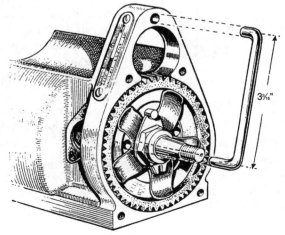

3³⁄₁₆"

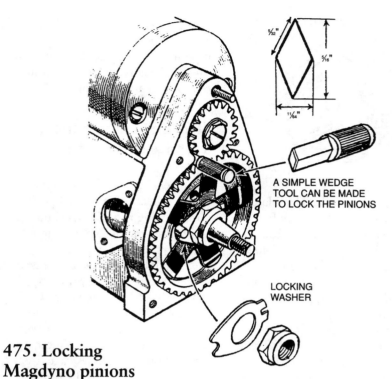

A SIMPLE WEDGE TOOL CAN BE MADE TO LOCK THE PINIONS

LOCKING WASHER

475. Locking Magdyno pinions

Wedging the pinions with wedges or a screwdriver to remove them risks damage. This simple diamond-shaped steel wedge can lock the pinions without damage while the nuts are loosened.

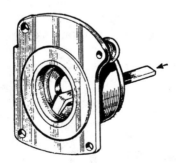

476. Removing and replacing Magdyno bearings

When removing the ball bearings which carry the Magdyno's armature this little tool makes a tricky job quite easy.

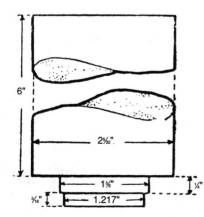

When replacing armature ball bearings a tool to these dimensions is recommended. It is best used in a hand press.

477. Magdyno ignition

One reader in 1956 suggested that it was easier to set the ignition timing on the Magdyno of his single-cylinder Royal Enfield if he removed the idler gear instead of the Magdyno gear. Royal Enfield, though admitting the system was quicker and easier, couldn't recommend it because of lack of accuracy.

'In general it will be found necessary to move the Magdyno gear slightly before the idler gear teeth drop into mesh; as there are 40 teeth on the Magdyno gear the movement necessary (plus or minus half a pitch) could be 4½ degrees, which is equal to 9 degrees of crankshaft rotation.'

You have been warned!

478. Contact breaker gap settings

Correctly set contact breaker gaps are important for the efficient and economical running of any engine. The correct gap settings for Lucas magnetos and distributors are as follows: rotating armature magnetos, 0.012–0.015 in.; rotating magnet magnetos, 0.010–0.012 in.; coil ignition contact breakers, 0.014–0.016 in.

When setting the contact breaker gap of a twin-cylinder magneto, measure the gap at both positions of the opening cam. The measurements may vary, and the smaller of the two gaps should be set to 0.012 in.; the greater gap should then be between 0.012 and 0.015 in. By setting the gaps in this manner the magnetic timing of the magneto is preserved.

479. Contact breaker removal

When dismantling the contact breaker the unit is often still tight on the taper after the stud has been removed. The taper seal can be broken without damage by pushing the fixing stud back in and wiggling it from side to side.

480. Lucas contact breaker units

Lucas contact breaker units, as fitted to most 60s twins are insulated from the surrounding casing by two pieces of thick black paper. These are often overlooked, but they must be in good condition and positioned correctly.

481. Lucas automatic advance and retard

The magnetos fitted to some motor cycles are provided with automatic timing control. This mechanism automatically varies the firing point according to the speed of the engine, thus relieving the rider of the necessity for adjusting the ignition timing. Its advantages are particularly evident when accelerating and during hill climbing, the danger of pre-ignition, pinking or knocking being very much reduced.

The control consists of a driving gear carrying a plate fitted with two pins. A weight is pivoted on each pin and the movement of the weight is controlled by a spring connected between the pivot end of the weight and a toggle lever pivoted at approximately the centre of the weight. Holes are provided in each toggle lever, in which locate pegs on the under-side of a driving plate secured to

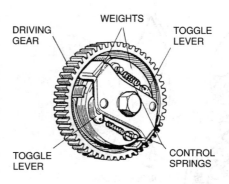

the magneto spindle. This plate is also provided with stops which limit the range of the control.

When the magneto is stationary the weights are in the closed position, and the magneto timing is retarded for starting purposes. As the speed is increased, centrifugal force acting on the weights overcomes the restraining influence of the springs and the weights move outwards, causing relative movement to take place between the driving gear and the magneto spindle, so advancing the timing. By careful design of the control springs, the control is arranged to conform closely to the engine requirements. When setting ignition timing with machines fitted with automatic advance and retard units, they should be wedged

gently in the fully advanced position. If the design of the machine disallows this, the manual should give a separate static (fully retarded) ignition setting.

482. BTH automatic advance and retard

The automatic ignition control mechanism is shown in the sketch where (1) is the self-withdrawing nut with its shoulder against the moving cage plate; (2) is the circlip to locate the oscillating hub relative to the gear wheel; and (3) is the spring to ensure that the moving cage returns to the full retard position.

The BTH unit was popular with Triumph, Velocette and Vincent. This is how it works: A cage, free to oscillate relative to the timing gear wheel, is attached to the armature shaft. Five rollers are interposed between five curved ears on the outer edge of this cage, and five corresponding ears on a cage riveted to the gear wheel. A spring inside the oil slinger pulls the oscillating cage (and, therefore, the armature shaft) backwards when the engine is stationary or

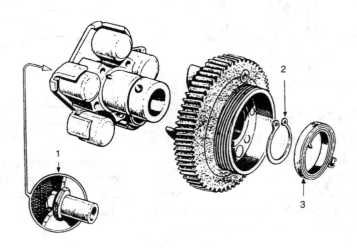

running slowly. When the engine speed reaches 1000 rpm, the rollers, or bob weights, are flung outwards causing a wedging action between the ears of the two cages, and moving the armature shaft forward relative to the driving gear, until the fully advanced position is reached at 2000 rpm.

Replacements were supplied as complete units. However, the outer cage and roller assembly can be separated from the timing wheel, if by any chance the timing wheel becomes damaged, by removing the coil spring and circlip inside the oil slinger from the hub of the oscillating cage. The timing wheel is riveted to the oil slinger and one half of the roller cage, and no attempt should be made to dismantle this sub-unit. A pair of circlip expanders are highly desirable for removing the circlip, which is too strong for the successful application of electrical screwdrivers.

On reassembling, the oscillating cage must have a little end float, likewise the rollers must also have end clearance. Great care should be taken of the cage ears which, if bent, will upset the amount of advance and retard automatically provided.

483. Contact breaker cam

A high pitched squeak from the timing side of a coil ignition Triumph twin could be caused by a dry contact breaker cam. The cure is a thin smear of high melting point grease (not ordinary grease) on the surface of the cam.

484. Coil protection

Never mount a coil in an exposed place, as water ingress will cause a short circuit. Under the petrol tank with the HT lead pointing backwards, or vertically under the seat, is ideal. Models with coils mounted on the saddle tube can suffer in heavy rain, or if left outside, from water running down the HT lead and into the coil. A neat cure is to fit a rubber boot used to seal HT leads on a magneto over the end of the coil.

485. Coil failure

The strap which secures an ignition coil should be just tight enough for the purpose – and no more. The coil windings are enclosed in an aluminium casing which, if distorted, could cause an internal short.

486. Warning light

On a machine equipped with coil ignition there is always a chance that the ignition switch will be left on inadvertently, particularly if the switch is positioned on the toolbox or somewhere equally out of the rider's view. To minimize the risk of a flat battery the speedometer bulb can be wired to the switch-wire (SW) terminal of the coil. The result is that when the ignition is switched on the speedo bulb lights and acts as a warning lamp. The extra consumption of current is negligible.

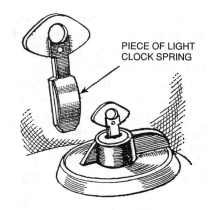

PIECE OF LIGHT CLOCK SPRING

487. Tight spade key

Spade keys for machines supplied with early coil ignition are notorious for their loose fit, and consequent loss mid-journey. To overcome the trouble, rivet a small piece of clock spring to the side of the business end of the key.

488. Conversion of flywheel magneto to coil ignition

The flywheel magnetos of Villiers two-strokes can be converted to coil ignition quite easily. This method was suggested in 1956 when the owner suspected loss of magnetism in the magneto. Extra items required are a single pole switch and a six-volt coil. Fit the switch to the headlamp to function as an ignition switch, and clip the coil to the frame. A terminal box big enough to house two terminals can be fixed to the magneto armature plate, out of the way of water or oil.

The wiring is simple. The lead from the flywheel magneto primary winding is disconnected from the insulated terminal of the contact breaker, and lengthened for connection to one terminal of the box. The other terminal of the box has a lead to the contact breaker insulated terminal, and a second lead to the CB terminal of the coil. (To pass the second lead out of the magneto, drill the armature plate and fit a grommet.) From the SW terminal of the coil run a lead to one side of the ignition switch. The other side of the switch is connected to the dynamo side (as opposed to the battery side) of the ammeter. The HT lead is, of course, connected to the spark plug.

The advantage of this conversion is that it has not destroyed the original ignition system. If the magneto is needed in an emergency, swap the HT leads and short-circuit the terminals in the box, leaving the ignition switch in the 'off' position.

489. Flywheel magnetos

In wet weather, water may run down the HT lead and enter the pick-up at the back of the generator. Re-route the lead so that it loops below the level of the terminal an inch or so from the back of the generator. Water will then drip off the lead at the bottom of the loop.

490. Maglita wiring diagram

Maglita lighting systems do not have a happy reputation. Nevertheless they were fitted to a wide range of British motor cycles in the 20s and 30s. This generally applicable wiring diagram comes from 1926.

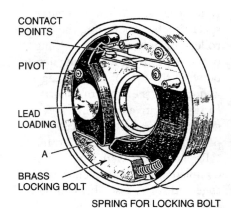

SPRING FOR LOCKING BOLT

491. Maglita cut-out

This drawing shows the construction of the centrifugal cut-out. The brass locking bolt should have highly polished bearing surfaces and be smeared with a trace of light oil, so that there is no possibility of it sticking. It is desirable that the curve at point A be nicely radiused.

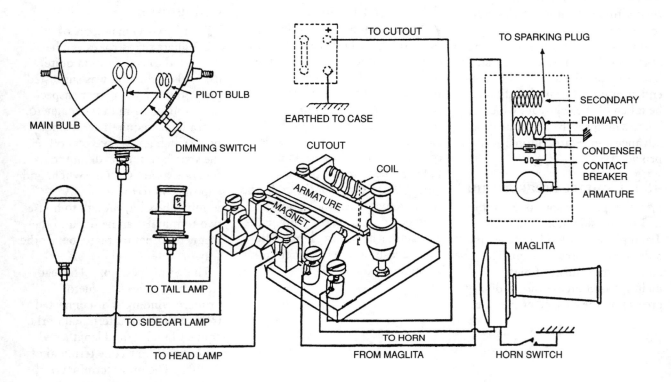

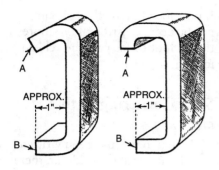

492. Maglita keeper

A special form of soft-iron keeper has to be used in connection with a ML Maglita. The sketch on the left shows a keeper suitable for later-type instruments. Face A has to mate with the bevelled upper surface of the magnet, while Face B is arranged to make contact with the laminations immediately below the magnet. In the case of the older type Maglita, the laminations at the top of the instrument are accessible once the top cover has been removed, and a keeper in the form shown on the right should be employed.

493. Careful with that plug thread!

In a light alloy cylinder head care must be taken when replacing a spark plug, or the result could be a crossed or stripped thread. Often the cause of the trouble is trying to start the thread by using a box or plug spanner. The plug should always be started by hand (use a rag if it's hot) and the spanner reserved for the final tightening only.

494. Clean spark plug threads

Fouling of the threads of a spark plug tends to retard heat flow from the plug to the cylinder head. Clean the threads with a brass wire brush every time the plug is removed. Dress the end of the electrode with a fine file or emery paper at the same time to remove encrusted carbon deposits. Keep the external surface of the insulator clean and dry to prevent loss of high tension energy.

495. Spark plugs – on the other hand

Graphited grease on the threads of a spark plug is an aid to easy removal, and is particularly desirable with light alloy cylinder heads.

496. Plug dismantling – cold

If care is not taken when dismantling a detachable spark plug it is easy to damage the gland nut. Instead of holding the nut in the vice while the plug body is unscrewed, it is better to clamp a suitable box spanner in the vice, insert the gland nut, and then undo the plug body. A ring spanner should be used in preference to an open-ended.

497. Plug dismantling – hot

Better still is to heat the plug up first before attempting to unscrew the gland nut. This could prevent damage from excessive force exerted on a cold plug.

498. Spark plugs on twins

Spark plugs on twins with magneto ignition receive spark discharges of alternate polarities, leading to unequal erosion of the electrodes. If the plugs are swapped over every 500 miles or so, their condition will remain more even and they will last longer.

499. Spark plug gap

The spark plug gap should be checked periodically on all machines. Check the manual, but it is usually between 0.018 in. and 0.025 in. On two-strokes the gap is critical, and should be checked regularly.

500. Wrong plug

Pre-ignition, bringing a rise in cylinder temperature which could result in burnt out valves or pistons, can often be caused by faulty or unsuitable spark plugs. Check for pre-ignition by pressing the cut-out button or switching off the ignition. The engine should cut cleanly, without any tendency to run on.

501. Further tips on ignition problems of a get-you-home nature are listed in 'The Road' section.

Sidecars

502. Sidecar alignment – fiction

In the UK it is usually assumed that sidecars are mounted on the left-hand side of a machine because of laws relating to driving on the left-hand side of the road. Not so. Before the First World War *The Motor Cycle* reasoned thus:

'The sidecar is preferably fitted to the left-hand side of the machine as ladies dislike being too close to approaching traffic.'

503. Sidecar alignment – fact

It is important, for reasons of safe steering, that the sidecar is aligned properly to the machine. As with most adjustments, optimum figures vary from machine to machine and type of sidecar. But the layout described below is a good enough general rule. The three factors to remember are toe-in, lean out, and lead.

1. Toe-in – with the motor cycle wheels pointing in line straight ahead, the sidecar wheel should toe-in about ¾ in. This is best measured by placing boards along either side of the outfit and taking a measurement front and back. The measurement between the two boards should be ¾ in. less at the front than at the back.
2. Lean out – with the sidecar chassis horizontal to the ground, the motor cycle should lean away from the sidecar by about an inch from the vertical between the handlebars and the ground. If the outfit drifts to the left on normal road cambers it is usually a sign that the motor cycle is not leaning away from the sidecar sufficiently.
3. Lead – the line of the sidecar axle should be in front of the motor cycle's rear wheel spindle. Recommendations vary from zero lead to 9 in. I would start with a 6 in. lead, and try the outfit.
4. Because, on an outfit, the handlebars are used as a tiller and not just somewhere to dangle the levers and switches, it is a good idea for some sort of steering damper to be fitted. Drive with the damper screwed on slightly all the time. This will prevent low speed wobble and severe jarring over rough surfaces.

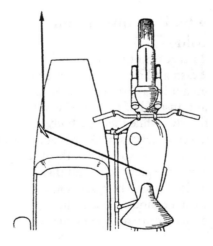

504. Alignment with Europe

Before crossing the Channel to the other side of the road, it is best to realign the sidecar so that the motor cycle is upright instead of leaning out. To permit safe overtaking a mirror can be fixed to the left-hand side of the sidecar. If positioned correctly it should not be necessary to pull out more than a foot to see past the vehicle in front.

505. Cornering with a sidecar

Though much has been written about handling a sidecar, there is no substitute for a lot of practice. This brief item from 1923 demonstrates that geometry hasn't changed since Pythagoras. On left-handers in Ancient Greece the horse still had to run round the outside of the chariot:

'Because of a one-sided drive, cornering on a sidecar outfit presents problems which do not arise in the case of other three- and four-wheelers. These problems once appreciated, the driver finds that he can round corners at a higher speed than the inexperienced would believe possible. The explanation lies in turning to account the inertia and the momentum of the two components of the sidecar outfit.

'A right-hand corner is approached at speed, the front wheel turned and simultaneously the engine shut down, and perhaps the rear brake applied. The momentum of the sidecar, tending to travel forward, produces a swinging effect to the right, the motor cycle's rear wheel acting as a pivot.

'Conversely, on a left-hand bend, the procedure is to slow down slightly before the corner is reached, and to accelerate the engine as the corner is rounded. In this instance the drag of the sidecar tends to cause the machine to swing to the left. The great point to remember is to

accelerate when actually on the bend; and it is best to turn on a fixed radius.'

506. Sidecar skills

According to this advice from the 30s, 'sidecars are all but immune from skids. They will in exceptional circumstances slide bodily when a greasy corner is taken recklessly, and if greasy hills are descended too fast the back wheel will sometimes swing across the track a little.' They may try to throw you into a hedge, 'but providing they are properly handled, there is no vehicle on the road so proof from skidding.'

507. Sidecar handlebars

If a machine is converted from solo to sidecar use, it may be a good idea to fit a longer pair of handlebars. The steering on an outfit is more like a tiller action, and the extra leverage afforded by the longer bars will mean a less tiring ride.

508. Emergency braking

In an emergency the braking distance of an outfit can be reduced by swinging the handlebars from one lock to the other as the brakes are applied.

509. Turning circle

The turning circle of an outfit is much smaller when the machine is driven round the sidecar.

510. Sidecar pivot mounting

This is a modification to cure body sway, and though intended for a Watsonian Albion, it could well apply to many other early 50s makes. The problem was put down to the four coil springs at the front chassis mounting; these were replaced by rubber bushed bearings. First, the front springs and bearer bar were removed. Two mountings to incorporate the rubber bushes were fabricated from two short lengths of steel tube of one inch internal diameter, to each of which were welded two struts cut from ¼ in. x 1 in. mild steel strip. The struts were drilled to register with the original spring retaining bolt holes on the chassis lugs.

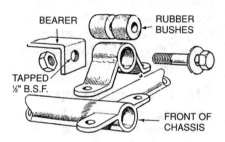

Four rubber bushes were chosen with an outside diameter of one inch, two being fitted end on in each mounting. The length of the bushes should be such that they project a little beyond the ends of the mounting. A new bearer bar was made from ¼ in. x 1½ in. mild steel strip. Each end was bent down at right angles, and drilled and tapped to take the bearer bolt. The assembly was completed by the bearer bolts being inserted through large flat washers, the mounting bushes, the threaded bearer bar, and tightened up with a locknut. As the bolt is tightened, the rubber bushes are compressed axially and therefore expand radially to grip the bolt and the housing.

511. Swan-neck solution

One way to free a front swan-neck on a sidecar chassis is to drill a tiny hole in the rear of each brazed connection on the front cross tube, and fill with penetrating oil. After leaving for a day or so, warm slightly and give the swan-neck a sharp blow across the axis of the pivot.

512. Special sidecar components

When the use of sidecars was widespread, many factories supplied special components to make their motor cycles more suitable for sidecar use. Usually a range of different-sized gearbox or engine sprockets were available to alter the gearing to increase the machine's pulling power at the expense of top speed. Front forks were altered to reduce front wheel wobble, either by increasing the trail or by fitting heavier gauge parts. Heavier fork springs were also available. If a solo machine is being rebuilt as a combination it is worth researching into what was originally available from the manufacturers.

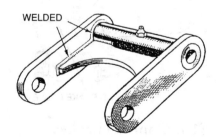

513. Girder fork strengthening

Some machines with girder forks may find sidecar work too

strenuous. The forks can be beefed up by fitting heavier duty links and even by brazing in a strengthening web. In this sketch the new links are the same thickness as the originals but ¼ in. wider, giving valuable extra meat around the spindle holes. The web is cut from ¼ in. thick steel plate and electrically welded.

514. Sidecar wheels

The wheel bearing arrangement in some early sidecars left a lot to be desired. *The Motor Cycle* recommended in the 20s that:

'When taking delivery of a new sidecar, it is not inadvisable to remove the hubcap and to make quite sure that some method of preventing the cone unscrewing itself from the spindle has been incorporated. This is often a split pin in the wheel spindle, and its absence may result in the complete wheel removing itself from the sidecar.'

And I thought it only happened in films!

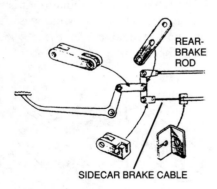

REAR-BRAKE ROD

SIDECAR BRAKE CABLE

515. Coupled brakes

This suggestion for a compensating mechanism comes from 1955. The system comprises four main parts. A piece of steel measuring 2½ in. x ⅝ in. x ⅝ in. is drilled and slotted at each

end. One slot accommodates the brake rod attachment eye on the pedal; the other receives a strip of steel (size 3½ in. x ⅝ in. x ³⁄₁₆ in.) drilled at each end and arranged vertically to pivot at the middle.

To the lower end of this second strip is fixed a small yoke to retain the nipple of the sidecar-wheel brake cable; a cable stop is fitted to the chainstay. The brake rod is shortened and fitted to the upper extremity of the vertical pivoted member.

Owing to the fact that the return spring of the sidecar-wheel brake is weaker than that for the rear brake, the sidecar brake is applied first, and thus the outfit can be assisted through left-hand corners by delicate use of the pedal.

516. Rear brake stop

A wedge can be placed between the rear brake lever and its stop to hold the brake on while parked. It is suggested that this can be used on gradients when, if merely left in gear, the outfit's engine may go over compression. Though a neat idea, this wedge should be used in conjunction with the gearbox, and on steep hills don't risk it. Turn the front wheel into the kerb, and borrow a couple of bricks as well!

517. Front brake stop

Wrap a rubber band made from an old inner tube round the front brake lever and the handlebar twistgrip.

518. Front wheel stand

How do you lift the front wheel of a heavy outfit on to its front wheel stand?
1. Wedge a wooden roller behind the front wheel. Standing in

front of the machine, grip the wheel at the bottom, and pull forwards and upwards. The wheel mounts the roller allowing the stand to drop into place, and a slight turn of the wheel will release the roller.
2. Roll the front wheel backwards up a plank with one end resting on a brick. This method also suits machines without front wheel stands which need to be supported by a block under the crankcase.

519. Sidecar wheel removal

Some machine's wheels can be loosened merely with a tommy-bar. If your sidecar is attached to such a machine why not alter the sidecar wheel fixing to match? By welding a short extension onto the wheel nut and drilling it to take a tommy-bar, all three wheels can be removed with one tool, and bulky spanners can be left at home.

MILD STEEL HOOK

10"

3" X 2" BASE

520. Sidecar wheel jack – Mk 1

A wooden board just long enough to raise the sidecar wheel off the ground, and with a V cut in one end, will be quite sufficient to act as a jack in an emergency. Alternatively, a simple jack can be made from a hardwood block and a mild steel strip. Shape the block into a slight taper and, in its top, form a curved groove suitable for the sidecar frame tube. Bend the steel strip into a hook at one end, and screw the other end to the top of the block. The dimensions shown on the sketch may not suit every sidecar; obviously the block has to be tall enough to lift the wheel off the ground.

To use, hook the jack onto the frame rail near the tube, lift the wheel and the jack will swing into position. Wheeling the outfit forward disengages it.

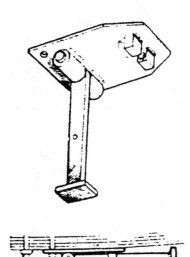

521. Sidecar wheel jack – Mk 2

This permanent jack-cum-leg from 1955 will suit many sidecars and may appeal to the more ambitious. The stand consists of an anchor plate of mild steel to which two short lengths of heavy gauge steel tubing were welded in line with their ends

$\frac{5}{16}$ in. apart. The plate was drilled and attached to the left underside as near as possible to the wheel. The leg of the stand was made from a length of ¼ in.-thick steel strip long enough to lift the sidecar wheel well off the ground. One of the corners of one end of the leg was radiused, and that end drilled to take a bolt which, when passed through the tubes and leg, formed the pivot. A rectangular steel pad was welded to the other end of the leg to give it a foot, and a spring clip was welded to the anchor plate to hold the leg in the raised position when it wasn't in use.

522. Sidecar support

If a machine is used regularly for both solo and sidecar work, it is handy to make up some wooden blocks capable of supporting the sidecar. These can be shaped to seat the chassis spars comfortably when removing the sidecar, and be cut to the exact height for fitting the lugs on the machine when refitting.

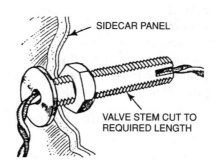

SIDECAR PANEL

VALVE STEM CUT TO REQUIRED LENGTH

523. Sidecar wiring

Valve holders cut from old inner tubes can be used to thread cables through sidecar panelling.

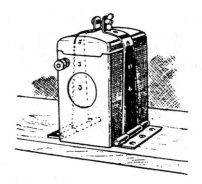

524. Sidecar-mounted battery

Batteries mounted in sidecars can be held in place neatly and securely by a pair of ordinary gate hinges drawn together at the top by a bolt and wing-nut.

525. Self-tapping screws

When using a self-tapping screw, it is better to punch a hole in the metal rather than drill it. A punched hole will permit the screw to grip the metal with two or three threads, whereas a drilled hole will only give an edge contact.

526. Sidecar hood care

Sidecar hoods should be kept buttoned to the sidecar when they are wet. Should they be rolled up before fully dry, they are likely to shrink or rot.

527. Eyelet fixing

Fixing eyelets in canvas can be done without special tools. First cut a hole of the correct size in the material and insert the eyelet. Pass a bolt through the eyelet with the bolt head against the smooth side. Clamp a nut in the vice large enough for the bolt to be a sliding fit. Place the bolt through the nut so that it is against the serrated edge of the eyelet. It remains only to give a few light taps with a hammer on the bolt head to turn and flatten the serrations.

528. Sidecar screens

Joining a transparent plastic screen to hood material can be done with boot eyelets available from any cobbler. They are easy to rivet with a centre punch, finishing with a light tap direct from the hammer. Select eyelets deep enough to take the screen and apron in addition to a thin strip of sheet steel used as a stiffener.

529. Hood protection

To prevent sidecar hoods from chafing on the angles of their framework, apply rubber patches to contact points between frame and hood.

530. Fitting a Perspex windscreen

Position the rubber H-section moulding around the window frame, and place a length of cord into the groove which is to accept the Perspex. The cord should be slightly longer than the periphery of the window and the two ends should be allowed to hang free.

Place one edge of the Perspex into the groove from which the ends of the cord are hanging. Maintain steady pressure against the rubber moulding by pressing on the Perspex with one hand, and with the free hand grip both ends of the cord and pull steadily. As the cord is drawn free of the groove it will peel open the outer flange of the moulding and allow the Perspex to slide into place.

531. Cutting Perspex

A good way to cut a hole or a slot in Perspex is to mount a ¼ in. diameter bit into an electric drill, and use the side of the drill as though it was a milling cutter. Take care not to press too hard against the Perspex, or it may fracture.

532. Screen cleaner

Shabby sidecar screens can be cleaned with liquid metal polish. Quite deep scratches in Perspex can be removed with the aid of fine grinding paste mixed with a little machine oil, and rubbed firmly along the scratch with cotton wool. When the scratch has almost disappeared, continue the process with metal polish, and finish with a proprietary Perspex cleaner.

533. Screen protection

Before undertaking a wet journey, apply two or three drops of glycerine to the windscreen with a damp cloth. This will lower the surface tension of the rain striking the screen, keeping it clearer for longer. In cold weather an application of glycerine will keep the screen frost free for several days.

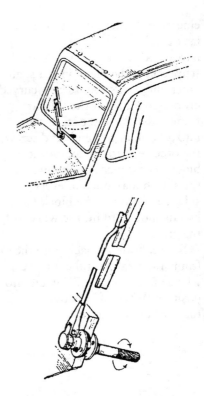

534. Windscreen wiper

This suggestion comes from 1954. Two flanged bushes were made from 1 in. Duralumin. One was drilled and tapped to accommodate three 4BA bolts at equidistant intervals around the circumference of the flange; the flange of the other was drilled with three clearance holes. The sidecar's fascia board was drilled halfway along its length and the bushes were bolted together, one on each side of the hole. A suitable spindle was filed square at one end to take an ordinary car windscreen wiper, secured with a grubscrew. Once in place, the other end was finished off with a small handle.

535. Fitting celluloid windows

When fitting celluloid windows to a sidecar, warm the celluloid first in front of a fire (not that close!). When the sheet is quite limp, lay it on a flat surface, place the window bead over it and mark off with a scriber. To make the holes for the rivets, heat the point of a large needle held by pliers, and pierce gently where the holes are required.

536. Celluloid cement

Celluloid cement can be made by dissolving celluloid in amyl acetate or cellulose thinners. It is ideal for mending windscreens. At a pinch it can be used to stop up redundant drill holes in mudguards and other tinware, though modern proprietary metal fillers are probably better.

537. Easy maintenance?

While solo riders may struggle with withdrawal of the clutch from the gearbox mainshaft, it can be carried out

without special pullers on an outfit. Simply loop a length of rope around the back of the clutch body and the adjacent sidecar frame rail. Tighten up the rope with a tyre lever tourniquet-fashion to pull off the clutch.

538. Norton clutch

Any work involving the primary drive is more awkward with a sidecar fitted. This tip to ease work on the clutch of a 16H Norton outfit had factory approval. Three screws hold the springs and spring boxes in position, which need a socket spanner for their removal and replacement. In the confined space between machine and chair it's difficult to get the required purchase on the socket spanner. By cutting slots in the ends of the clutch screws, a screwdriver can be used instead. Final tightening should be done with the spanner.

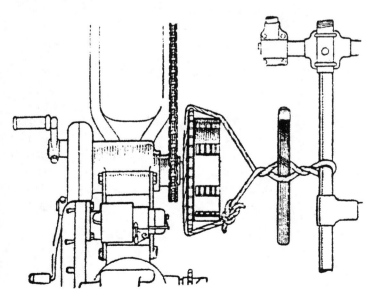

539. Foot warmer

To keep your passenger's feet warm, heat up thoroughly a couple of house bricks, wrap in a towel, and place in the nose of the sidecar. The storage heating principle means the bricks retain their heat for a long time.

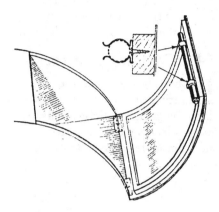

540. Pump storage

Tyre pumps on solos are usually stored directly in line with oil and road dirt. In a sidecar they can be stored out of the way, neatly clipped to the inside of the boot lid.

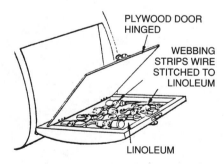

PLYWOOD DOOR HINGED

WEBBING STRIPS WIRE STITCHED TO LINOLEUM

LINOLEUM

541. Sidecar tool kit

Many sidecar riders just keep their tools rattling about loose in the boot. This sketch from 1959 shows how the boot lid of a Watsonian Warwick can be adapted as a tool tray, an idea which could be used for many different types of chair. The plywood cover from inside the boot lid was removed and refitted with a pair of hinges at the bottom and a fastener at the top. A piece of vinyl floor covering was cut to fit the shallow cupboard thus formed. Two strips of webbing were then attached to the vinyl by stapling with copper wire in such a way that they formed loops into which the tools could be held firm.

542. Camping gear rack

If you've ever endured the sensation of packing wet camping gear, this tip is a must as most sidecars will be able to accommodate some form of rack.

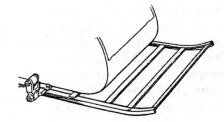

The one shown is made from two longitudinals of ⅜ in. angle iron connected by welding flat cross members of strip steel. The frontend of the carrier was bolted to the chassis rear bearer bar. A rear fixing was constructed by drilling holes in the floor of the sidecar boot, and bolting a spare length of strip steel to one of the cross members with ⅜ in. bolts.

543. Pillion handgrip

For a pillion rider on a sidecar outfit a safe and comfortable handgrip is made by fixing a leather strap to the sidecar body. The strap should be at least 7 in. long and fixed to a convenient structural part of the sidecar, such as a frame member.

544. One-way intercom

'Recently I fitted a sidecar to my machine and found that I could not hear my wife speaking, though she could hear me. I made a simple one-way intercom from a length of rubber tubing – of the type used for gas pokers – and a couple of polythene funnels. One funnel fits into the left earflap of my safety helmet and the other forms a mouthpiece for my wife.' Gas tubing? It would be, wouldn't it!

THE WORKSHOP

The Motor Cycle reckoned that the three essential features of any workshop are a good light, a sturdy and rigid bench and a suitable vice set at the right height. This is true whether the workshop is purpose-built with piped music and an oxy-acetylene welding set, or just a garden shed.

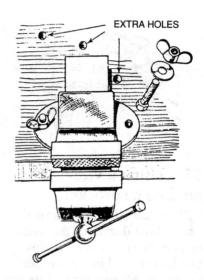

EXTRA HOLES

Workshop practice

545. Fire precaution

Whatever your workshop is like, and wherever it is, it should have a fire extinguisher capable of dealing with burning petrol. And don't forget, water spreads a petrol fire, so a bucket of sand is better than the wrong type of extinguisher.

546. Workshop organisation

Just because the workshop is large, doesn't mean there'll be plenty of space. Conversely a lot can be stored in a small shed if it is done thoughtfully and kept tidy. No one needs reminding how much floor space can be saved by extensive wall storage and adequate shelving. But have you ever thought of using both sides of the shelf?

547. Useless waste?

Those with pristine, temperature-controlled workshops will want to skip this paragraph. But for most of us in our damp sheds, where the tools share space with garden spades and chicken wire, this tip kills two birds with one stone. Neither soiled cleaning rags nor old engine oil present a picture of usefulness on their own, but together they can. Soak the rags in the oil, squeeze them out, and use them over tool trays and nut and bolt tins to keep both damp and dust at bay.

548. The height for a vice

A vice is at the correct working height when the top of the jaws are level with the user's elbow. A vice can be raised by packing the underside with a steel plate.

549. Swivelling vice

The utility of a swivelling vice cannot be denied, but is probably too expensive for most workshops. However, additional holes can be drilled in the workbench surface to allow the vice to be moved to different angles.

550. Soft jaws

The jaws of an engineering vice are too hard for many motor cycle engineering tasks. One way to soften them when working with alloy and the like is to cover them temporarily with an L-shaped strip of lead, copper or aluminium sheeting. Alternatively make up two jaws of hardwood to screw in place of the metal originals when required.

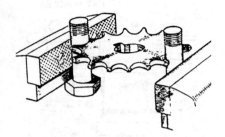

551. Using a vice – holding a sprocket

To hold a sprocket in a vice without damaging the teeth, tighten the vice jaws up against two bolts placed in the sprocket's serrations. Magneto sprockets can be fixed to a wooden block with two screws set between the teeth, and the block held in the vice.

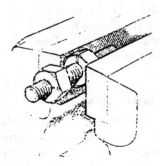

552. Using a vice – removing a seized nut

When removing a seized nut from a stud, the good end of the stud can be preserved from the vice jaws by splitting another nut of the same thread down one side. This is then threaded onto the stud and tightened into the vice, leaving the seized nut exposed ready for removal.

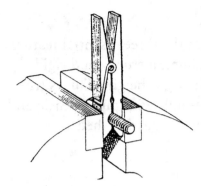

553. Using a vice – without damaging a thread

To protect the thread from the vice jaws, apart from the split nut method above, wind copper wire into the thread pitch. As long as the wire thickness is greater than the pitch, the thread will be protected. Or hold it in a wooden clothes peg.

554. Using a vice – shortening a bolt

If a bolt is being shortened with a hacksaw, screw the nut onto the bolt before cutting it. Then the nut can be wound backwards and forwards over the cut to clear the thread and provide a good lead.

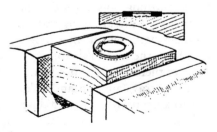

555. Using a vice – reducing a washer

To work on washers (e.g. reducing their thickness) grip a softwood block in the vice jaws, and tap the washer onto the block.

The indentation in the softwood will be enough to hold the washer while working, without taking the skin off your fingers.

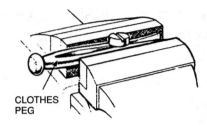

CLOTHES PEG

556. Using a vice – Cutting a slot

Cutting a slot in a small cheesehead screw is difficult to achieve without damaging the threads in the vice jaws. A simple solution is to place the screw between the legs of an ordinary wooden clothes peg, thus protecting the thread – only a small amount of pressure is needed to hold the screw securely.

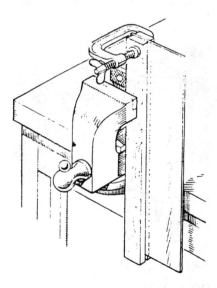

557. Using a vice – cutting thin sheets

If using tinsnips, sheet metal can be cut easier if one arm of the snips is gripped in the vice. The tin can be fed through, more pressure applied to the other arm, and a straight, even line followed. Thin sheets of timber or metal cut with a saw are best held in a vice between two stout battens. Depending on the length of the sheet, a G-clamp can be used as an additional grip.

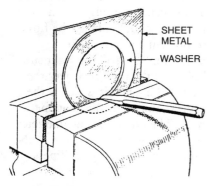

SHEET METAL

WASHER

558. Using a vice – cutting a hole

To cut a hole in sheet metal, place the sheet of metal in the vice together with a washer with the same inside diameter as the required hole. Keep the inner edge of the washer level with the top edge of the vice jaws. Cut the hole with a sharp cold chisel and a hammer, working the sheet round in the vice so that the cutting is always done near the top of the vice jaws.

559. Using a vice – drilling thin sheets

When drilling thin materials such as gaskets, celluloid or tin, place the material between two pieces of wood, and grip vertically in the vice. One piece of wood should be taller than the other and act as a backing to the material being drilled. In this way

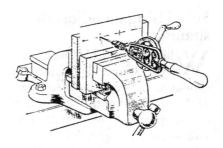

the drill will run straight through the thin material into the backing, without tearing or bending it.

560. Using a vice – filing a shoulder

To file a shoulder on a rod, place the rod vertically in a vice and slide a washer over the end of the rod to rest on the vice jaws. The rod should be adjusted so that the limit of the required shoulder is exactly in line with the upper face of the washer. Use a safe-edge file working evenly round the rod with the safe edge resting on the washer. The washer will protect the vice and provide an accurate and level working line. If filing a soft metal such as aluminium, coating the file with chalk will help prevent clogging.

561. Tap turning

Tapping a hole in a confined space can prove awkward if an obstruction makes it impossible to use a conventional tap wrench. In some circumstances the problem can be overcome by holding the tap in a carpenter's brace. Because of the length of the brace, extra care is necessary to ensure the tap is vertical in the hole.

562. Threading holes

There is a simple way to gauge the right size drill before tapping a hole. Take a nut which has the same size and type of thread as the hole to be tapped, and select a drill which will pass comfortably through the nut. This will ensure that only so much metal is removed before tapping the thread.

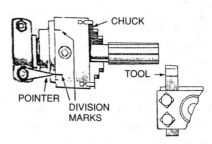

CHUCK

TOOL

POINTER

DIVISION MARKS

563. Cutting splines with a lathe

If the splined portion of a kickstarter shaft breaks off, a new shaft can be fashioned on a lathe from a length of 60-ton steel. Place the original shaft in the lathe with the splined piece protruding. Grind a tool to suit the shape of the spline, and use the tool to divide the lathe's chuck into the number of splines, each being marked on the chuck with a scriber. Having fixed a pointer on one of the bearing cap nuts to coincide with the divisions marked on the chuck, put the new blank in the chuck and cut the splines by moving the saddle to and fro. Take only small cuts, turning the chuck after each cut to the next division. Continue rotating and cutting gradually until the required depth of the spline is reached. Tidy up the new shaft with a file before refitting the quadrant.

564. Turning without a lathe

A metal rod can be reduced in diameter by cutting a thread and filing it off. If you have enough dies, thread cutting and filing will reduce the rod by as much as needed.

565. The Diabolo method

A high polish on a spindle or valve stem can be accomplished by what is known as the Diabolo method. Mount the spindle rigidly in the vice, using the jaw protectors to prevent damage. Wind a strip of fine emery paper round the shaft twice, and overwrap the emery with a length of cotton tape. The tape should be wrapped round the emery three or four turns, leaving the two ends of the tape free. By pulling alternately on the two ends one automatically spins the emery at high speed, at the same time exerting an even pressure. If the tapes are worked steadily from end to end along the shaft, the result will be excellent.

566. Clean piston ring grooves

After scraping out piston ring grooves with a piece of discarded ring, there are usually small patches of stubborn carbon remaining. To finally clean up, soak a piece of thick string in oil and work through each groove 'diabolo' fashion. That is with the string looped round the piston one and a half times, so that when each end is pulled the action on the groove is constant all the way round. This will take out the carbon and leave a polished groove.

567. Using an adjustable spanner

Whenever possible, the handle of an adjustable spanner should be turned in the direction of the open end of the jaws; if used consistently the other way the jaws will become strained. An adjustable spanner can be used to measure anything circular if callipers are not available or the object is inaccessible. Tighten the jaws around the object to be measured, remove the spanner, and measure the width of the jaws with a ruler.

568. Useful electrical aids

The list of items to improve the stock of the workshop is more or less endless and, let's face it, all part of the hobby. But some tools are indispensable, and electricity is an essential medium:

1. A good electric drill.
2. A drill stand.
3. A lead light.
4. An extension lead.
5. And while we're on the subject of electricity, it won't do any harm to splash out on a power breaker.

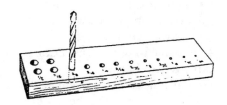

569. Drill bit storage

If not properly stored, drill bits can become lost and damaged. A stand can be made quite simply from a piece of hardwood drilled at intervals to a depth of about ¾ in. with each appropriate drill size, and the holes marked accordingly. The advantage of this over a bought drill stand, apart from being cheaper, is that if you have more than one drill bit of the same size, you can drill an extra hole beside the first.

570. Grommet gauge

Where an electric wire passes through a metal panel, such as a nacelle or mudguard, a rubber grommet should always be fitted to prevent chafing of the insulation. To drill the right size hole, slip the grommet over the shank of a drill bit which is the same diameter as the grommet bore. Then measure the diameter of the grommet at the base of the groove with a pair of callipers.

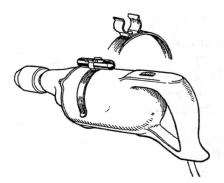

571. Accuracy in drilling

A good way to maintain the horizontal when using an electric drill is to attach a spirit level to the body of the drill. Wrap a large worm screw clip round the body of the drill (an ordinary bicycle clip fits some drills) and rivet to it a spring clip capable of gripping firmly a small spirit level. The rivet should be tight enough to hold the two clips firmly together, but still allow them to rotate stiffly. When using the drill horizontally, align the level along the axis of the drill. When using it vertically, turn the level across the axis and adjust it in the clip so that the glass panel is uppermost.

572. Heat

A source of heat is extremely useful in a workshop. Oxy-acetylene will give the hottest flame and is best for dismantling a rusty wreck with the minimum of damage, but it is expensive and dangerous without some basic training. For most ordinary tasks involving alloy a little butane or propane gas blow torch is quite adequate.

573. All over warmth

When removing a bearing from a light alloy casting, a good method is to use heat, because it doesn't take a lot of heat to expand the alloy sufficiently and it avoids the risk of damage caused by hammering or levering. But it is important that the casting is heated uniformly, not just in the region of the bearing. A blow-lamp flame should flicker over the whole surface, bringing the heat of the alloy up gently. Over a gas ring the casting should be revolved regularly. An oven is the best solution of all, adding a delicate flavour to the Sunday joint into the bargain.

574. Safe tank welding

Welding up petrol tanks fills most us with the fear of a blow-up. This method suggests the help of a vacuum cleaner. After draining all the petrol from the tank, fill it to overflowing with boiling water. When the tank is quite hot, empty out the water and leave the cap off and taps open.

Finally, use the vacuum cleaner to blow out any vapours that may still be trapped in nooks and crannies. As an added safeguard, ask someone else to do the welding!

575. Fuel pipe joint – plastic

Plastic fuel pipes will push home more readily over their unions if the ends are first softened by warming. The best way of doing this is to immerse the ends of the pipe in a cup of hot water. Warming, however, is not a cure for age-hardened pipes, which should be discarded and replaced with new.

576. Fuel pipe joint – plastic to copper

If a flexible fuel or oil pipe is loose where it joins onto a copper pipe, the joint can be sealed by belling out the end of the copper pipe with a taper punch.

577. Portable work-bench

Even if the workshop is equipped with a work-bench, a portable Black and Decker Workmate will more than pay for itself. Not only is it an extra work surface, but its movable boards can grip almost as well as, and much larger items than, a vice. And because it is portable and lower than the standard bench it can be used even as a machine stand. In small sheds and indoor workshops it is a must.

578. Home-made electric bench grinder

This ingenious yet simple grinder-cum-buffer comes from 1954. The main components used are a cycle spindle and hub, a spare drill chuck from an old hand drill, and a block of wood. The wood is cut to shape to form a suitable mounting block and is screwed to the work-bench. The spindle and hub are mounted on the block and held in place by a pair of pipe clips. Screw the chuck onto one end of the spindle (the threads matched!), and a pulley wheel onto the other. This is connected to a belt-driven electric motor. No provision for protection is included in this design. I would suggest some sort of belt guard should be added, and goggles must always be worn.

579. Garage turntable

This idea emanates from the age of steam, but there's no reason why it's not still relevant today. A turntable was installed in a garage which, though amply big enough itself, was approached by a long narrow passage. Made from ¼ in. steel plate welded to a collar which turns in an old large bearing, the turntable is just big enough to accept comfortably a machine's centre stand legs. Though the centre stand lifts both wheels off the floor, it requires no small effort to bring it into use. So a ramp has been placed on the floor ahead of the turntable. When the machine is run into the garage, the front wheel mounts the ramp, and the stand legs are lowered onto the turntable. Gravity does most of the work pulling the machine back onto its stand.

580. Tidy oddments

This tip comes from 1959. Most amateur restorers squirrel away nuts, bolts and washers in a jealously guarded collection of old tins. When a bolt is needed, instead of tipping the lot out onto the floor, line the tin with a rag and remove and replace the collection in a bundle.

581. Keeping grips and seat clean

When doing maintenance work it is a good idea to protect the handlebar grips from oily hands with a pair of plastic bags taped in place. The seat can be protected as well, before it's used as a tool tray!

582. Plastic protection

When cleaning a machine with a hose it's easy to let water into exposed carburettor intakes or magneto covers, especially with modern high-pressure steam washes. A plastic bag pushed over items most at risk and secured with a rubber band will keep even high-pressure water out.

583. A paraffin bath

Paraffin can be kept cleaner for longer, either by mixing it 50/50 with water (as the water retains all the grit), or by standing a drainer in the base of your paraffin tin to act as a sludge trap. (Newspaper placed in the bottom

of the paraffin bath is quite an effective sludge trap.) Paraffin is ultimately an abrasive, and all cleaned parts should be rinsed in water and be thoroughly dried. Delicate components should be washed in petrol.

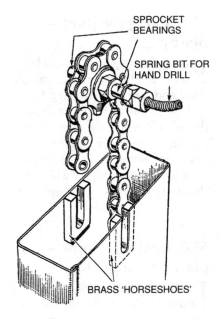

SPROCKET BEARINGS

SPRING BIT FOR HAND DRILL

BRASS 'HORSESHOES'

584. Cleaning chains

This chain cleaner has the advantage of running a chain through paraffin at five feet per second, and flexing each joint twice per second as it does. It was made from tin sheet formed into a tube 2½ x 1 x 36 in. long. One end was blanked off, and two brass 'horseshoes' were soldered at the other midway along the 2½ in. sides. The sheet was cut out from the inside of one of the horseshoes. Into this bearing drops a spindle carrying a six tooth sprocket, upon which the chain is already looped. The tin tube is half filled with paraffin, and the spindle rotated by means of a hand drill using an inch of spring curtain rail as a bit.

The rotating assembly consists of screwed rod and nuts, and rollers from a scrap duplex chain. The six tooth sprocket was fashioned from a plastic disc by drilling six equidistant holes to suit the chain roller diameter (in this case ⅜ in.) on a radius again to suit the chain (here ⅝ in.). Cleaned up with a file, the holes became the valleys of the sprocket with the teeth in between. A tin lid is necessary to prevent the paraffin from spurting about. And a sump plate of drilled tin in the base trapped the dirt washed from the chain, stopping it from re-entering the paraffin cleaner.

585. Filter rejuvenation

If filters of the wire-mesh-and-fabric type can't be obtained, they can be cleaned as follows. Fill an old saucepan with a solution of a pint of water and one tablespoonful of household detergent. Slide in the element and bring to the boil, keeping the pan just boiling for about 15 minutes. Then remove the element and rinse thoroughly to remove all traces of detergent. Dry out the element completely before refitting.

586. Oil tank sludge

One way to remove the sludge from the bottom of an oil tank is to detach the tank and pour in some petrol or paraffin. Add a collection of old nuts and bolts, and shake the tank vigorously for a few minutes. This action should dislodge the sludge, which can be poured out of the tank with the petrol. Repeat until the petrol poured from the tank is clean.

The nut and bolt trick is also a good way of removing loose rust from inside a petrol tank, to prevent it finding its way into the carburettor.

587. Clear oilways

Pipe cleaners are quite effective for cleaning oilways. For stubborn grit, feed an old Bowden inner cable down the oilway and splay the end. Draw it back slowly through the oilway, rotating the cable constantly to dislodge the grit. Finally blow clear with a compressed air line (if you are fortunate enough to have one).

588. Paint brush from a pipe cleaner

If you are an obsessive concours fan, pipe cleaners bent double are excellent for cleaning between cylinder head and barrel finning. They can also be used for painting between fins.

589. Rust prevention

It is fashionable nowadays to replace fasteners on restored motor cycles with stainless steel to the extent some machines look more like kitchen appliances. But one of the first places rust appears is between bolt heads and tinware, such as mudguards. A dab of grease will prevent this happening, as it forms a non-rusting insulation between bolt and mudguard.

590. Rust under mudguards

Painting the underside of mudguards with boiled linseed oil stops mud and grit sticking, reducing the chance of rust forming.

591. Rustproofing

Keeping the major parts of a machine rust-free is not too hard, given a little time and effort. But details such as exposed threads, clevis pins and bolts are easily missed. A weekly wipe with a rag soaked in light oil will keep them clean and replace the oil film. A spray from an oil aerosol can is almost as good and less time consuming.

592. Rust-proofing nuts and bolts

Heat the nuts to a dull red and plunge them into old engine oil. Withdraw them immediately and burn off the oil. Repeat several times for a lasting black finish. Alternatively, heat up the articles to a dull red, and plunge them in a mixture of black lead and linseed oil. Remove when cool. Note that an aluminium pan will melt if steel is heated to a dull red.

593. Cylinder black

It pays to keep the cylinder fins free from mud, rust, oil or scale, as any build-up in the fins will hamper cooling. If made of cast iron it is a good idea to keep the barrel coated with cylinder black paint even if you don't wish to fork out for a proper paint job. The black paint will dissipate the engine heat quicker.

594. Delicate rust removal

The treacle bath recommended by *The Classic Motor Cycle* is famous, and particularly useful for de-rusting delicate items which won't take severe modern chemicals. Dissolve a 1 lb tin of black treacle in about a gallon of

water. Clean loose flakes and surface rust off the components, drop into the tank and leave them for a week (longer if required). The residue can be washed off with water and, unlike modern chemicals, will not lead to subsequent paint damage.

595. Black polish

A pleasing black polish on iron and steel parts can be obtained by applying, as thinly as possible, a solution of sulphur and turpentine. The proportion should be one part sulphur to 10 parts turpentine. Once the articles have been coated, hold them over a flame until the black polish appears.

596. Temporary touch-up

Scratches and chips are inevitable if a motor cycle is used as it should be. These can be prevented from rusting or deteriorating further by applying a dab of clear nail varnish straight away. The bottle is provided with its own little brush, and the lacquer dries fast and will easily last until a proper touch up can be carried out.

597. Mixing top coats

Make sure that the top coat of paint is compatible with the others. Cellulose paints will react against oil-based undercoats.

598. Paint suspension

When hanging painted items to dry, always use wire. String will shed dust and bits every time you move something.

599. Old brush

For top coats use a brush that has been well broken in. New brushes, even of good quality, are bound to shed some bristles for the first few applications.

600. Mixing undercoats

The first undercoat applied should be in a striking colour. When rubbing down, it will warn how close you are to bare metal. Succeeding undercoats can be in different colours (or at least alternate) to identify them when rubbing down.

601. We can go on meeting like this

When applying paint, think first where you want the paint to meet. For frames and the like make the meeting point at an out of sight place such as under the petrol tank or below the engine. For tinware painted in two stages, the paint should carry over the whole of the top or outside to just underneath out of sight. Then the meeting point will be along the edge of the unexposed face.

602. Painting small items

Small painted parts can be dried quickly if they are suspended in a syrup tin placed over a candle flame.

603. Second coat

When applying a second coat of paint to small, awkwardly shaped items it is often hard to tell whether the second coat has covered completely – especially if the colour is black! If you breathe lightly on the article the freshly painted part will remain bright while the first coat will go dull momentarily.

604. Cellulosing tip

Spray painting on large curved surfaces, such as sidecar bodies or engine enclosures, can present problems of the paint running before it has had a chance to dry. Apart from the obvious tip of choosing a warm day, it can be overcome by playing a domestic hairdryer over the paintwork immediately after spraying. It not only dries the cellulose quicker, but minimizes the risk of dust as well. It is better to apply several thin coats than one thick.

605. Paint storage

When a tin of enamel is only half used and the remainder stored for a time, a skin forms on top of the paint. When you need to use the paint, pieces of broken skin can contaminate the brush. This can be avoided by storing the tin upside down. Just remember to make sure that the lid is tightly shut, and to turn the pot the right way up an hour before you need it to allow the paint to drain away from the lid.

If paints, especially varnishes, are going to be used in winter, stand the pot in a bowl of hot water for an hour before use. Remember to loosen the lid first. The paint will be easier to brush, and will dry to a smoother finish.

Tubes of sealing compound also benefit from the upside down treatment. The base fluid tends to separate and rise to the top. Removing the cap of an upside down tube will produce only compound every time.

606. Natural cleaners

Petrol is a good agent for removing oil stains from crankcases. Alcohol fuel is even better, particularly at removing castor based oil. Butter is quite good at removing tar stains from clothing if special cleaners aren't available.

607. Chrome cleaning

A nylon pot scourer dipped in a degreasing solution allows any amount of vigorous rubbing without risk of damage to plating. For more serious rusting, mix household scouring powder with light engine oil to form a paste, and apply as a normal chrome cleaner.

608. Fixing varnish transfers

Apply a thin coat of varnish to the transfer and the surface to which the transfer is to stick. Do not use polyurethane varnish, as this forms a skin as it dries, making it impossible for the transfer to stick to the tank. Give the varnish time to become tacky, then press the transfer home, rolling it quite flat with the aid of a pencil. After a couple of hours, thoroughly soak the paper backing of the transfer with water, and then carefully peel off the backing. The paper must be absolutely sodden. Then wash the surface of the transfer lightly with water and, after allowing it to dry, apply a final coating of varnish.

609. Motif fixing

Fixing maker's badges onto a petrol tank can be awkward if the original screws have rusted and broken off flush with the metal. One solution, to avoid the risk of puncturing the tank by drilling them out, is to cut a piece of rubber to match the badge. First stick the rubber to the tank with latex adhesive, then stick the badge to the rubber. The advantages of using this method instead of gluing the badge straight onto the tank with a metal glue are twofold. If the badge has been stamped out leaving a crenellated back, the rubber will stick to all of the badge, not just the raised points. And if the badge ever has to be removed, the rubber can be destroyed without harming the badge or the tank.

610. Insulating tape – sealing with glue

Plastic insulating tape is useful for protecting cables and can be wound neatly, but often the end refuses to stick down either because of a thumb print or awkward positioning. A drop of balsa wood cement will hold it in place. Appearance and waterproofing are further enhanced if balsa wood cement is applied as a coating along the length of the tape.

611. Insulating tape – sealing with heat

Another way to prevent the ends of insulating tape from coming loose and looking untidy is to heat the last inch with a match before fixing. After a few seconds the tape will become tacky, and can be pressed into place permanently.

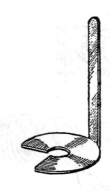

612. Filling a grease gun

It's easy to fill a modern grease gun from a modern tin which has a plate inside, but I have a couple of those old Tecalmit guns of the simple 'push' type, one of brass only six inches long and ideal for my toolkit. For years I've struggled to fill them with grease, usually leaving all the air on the inside and all the grease on the outside. A screwdriver pushed down one side of the gun will help air escape, but this tool from 1950 is ideal. Cut a section out of a plain washer, which is the same diameter as the inside of the gun, and weld a handle to it opposite the cut-away. The cut out section is for air to escape as the grease is pushed down.

613. Grease gun filling pump

Another way of filling an old-fashioned grease gun is to make up a small pump to inject the grease directly into the barrel of the gun. The pump consists of a 6 in. length of thin metal tubing with an external diameter slightly

less than the internal diameter of the grease gun barrel. The plunger is made by screwing a suitable diameter cork to one end of a 7 in. long wooden dowel. The pump is primed by placing the open end in a tin of grease and slowly withdrawing the plunger.

614. Toolbox grease gun filling

The small type grease gun, so useful for carrying with the tools for girder forks and exposed rockers, is also difficult to fill. One tip is that when the gun appears to be full, tap the bottom end smartly on the bench or floor. The grease is jerked down into the body of the gun, the air expelled and room left for more grease.

615. Efficient greasing

A thin piece of clean rag placed between grease gun and nipple will make a better seal, and ensure all the grease goes where it is intended and prevent grease from squeezing out the sides.

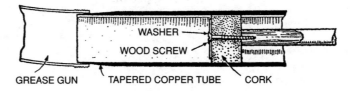

GREASE GUN   WASHER   WOOD SCREW   TAPERED COPPER TUBE   CORK

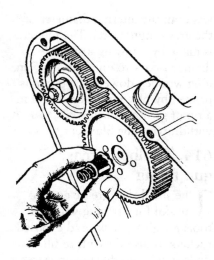

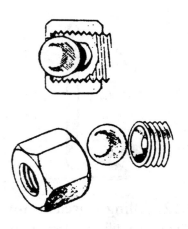

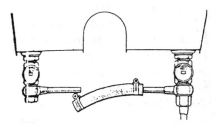

616. Grease glue

Thick grease acts as a useful temporary adhesive during assembly, such as keeping the lower ends of pushrods in place on the tappets, or retaining a pump plunger while the timing cover is replaced (as illustration of Panther 100 shows). Where pushrods are enclosed, as on the Triumph Tiger Cub, a thick blob at each side at the top of the tube keeps the rods separated while the head is lowered into place.

Ball bearings can be held in place with grease while casings or cups are replaced.

A screwdriver with heavy grease on the blade can be invaluable for fishing out odd items from awkward corners, such as a washer or ball bearing which has slipped out of place.

617. Temporary oil seal

A neat method of temporarily sealing an oil or petrol union is to fit an appropriate ball bearing inside the union nut. This will prevent unnecessary spillage on the workshop floor.

618. Temporary fuel tank

Some petrol tanks are quite fiddly to fit, and each refitting risks another chip to that expensive paintwork. During a rebuild it is a good idea to have a temporary tank so that engine checks can be made without the need to risk constantly the real tank. Wash out an empty gallon oil can and drill a 3/16 in. diameter hole in its base. Solder over the hole a petrol union capable of holding a petrol tap. Fixed loosely to the machine, the temporary tank can be connected to the existing carburettor petrol pipe union. For safety reasons puncture a vent in the temporary tank's filler cap, and store it empty. Oil cans are not suitable for storing petrol.

619. Quick tank removal

Many saddle petrol tanks have twin taps and a connecting pipe between the two halves running below the line of the frame tube. When the tank has to be removed this pipe must be disconnected, which entails a lot of extra spanner work, as well as disturbing leak-free joints. If the centre section of this pipe is cut out, it can be replaced by a short length of flexible petrol hose connected either end by worm screw clips, thus saving time and extra work.

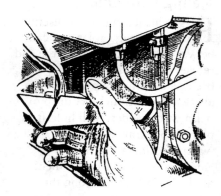

620. Makeshift funnel

To pour oil into awkward or vertical openings, tear a piece of cardboard into an oblong, cut one end to a V-shape, and fold in half to form an oil feeder.

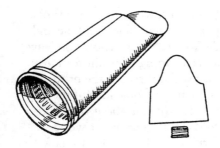

621. Less makeshift funnels

A cone rolled from a sheet of plastic is good for gearboxes and primary chaincases. It is strong enough and flexible, and it can be reused. Another tip is to knock the top out of the oil can cap, and solder in place a cone of thin sheet tin. This funnel will now screw onto any 5-litre oil tin. Nowadays the best method of the lot is to use a refillable fork oil bottle, which has measurements up one side and a thin plastic tube extending from its cap.

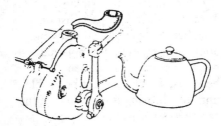

622. Gearbox oiling

Feeding oil into an awkward orifice is a perennial problem. Simple disposable funnels are sometimes the best, either made of cardboard or silver foil. This suggestion from 1956 finds the spout from a teapot the ideal shape and angle for the gearbox. Make sure its an old one, though; I don't suppose the oil will make the tea slip down any easier.

623. Penetrating oil

Ordinary household vinegar makes a good substitute penetrating oil.

624. Washing-up bottle

Empty washing-up liquid bottles can be mighty useful in the workshop. Fill one with light oil or cutting oil to cool a drill bit. Cut the base off a second to make a neat funnel. Push a small bore plastic pipe onto a third to top up the battery. And the fourth can be converted into a cable oiler by cutting it in half and fitting a drilled cork in place of the cap.

It's worthwhile hanging on to many of the specialist bottles produced nowadays. Fork oil usually comes in a bottle with a plastic pipe fitting for the cap, and a volumetric measure up one side, which can be used for many liquids other than fork oil. And household spray bottles which garden centres sell for house plants are ideal for applying thin protection oil under a bit of pressure.

625. A magnet as a useful tool

A magnet is a useful tool to have around the workshop. It can be used for retrieving circlips from the bottom of crankcases, swarf from the bottom of oil tanks, and washers from those inaccessible corners between engine and gearbox. If the magnet is too bulky, a flat-headed nail can be stuck to it as an extension piece. Indeed, I have a magnetized screwdriver in my toolbox which can pull loose screws out of recessed holes and ball bearings out of clutch housings. Attaching a magnet permanently to a dipstick in the oil tank will keep the oil free from metal particles.

626. Tinning a soldering iron

For efficient conduction of heat, the soldering iron should be completely free of dirt or oil, and tinned by coating with a film of solder.

627. Soldering small items

Small awkward items to be soldered together can be held in the correct position relative to each other if they are pressed into a piece of potato.

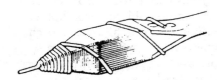

628. Small soldering iron

Sometimes when carrying out fiddly soldering tasks the point of the soldering iron is too clumsy. This can be reduced to a neat point by wrapping heavy-gauge copper wire round the iron and extending it beyond the tip. Though this sketch shows an old fashioned iron, the tip could easily be applied to a modern electric one.

629. Solder tip

Often when soldering up a small hole the solder has a habit of floating round the edges instead of running into the hole. This difficulty can be overcome by pressing a piece of cloth hard up against the back of the hole, and dropping the solder into the required position.

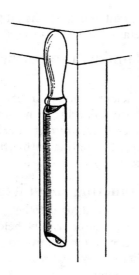

630. Hot iron holder

This sketch from 1959 shows a simple soldering iron holder to put an end to all those scorch marks on the worktop. Cut a piece of steel tube slightly longer than the shank and bit of the iron. The tube's diameter is less than the handle, to prevent it slipping through. The ends of the tube are cut at an angle to allow fixing holes to be drilled and screwdriver access. In the sketch the tube is screwed to the workbench leg to house a non-electrical iron. Nowadays, knowing how short most electric soldering iron cables are, it might be better mounted on the wall not far from the power point.

631. Annealing copper

Before bending copper tube for a fuel pipe, the part to be bent should be annealed to make it pliable (copper head gaskets should be treated the same way). This is done by heating the copper until it is red hot, and allowing it to cool. Plunging it immediately into a bowl of clean cold water speeds the process and descales the copper.

632. Bending copper tube

When bending up small gauge copper tube for oil or petrol pipes, annoying kinks can be avoided if a length of discarded speedometer drive cable is inserted into the bore of the pipe first.

633. Annealing steel

Quenching in water will harden steel. To anneal, heat the steel until red hot, but then allow it to cool slowly.

634. Working with silver steel

Silver steel is a most useful substance for manufacturing tools as it can be bought in dead size bar in a range of regular sizes. When hardening, it is most important not to overheat; 750°C (1382°F) is correct, and 800°C (1472°F) the absolute maximum to guarantee good results. It is difficult to describe the colour at which it should be quenched, but it is well below cherry red. What is known as 'nascent cherry' – that is, when dull red begins to turn to cherry – indicates the 800° mark, and a little practice will be required before perfect results are obtained.

635. Tempering steel

After a tool has been hardened it should be tempered to reduce its brittleness. Once polished and freed from all traces of oil, the body of the tool – some way from the point – should be reheated in a gas flame, when colours, which are actually caused by a film of oxide, will start to run towards the point. When the desired colour is obtained, the tool should be plunged immediately in clean water.

The colours start with pale yellow and get gradually darker to brown, brown with purple spots, purple, bright blue, full blue and dark blue. Straw yellow will leave a keen cutting edge but for most jobs will not reduce the brittleness enough. For some idea of the range, brown is about right for cold chisels, purple for wood-turning tools, and blue to dark blue for screwdrivers and punches.

636. Grinding steel

When grinding any tool to a sharp point, be careful not to let the point become too hot, as there is a danger it will lose its temper (who wouldn't?). To avoid overheating, regularly dip the tool in clean water

Machine maintenance

637. Hidden connections

Before starting to strip an engine, have a look at a parts list or, even better, an exploded drawing. Sometimes a circlip is employed between pairs of crankcase bearings, which may not be visible until one bearing is extracted. If the casing is warmed the bearing should drop out, so don't start tapping until you're sure.

Check also for concealed grub screws. Some Triumph twin crankcases have them just inside the mouth. And while you're at it, see if there are any left-hand threads. Favourite places are in the timing side of the engine where there would otherwise be a danger of revolving parts unscrewing themselves.

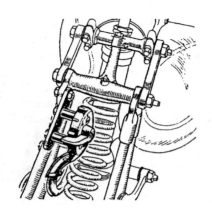

638. Switchgear retainer

If the headlight needs to be removed for any reason, it is useful to be able to mount the switch safely out of the way, not only to prevent damage to the switch but also to avoid tangling or straining the wiring loom. A switch mounting bar can be made from a strip of metal, drilled to take the two switch fixing screws. Spacers are cut to hold the body of the switch clear of the metal strip. A third hole is drilled to attach the assembled unit to an appropriate fork bolt.

639. Fitting plain bearings

It is often difficult to start a plain bearing in a housing, and ensure that it is square. The sharp edges of both metal faces and the exact fit of the bearing usually mean the first tap skews it at an angle. One way to overcome this problem is to lightly chamfer the outer leading edge of the bush, so it can be started true, and then tap it home in the normal way using a wooden block and hammer.

640. Engine compression

After an overhaul it is not unusual to find that there is little compression. This is nothing to worry about unless the trouble persists, as the oil film on the cylinder walls won't be perfect until the engine has run, despite oiling the piston and bore prior to reassembly. If lack of compression does persist, items to check are decompressor adjustment, valve clearances and timing, piston ring position (or the possibility that one snapped on reassembly), and the tightening down of the cylinder head.

641. Testing for compression

On a big single, if the compression is good it should be possible to stand on the kickstarter for two or three seconds before compression is overcome. On a multi-cylinder machine the compression is likely to feel less even when it is perfectly satisfactory; on a Panther single you should be able to stand there all week. The test must be made with the throttle open, and a steady pressure exerted on the pedal. The fact that it is possible to kick over the engine without using the exhaust lifter does not necessarily mean that the compression is poor, since with a vigorous kick the impetus given to the flywheels may be sufficient to carry the piston over compression.

642. Compression plates

When lifting a cylinder barrel, check if compression plates have been fitted at the base. If so, ensure that they are put back on reassembly to maintain the correct tolerances. If compression is being lowered, it is better to fit one thick plate rather than several thin ones, as a number of thin plates will tend to bulge where they are not under direct pressure from the cylinder base nuts, and may cause the cylinder flange to crack. Check that oil holes between the crankcase and cylinder are not covered by the compression plate.

643. Running in

Do not run the engine either fast or for long periods when the machine is stationary, and avoid accelerating hard when the engine is cold. Allow the engine to turn over evenly and sweetly by extra use of the gearbox. It is better, within limits, to rev the engine in an indirect gear than to allow it to slog or labour. Over the first 500 miles various parts of the machine, as well as engine components, will bed down. Therefore, make regular checks on all mechanical adjustments and the tightness of nuts and bolts.

644. First oil change

After a major rebuild, change the oil once 500 miles have been covered. This will remove any small particles of metal, fluff, or dirt, resulting from the bedding in of new parts, from the lubrication system.

FEELER
SOLDERED TO
STEEL STRIP

645. Tappet adjustment

On some types of overhead-valve engine, when the rocker ends are deeply recessed in the rocker box, it is awkward to adjust the valve clearances with any degree of accuracy owing to the difficulty of inserting a feeler

109

gauge between the rocker end and the valve stem. To make this task easier, bend to shape a strip of 1/16 x 3/8 in. steel. Solder onto each end a short length of the correct thickness feeler for the inlet and exhaust. The sketch shows a gauge suitable for an early 50s Triumph.

646. Clutch slip cure

Cleaning oil out of clutch friction plates is a perennial problem. One BSA M20 owner, fed up with persistent clutch slip, boiled the clutch plates in a solution of washing soda and water, (two tablespoons of soda to two pints of water). The water was changed several times until it remained clean. To prevent burning, lengths of mild steel rod were placed in the bottom of the pan and between each friction plate.

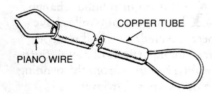

COPPER TUBE

PIANO WIRE

647. Retrieving a nut

A useful gadget for removing nuts and washers from inaccessible places can be made from a length of 1/4 in. bore copper tubing and a piece of piano wire. Loop the wire in the middle and push the ends through the tube, leaving a loop of about 2 in. at one end. Shape the wires at the other end into claws. When the loop is pushed into the tube the claws open, and when the pressure is released the claws automatically close.

648. Retrieving a circlip

Incidentally, if a circlip falls into the crankcase of a machine with no room for a magnet (and no sump plate either), it may be possible to remove it by dabbing a blob of grease onto the top of the flywheel and slowly rotating it through 360 degrees. With luck, the circlip will stick to the grease and be lifted back up.

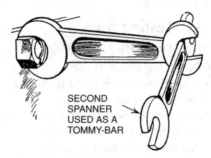

SECOND SPANNER USED AS A TOMMY-BAR

649. Inaccessible bolts – T-spanner

Using two open-end spanners as a T-spanner can be useful for inaccessible nuts perhaps too close to a casing to accommodate a socket or too deep for a box spanner. (For example, some gearbox mounting bolts loosened to adjust the primary chains.) The open end on the nut must be a good fit or it will soon round it off. Box spanners can be sometimes lengthened by sliding the hexagon of another either inside or over the one in use.

650. Inaccessible bolts – screwdriver slot

Inaccessible bolts, such as crankcase drain plugs, may benefit from a screwdriver slot. Insert two hacksaw blades into the saw frame to make a wide cut that will suit a standard screwdriver.

651. Nut refitting

Another way to overcome the old problem of replacing small nuts in confined spaces is to use a length of Sellotape and a pencil. The tape is placed adhesive side outward across the blunt end of the pencil, its ends twisted to hold it onto the pencil. The nut is held onto the sticky tape across the pencil end, and started on its thread by rotating the pencil.

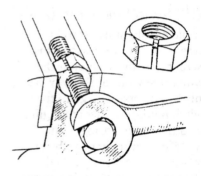

652. Easing tight threads

Tight threads, or even slightly damaged ones, can be eased by smearing them with fine valve grinding paste and working repeatedly to and fro. Once eased, remove all traces of grinding paste before final reassembly. The same method can be used to true an olive of a petrol or oil pipe union. Alternatively, cut a nut of the correct thread radially through one of the hexagon flats, clench it in a vice, and work the bolt slowly through the nut.

653. Unscrewing a union nut

Never attempt to loosen a petrol or oil union nut unless the body nut is firmly held by a second spanner at the same time. Otherwise the body may be unscrewed too, and the pipe damaged. Once the body has become loose it is much more difficult to undo the union nut, and to reseal the joint.

654. Unscrewing corroded threads

Tight or corroded threads, particularly of large flat items such as inspection covers, can often be freed by tapping vertically with a hammer. Avoid hammer marks by placing an aluminium or hardwood block on the cover. The same rule applies to screws: giving a light hammer tap on the end of the screwdriver should free the thread.

655. Jarring a nut

Stubborn nuts can be shifted more easily by jarring the end of the spanner with a hammer than by simply applying more brute strength. And, however odd it seems, a light blow with a heavy hammer is far safer than repeated heavy blows with a light hammer.

656. Removing nuts logically

Many suggestions were submitted for special jigs to undo large nuts securing rotating parts like primary drive sprockets or timing pinions. The best advice is to think ahead of the work to be conducted, and loosen as many of these nuts as possible in advance of dismantling other components. For example, leave the primary chain on until after the primary drive sprockets have been freed, and leave the rear chain on likewise for the gearbox sprocket. Most of these nuts can be undone if the rear wheel or the crankshaft is prevented from rotating by selecting first gear and applying the back brake.

657. Removing a sprocket nut

Many have suggested locking sprockets by wedging them with screwdrivers, but this is best avoided if possible. Here is a suggestion for a sprocket holder. A length of old chain of the correct size is put round the sprocket with the ends of the chain then fed into a 12 in. length of copper pipe hammered into an oval shape. The pipe is then pushed towards the sprocket until the chain grips it firmly, at which point a metal rod or bolt is pushed through the chain at the other end of the pipe to secure it.
Remember that light sharp blows on a spanner will move a tight nut far easier than sustained heavy pressure.

658. Removing a sprocket

Time spent on working out ways to remove sprockets carefully is never wasted. Not only will damage to the (perhaps irreplaceable) sprocket be avoided, but also to the shaft that it's attached to. A universal puller is useful in any tool collection, and preferably with three legs for a more even pull. However, many universal pullers are too bulky to use around compact motor cycle casings, so it is a good idea to build up a collection of factory tools for sprockets removed often. If factory pullers can't be found, the following selection of home made devices may be useful.

659. Clamping a sprocket puller

Sometimes, owing to lack of space at the back of a sprocket, the legs of the puller tend to slip off the sprocket when pressure is applied. To overcome this, get the puller in position, then tighten a worm screw clip round the legs.

660. Sprocket puller Mk 1

Take a strip of steel 5 in. x ¾ in. x ¼ in., and drill and tap a ⁵⁄₁₆ in. hole in the centre. Other ⁵⁄₁₆ in. holes, untapped, are drilled in the strip at the necessary distances for the various sprockets which are to be handled. Two lengths of steel bar 3 in. x ⁵⁄₁₆ in. are heated, flattened at one end, and bent round into claws. Threads are cut onto the other end, and they are fixed to the strip

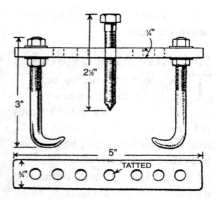

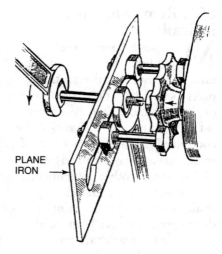

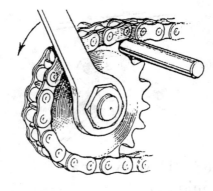

by the appropriate nuts and washers. The tool is completed by tapering the end of a 2½ in. x 5⁄16 in. bolt, and threading it through the central hole.

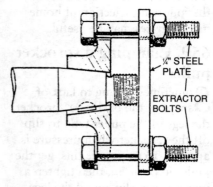

661. Sprocket puller Mk 2

Bolts are quite suitable to make the jaws of a puller. The puller shown here is less complex than Mk 1 above, but provides no adjustment in its length and little in its depth; perhaps a combination of the two would be ideal.

662. Sprocket puller Mk 3

The basis for this puller is an old blade from a carpenter's plane. The method of using the tool is clearly shown in the sketch, the slot in the blade providing a certain amount of adjustment.

663. Removing an engine sprocket

When removing an engine sprocket, never let the stud of the puller bear directly on the end of the engine shaft. It may damage the small indentation important for flywheel alignment. Always pack it with a shim of soft metal or hard wood.

664. Sprocket lock

A simple way of locking a sprocket when removing the shaft nut is to slip a length of rod between the sprocket and the chain. The rod diameter should be a snug fit as care must be taken not to damage the sprocket teeth.

665. Refitting a sprocket

When refitting a sprocket on a taper, see that the tapers are absolutely clean. Locate the sprocket on the taper by giving it a tap with a socket or tube placed over the shaft before tightening the nut. Having rotated the spanner as far as it will go by hand, give it a few light taps with a mallet to lock the nut. Should sprockets persist in coming loose, the tapers should be ground carefully with fine grinding paste until they bed down all round.

If a sprocket seems welded to a shaft, tighten the puller and then tap the end of the puller's central stud lightly with a hammer to free the sprocket.

666. Gearbox sprocket gauge

Most gearbox sprockets are so situated that it's difficult to measure their state of wear without dismantling the primary drive. One solution is to press a piece of white paper against the sprocket teeth with the fingers to get a clear imprint of the profile. A large number of teeth can be impressed if the chain is first removed.

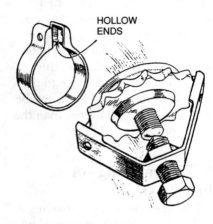

HOLLOW ENDS

667. Removing a magneto pinion

This is probably the one sprocket that is removed most often, so consider buying the proper tool. But here are two different makeshift ideas:

1. Bend open an exhaust pipe clip, and thread a hole through its centre for the threaded stud.

2. Screw two bolts into the

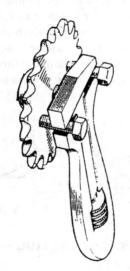

sprocket's threaded holes, and jar loose with a small adjustable spanner.

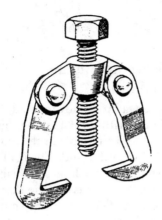

668. Magneto pinion puller – Mk 1

A thoroughly practical puller for removing magneto sprockets and the like can be made as follows. The body consists of a ⅜ in. Whitworth malleable iron wing-nut, the wings of which are drilled to retain the claws by means of ¼ in. shouldered rivets. Claws are made from ³⁄₁₆ in. mild steel, offset to bring the ends central, and case-hardened. The ends are drilled a loose fit to suit the shoulders of the rivets. The thrust portion is a ⅜ x 2 in. Whitworth hexagon-headed setscrew, the end of which is case-hardened after being tapered. For simplicity the claws could be secured by means of screws and locknuts, in which case the wings would have to be tapped out to take the screws.

669. Magneto pinion puller – Mk 2

An easy way to make up a sprocket puller in a situation with a protruding shaft, such as a magneto, is as follows: Make a template of the sprocket with a piece of paper and stick it to a 4 in. square steel plate ¹⁄₁₆ in. thick. Drill four ¼ in. holes in the steel plate between the teeth of the sprocket template. Make up three more identical plates to form one steel plate ¼ in. thick. Hook the heads of four ¼ in. bolts behind the sprocket teeth, and push on the metal plates so they butt up to the end of the shaft. Thread on four nuts, tightening evenly and gradually to pull off the sprocket.

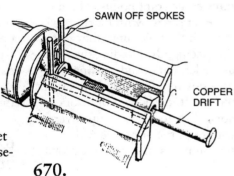

SAWN OFF SPOKES

COPPER DRIFT

670. Removing an armature inner race – with a vice

This is a similar method to the tip suggested earlier. Grip the inner race in the vice with the help of a pair of old spokes – taking care that the thickness of the wire is greater than the depth of the groove, so that the vice can grip without damaging the race. Place a nut between the other end of the vice jaws to act as a guide, and use a soft metal drift to drive out the shaft from the race.

113

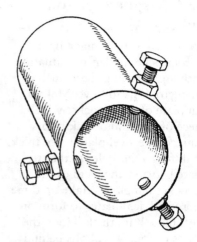

671. Removing an armature inner race – without a vice

Find a length of steel tube which fits snugly over the inner race, and radially drill and tap it at three equidistant points. Thread three set screws with locknuts through the holes until they grip the race tightly. Holding the tube in the left hand, slide a copper drift down the tube and knock out the armature shaft. If the work is done close to a bench top covered with rags, the armature will sustain no damage when it drops.

672. Removing a stubborn nut

One simple way of loosening a stubborn nut is to hit it with two hammers simultaneously on opposing flats. This method is not a guaranteed success, but often jars free any rust or grit stuck in the threads.

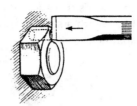

673. Removing a rusted nut

One way to remove rusted nuts without damaging their studs is to drill a hole in the nut parallel with the stud. The drill size should be the largest possible consistent with missing the thread of the stud. The nut can be split with a chisel.

674. Removing a stud

The correct way to remove a stud is to lock a second nut of the right size and thread onto the stud's original nut. Then by unscrewing the lower nut, the stud will be drawn out without damaging the thread. The stud should be reinserted by reversing this technique.

675. Removing a broken stud

For removing studs or screws broken below surface use a drill bit smaller than the diameter of the tapped hole, and grind the drill's cutting edges so that it will take a grip when rotated anti-clockwise. Once the drill bit has caught the end of the stud, by drilling anti-clockwise the broken portion should unscrew itself out of the hole.

676. Removing another broken stud

If this doesn't work, use an ordinary drill bit smaller than the tapped hole, and drill into the broken stud. Then an inserted screwdriver should unscrew it, or it may be possible to collapse the remains of the stud into the hole and fish out the bits. With this method beware of damage to the threads of the tapped hole, and be careful not to drill deeper than the depth of the tapped hole.

677. Removing son of broken stud

Another method of removing a sheared stud from a blind hole is as follows. Drill a hole into the stud of a slightly larger diameter than an Allen key measured across the flats. Tap the Allen key into the hole and unscrew the stud.

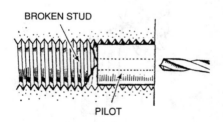

BROKEN STUD

PILOT

678. Drilling the stud – not the casing

When studs break off below the surface of the casing they usually leave a conical tip, making drilling out difficult. A wooden dowel knocked into the hole above the broken stud will act as a pilot for the drill bit.

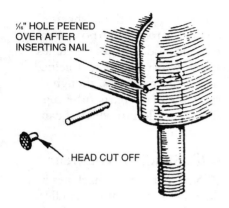

1/16" HOLE PEENED
OVER AFTER
INSERTING NAIL

HEAD CUT OFF

679. Repairing a stud

Specialist engineers are available for most types of repairs nowadays, but this suggestion for fixing a stud could still be useful. The threaded hole in the alloy casting had stripped, though the stud could be screwed in loosely. A 1/16 in. hole was drilled at right angles to the stud into the casting and through the stud. A steel nail, used as a dowel, was pressed tightly into the hole, its head cut off, and the end peened over to retain it in position. The nail prevented the stud from turning when the nut was tightened up. Using modern proprietary metal adhesive in the loose thread would make an even better job.

680. Stripped aluminium thread

In cases where helicoiling is inappropriate or just not possible, tapping holes out oversize can be a solution. This sketch demonstrates the art on the crankcase of an M series Velocette. Two of the hollow studs into which screw the cylinder head holding down rods had stripped their threads in the crankcase. The original stud threads were 5/16 in., so the crankcase stud holes were

retapped to 3/8 in. Oversize hollow studs were made from 2 in. long steel bolts with the heads removed. The bolts were ground down for half their length to allow them to take a 3/8 in. tap; the other half was finished off to form the collar, and drilled and tapped to take the cylinder holding down rod.

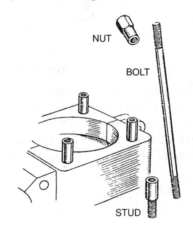

NUT

BOLT

STUD

681. Starting a nut

Always apply a smear of oil or grease to a thread before doing it up; it will delay corrosion and ease future removal. When a nut refuses to screw onto the end of its bolt, try turning it anti-clockwise for part of a turn before screwing it clockwise. It may help the two thread ends catch.

682. Replacing tricky nuts

Sometimes a nut or washer has to be replaced on an awkwardly located stud or bolt. One way is to place a length of stiff wire hard against the end of the stud, then thread the washer or nut (or both) over the wire so that it slides into place. Keep the wire in position until the nut is started on its thread to prevent it dropping into any tiny crevice.

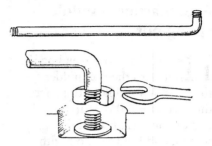

683. A tool for starting a nut

If a bolt is difficult to reach, make this special tool. A short mild steel rod is bent at one end, Allen key fashion. Then either or both ends can be threaded to take the awkward nut.

684. Another tool for starting a nut

Press the nut into a piece of plywood with the vice, and carefully chisel out the indentation so that the nut is a tight fit. This tool can either hold the nut in place long enough to start the thread, or be slid behind awkward faces to lock a bolt head.

685. And yet another tool for starting a nut

A long box spanner or socket with a blob of grease in the end will hold the nut while you try to start it in the thread. So will a nail pushed through a hole drilled the depth of the nut up the box spanner. This is particularly useful for spring loaded nuts, such as found in clutches.

686. Starting a saddle spring nut

Here is a way of inveigling the nut onto the bolt hidden in the coils of a saddle spring. Screw the correct nut three turns on the end of a longish bolt of the same thread, and hold the bolt with pliers up to and against the end of the bolt which is to receive the nut. A screwdriver or thin spanner will rotate the nut while it is biting on the first few threads, and the spanner finishes the job in the usual way.

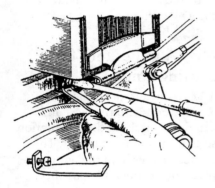

687. Starting small screws

Small screws, such as inside the headlamp shell, can be awkward to hold in place while started with a screwdriver. This difficulty can be overcome by pushing the screw through a piece of card. When the screw is part way home, the card can be torn away.

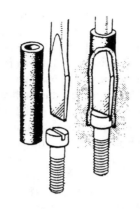

688. Starting large screws

Connect the screw to the screwdriver tip with a thin rubber tube. This will allow you to start the screw even at awkward angles.

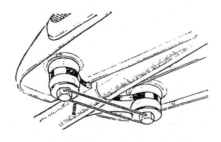

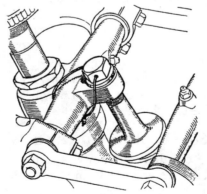

689. Locking wire

Locking wire is usually associated with racing motor cycles. It won't make your machine go any faster, but it can play a useful part in road reliability. Velocette used it in the screw fixings of the primary chaincase to the gearbox on most of their models. These sketches show two areas where it helped on certain machines, though there are many parts suffering from vibration to which it can be applied.

690. Saddle pivot wear

On rigid framed machines it is important that the saddle pivot hinges up and down for comfort, but does not rock from side to side. In this tip from 1947, the owner found that only the bush in the frame had worn oval. He replaced this with a tube of ⅜ in. inside diameter which extended right through the frame from one seat pivot to the other. He locked it in place with a grub screw drilled into the frame, and inserted a grease nipple along its length. The seat pivots were drilled to take a ⅜ in. bolt.

On one of my rigid framed machines both the frame and the seat pivots are worn, and I have made a pair of tube spacers, one for each side of the frame pivot. The worn holes were drilled oversize, and the spacer's outside diameter was bigger than the largest hole. Both ends of the spacer were reduced to fit the frame pivot at one end and the seat pivot at the other. They were bolted up with a single bolt.

691. Saddle spring renewal

Renewal of one or more saddle springs often presents a problem, undue force sometimes breaking the hooked ends. The best method on a seat with two spring lengths is to insert a

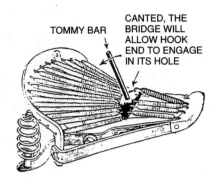

tommy-bar into the bridge separating the short and long springs (a convenient hole should already be drilled in it). To fit a short spring the front frame should be hooked and the tommy-bar pushed backwards, thereby raising the front of the bridge so that the spring hook will easily register in its hole. A gentle tap will hook it into position. To fit a long spring the tommy-bar should be pushed forward.

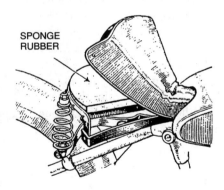

692. Saddle pad

To overcome saddle soreness slip a piece of sponge rubber one inch thick, cut to the shape of the saddle, between the springs and saddle top. The rubber will also reduce the wear of the springs on the saddle cover, delaying the contouring which eventually becomes apparent.

693. Cleaning oil from clothing

In the 30s it was suggested that oil stains could be removed from even the most delicate articles (Esmeralda's silk stockings, no less!) by applying breadcrumbs soaked in petrol. The outer ring stain caused by evaporating petrol could be avoided by vigorous rubbing with dry breadcrumbs. Nowadays Swarfega or other hand-cleaner and a washing machine will remove nasty stains from any material. My wife recommends rubbing the stain with Swarfega without wetting the material, and putting the garment straight in the washing machine. If the material is delicate (she will change wheel bearings in her nightie!), the Swarfega may need rinsing off before washing.

694. Acid neutralizer

The prompt application of liquid ammonia or baking soda will do much to neutralize the ill-effects of sulphuric acid on clothes and metalwork.

Home-made tools

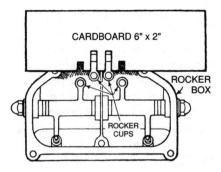

695. Pushrod guide

Reassembling the top end of many twins can be made easier with a pushrod guide to keep the rods aligned while the rocker box is fitted. BSA actually supplied one in the toolkit of their later A10 twins. Here is one for an A10 made out of cardboard. First the rocker box was turned upside down on the workbench and the rocker sighted in line with the cardboard. The board was marked and cut to shape. It can hold the pushrods in position while the rocker box is fitted, and be slid out prior to final tightening.

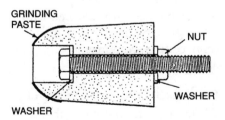

696. Port polishing tool

Port polishing always presents the problem of a fine finish without damage to soft alloy. This home-made tool was made from a cork and designed to be held in a drill. The cork was selected for size and one end shaped to suit the curve of the ports and combustion chamber. It was then drilled axially with a ³⁄₁₆ in. hole, and counter-bored for a third of its length to accept the head of a ³⁄₁₆ in. bolt. The bolt was inserted with a washer under its head and another at the base of the cork, and the whole was pulled up tightly with a nut. The protruding end of the bolt was attached to the drill chuck and the shaped cork face lightly smeared with fine grinding paste.

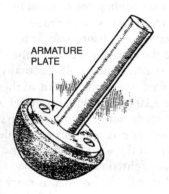

ARMATURE PLATE

697. Combustion chamber polisher

This alternative port polishing tool was made from a sock darning mushroom. The mushroom head was covered with a fine piece of emery cloth, and screwed to a scrap magneto armature spindle.

698. Exhaust port scraper

Scraping carbon out of exhaust ports could be made easier with this little tool fashioned from the discarded pushrod of a lorry engine. The pushrod was heated and bent to form an offset immediately below the tulip head. The other end of the rod was bent to form a handle. A half segment of the tulip head was then ground

away to leave a scoop shape ideal for tackling awkward ports.

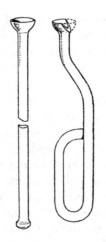

699. Carbon removal from piston

A good tool to use to remove carbon from a piston crown is the sharp-contoured edge of an old piston ring. It's hard enough to shift the carbon, but with care won't damage the piston in any way.

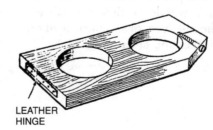

LEATHER HINGE

700. Piston ring clamp for parallel twin

The sketch shows a home made jig for compressing the piston rings on a Triumph 500 cc twin, but the idea will suit any parallel twin with the dimensions altered accordingly. The jig required one piece of wood 7½ x 3½ x ½ in. Two holes were made in the wood, 2½ in. diameter and ⅞ in. apart, to be a sliding fit on the pistons.

Then the wood was sawn lengthways across the middle of both holes. A piece of leather was tacked across one end for a hinge, and one of the other corners was cut off and a wood screw inserted to pull the halves together.

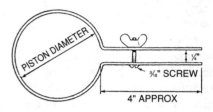

PISTON DIAMETER

¼"

³⁄₁₆" SCREW

4" APPROX

701. Piston ring clamp for a single

This piston ring clamp was made for a single-cylinder engine from a strip of hard-drawn brass sheet (size 18 x 1¾ in. x 14 swg). The shape was obtained by using a spare piston as a form, and the handles were drilled to take a screw and wing-nut. The clip is secured over the piston and rings by means of the screw. Once the rings are in the bore, the engine is turned over with the kickstart lever to raise the piston and allow the clip to be undone and removed.

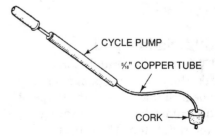

CYCLE PUMP

³⁄₁₆" COPPER TUBE

CORK

702. Gearbox lubrication

This suggestion is for a home made grease/oil gun to tackle an awkward gearbox filler cap. Made from an old brass cycle pump, the hole for the connector was drilled out to be able to take a length of 5/16 in. copper pipe. This was bent to the correct shape before being soldered into the end of the pump. A cork was fashioned to be a good fit in the gearbox filler hole, and drilled out to be a tight fit round the copper tube. To prepare the gun, first insert the cork firmly in the filler hole, then withdraw the plunger from the pump and fill the barrel with a mixture of oil and grease. Replace the plunger and apply pressure.

703. Wire brush from a Bowden cable

A small stiff wire brush can be made from a length of copper tubing and an inner Bowden cable. Bend the cable double, and push the bend up the tube leaving the bristly ends exposed. Secure by flattening the copper tube over the bend, and for neatness trim the bristles with a pair of pliers.

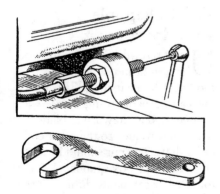

704. Cable adjuster spanner

Many cable adjuster locknuts are in inaccessible places, so even the correct size spanner may not be able to fit. To make up your own, cut the correct shape

from a piece of 1/8 in. thick flat steel. It is best to cut the gap in the jaws undersize and then file it to the right size to ensure a tight fit on the nut. The spanner can be case hardened but it isn't essential.

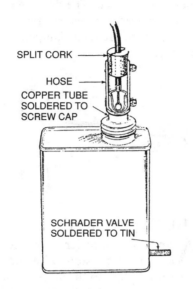

SPLIT CORK

HOSE
COPPER TUBE SOLDERED TO SCREW CAP

SCHRADER VALVE SOLDERED TO TIN

705. Home-made pressurized cable oiler

A cable oiler which will deliver oil under pressure can be constructed as follows:

Components consist of a small tin, a 2 in. length of hose, a 1 in. length of 3/4 in. bore copper tube, two worm screw clips, a cork and a Schrader valve. The oiler is made by cutting a hole in the cap of the tin and soldering in the copper tube. The hose is slipped over the tube and secured by a worm screw clip. Into the side of the tin, an inch or so from the bottom, is soldered the Schrader valve. The cork is bored through the centre (the hole is the same diameter as the outer casing of the cable) and then halved along its length.

To use the oiler, insert the outer casing of the cable in the end of the hose and fit both halves of the

cork around it to form a shoulder in the hose. Fit the other worm screw clip around the top of the hose, tightened so that the cork clamps the cable securely. Unscrew the cap, pour some oil into the tin, and refasten the cap firmly. Screw a tyre pump onto the Schrader valve and invert the tin. A few strokes with the pump creates sufficient pressure to push the oil right through the cable. It is essential that the nipple at the free end of the cable is pressed against its ferrule to prevent oil pressure in the hose forcing down the other nipple, and thus causing a blockage.

706. Spoke cleaning tool

An effective tool for removing paint from spokes can be made from a hacksaw blade broken across its fixing hole. The resulting semi-circle forms a perfect spoke-sized groove.

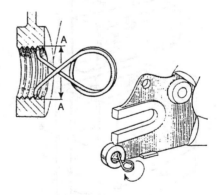

707. Thread cleaner

Bend some wire (sprung if possible) to the shape shown with length A-A slightly greater than the tapped hole. The wire ends will spring into the pitch and remove even old paint without damaging the thread.

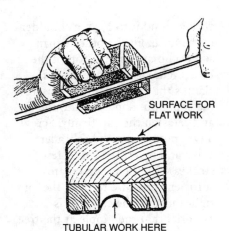

SURFACE FOR
FLAT WORK

TUBULAR WORK HERE

708. Sanding block

For sanding flat surfaces, wrap wet-or-dry paper round a block of wood or rubber. If two strips of batten are fixed to one side of the wooden block, leaving a gap between them, the sanding block can be used for tubes as well as flat surfaces.

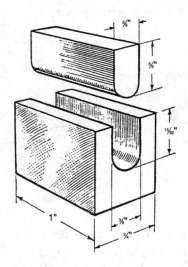

709. Damaged chaincase band

Banded chaincases on 50s singles are notoriously difficult to keep oiltight, often because age has distorted components. The tool shown in the sketch is to

reshape the alloy band, and is made from two pieces of mild steel, though hardwood would probably work just as well. The larger piece is drilled with a ⅜ in. diameter drill, then cut with a hacksaw and filed. The damaged band is placed between the two pieces, which are then clamped in a vice.

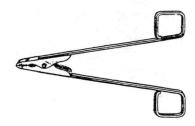

710. Finger pliers

A small pair of finger pliers can be made from stout wire and a crocodile clip. To the arms of the clip are soldered lengths of stiff wire, with loops formed in their other end like a pair of scissors.

711. Circlip pliers

A cheap pair of circlip pliers can be made from ordinary kitchen scissors. File the ends of the scissors to form a protruding notch able to fit into the hole in the circlip's ears.

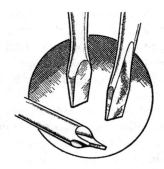

712. Screwdrivers that will not slip

Many screwdrivers are sold with unsuitably shaped blades, which cause them to slip out of a screw slot. In most cases it is quite easy to modify the shape, either to a long easy slope or to a short parallel blade. The latter is the nicer to use, but at least two sizes will be needed by the practical motor cyclist. Alterations may be made by grinding or with a fine cut file. Using a grindstone, remove only a small amount of metal at a time, or the blade will get too hot and lose its temper.

713. Collapsible screwdriver

Useful screwdrivers are often too long to fit into a normal toolkit. A home made collapsible one can be made from a box spanner and a screwdriver blade with a nut welded to the other end of its shaft. The nut should be a good fit in the box spanner. A tommy-bar can be used through the other end if need be, and both blade and tommy-bar will slide into the box spanner for storage.

714. Double-ended screwdriver

This neat little tool is ideal for awkward places, and jobs such as tappet adjustment which don't require a lot of pressure. A length of ¼ in. silver steel rod had 1 in. each end turned at right angles. The flats were ground at right angles to each other.

715. Screwdriver from an Allen key

Small scrapers and screwdrivers for awkward corners can be made from Allen keys with the ends ground flat.

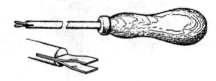

716. Small screw tool

This useful workshop tool was devised for holding a screw when fitting it in, or removing it from, an inaccessible hole. A ½ in. deep slot was cut diametrically across one end of a length of ¼ in. diameter mild steel rod. Into the slot was soldered two small strips of spring steel. The two free ends of the strips were opened out slightly, and the rod pushed into a file handle. The spring action of the steel strips is sufficient to retain a screw head enough for the screw to be started in its thread.

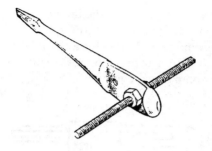

717. Tommy-bar screwdriver

Some types of screwdriver have a wide blade underneath wooden handles. If the handles are removed, a threaded rod can be bolted through the blade to form a useful tommy-bar.

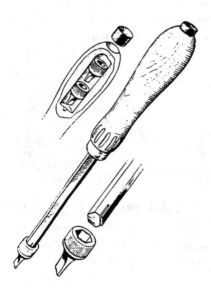

718. Ingenious screwdriver

This idea for a special tool comes from 1952. Components used were a wooden file handle, a 5⁄16 in. Allen key 6 in. long, a rubber cork, and three 5⁄16 in. Allen cap screws. Drill a ¼ in. hole in the ferrule of the file handle to a depth of 1½ in. In the opposite end of the handle drill a

⅝ in. hole 2½ in. deep, and close it with the rubber stopper ensuring it is a tight fit. Cut off the cranked end of the Allen key and drive the long straight portion into the ¼ in. hole in the file handle; again, ensure a tight fit. At the other end of the key cut a slit, slightly off-centre, about 5⁄16 in. deep.

The screwdriver heads are made by cutting down the cap screws to a suitable length and filing them to shape. These fit onto the hexagonal Allen key very firmly, and when not in use are stored in the wooden handle. Though similar proprietary tools can be acquired at some tool merchants, the advantage here is that particular heads can be made to suit specific applications.

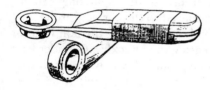

719. Comfortable ring spanner

Many older-type ring spanners which may be needed on vintage machines, such as the 18 mm plug spanner shown, have thin shanks. Not only are they uncomfortable to use, but by being so it is often difficult to undo tight nuts and to judge by feel the correct torque when tightening. A rag wrapped round the shank will do in most cases, but if there is a spanner that's often called upon, a more permanent solution like the one shown is preferable.

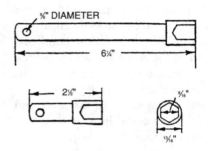

720. Spanner adaptation

There are many instances when bolt heads are fitted in recesses or tight places close to cylinder fins or other easily damaged components. Normal socket or ring spanners are too bulky, and the thinner box spanners distort or 'round off' before sufficient purchase can be applied. In these cases it is a good idea to adapt or make a spanner for the particular purpose, so that tightening can be achieved to the correct torque without damaging the bolt head or tearing the knuckles. Cylinder base nuts, some of which are set too close to the barrel, will benefit from a specially filed down ring spanner. The spanner sketched here was made to remove the cylinder head bolts from a 1953 BSA A7, but the idea can be universally applied as I have a similar tool for an OHC Velocette.

In the case of the A7 the bolts are recessed into the cylinder head leaving very little clearance. It is necessary to use a box spanner with a wall thickness of $3/32$ in. or less. And, owing to the different depths of the recesses in the head, spanners of two different lengths are called for. The idea is to use two large socket head screws of the correct size ($9/16$ in. across the flats of the internal hexagon) with the heads turned down to a diameter of $13/16$ in. Though not

strictly necessary, the threads can be turned off for neatness at the same time. A hole for a $5/16$ in. tommy-bar in the opposite end completes the job.

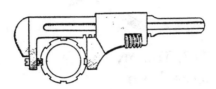

721. Adjustable C-spanner

This tip is only possible with certain types of adjustable spanner. Cut the end to form a flat. Drill an $1/8$ in. hole through the new flat, and pass through the hole a $1/8$ in. bolt of the correct length secured in place by a suitable nut.

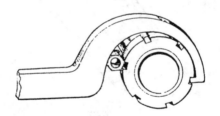

722. Adapting a C-spanner

A purpose-made C spanner can be reduced in size by packing one side out with a nut.

723. Spanner manipulation

A handy extension bar to give added leverage to spanners can be made from a strip of steel and a few nuts. Braze nuts of various sizes to each end of the steel strip. These can be placed

into the end of the spanner not in use for extra purchase and a wider variety of angles.

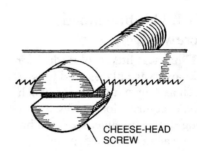

CHEESE-HEAD SCREW

724. Substitute Woodruff key

An effective Woodruff key can be made from the head of a cheesehead screw.

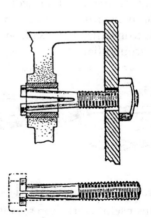

725. Removing cam wheel bushes

It isn't always necessary to split the crankcase to remove cam wheel bushes. A simple withdrawal tool can be made up as follows. Cut the head off a $1/2$ in. bolt and file it away down to a depth of about $1/8$ in. leaving an $1/8$ in. step at the end, as shown in the sketch. Cut a long slit up the centre of the bolt. To remove the bush, compress the split bolt, push it through and wedge a nail into the saw-cut. The nail will splay the end so that the steps come against the ends of the bush. Now place a plate suitably drilled and run a nut down the bolt, thus drawing out the bush.

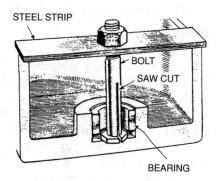

STEEL STRIP
BOLT
SAW CUT
BEARING

726. Blind bush removing tool

How can you remove an obstinate bush after heat treatment and other methods have failed? Take a suitable bolt and file down the head to a very thin section. Make a saw-cut about 1½ in. long down the middle of the bolt from the head end. Assemble the improvised withdrawal tool by passing the threaded end of the bolt through a strip of metal, and rest this across the casing, protecting the soft face with alloy or hardwood bearers. Tap a tiny steel wedge into the saw-cut, above the bearing, so that the bolt head is forced outward to grip the reluctant bush from below. Heat the case and withdraw the bush by tightening the nut on the bolt.

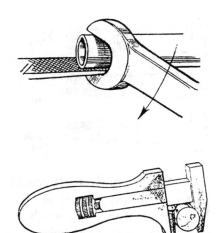

727. Makeshift pipe wrench

The difficulty of turning a shaft or pipe without a pipe wrench can be overcome by choosing an open-end spanner bigger than the pipe and packing the gap with a flat file or set screw. To tighten, turn in the direction of the file. The disadvantage of this method is that it will inevitably scratch the surface of the pipe.

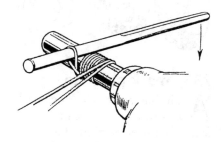

728. Pipe wrench tourniquet

An alternative pipe wrench that avoids damage can be made by using strong cord and a metal bar in tourniquet fashion.

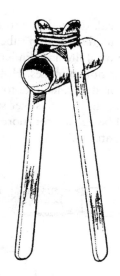

729. Improvized grips

A pair of grips can be improvized in an emergency by using two tyre levers back to back, bound at one end by stout wire.

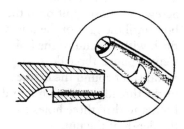

730. Hole punch from silver steel

Silver steel can be used to make a hole punch of the exact correct size by anyone with access to a lathe. Start work on a rod quite a bit larger than the hole required, and drill it endwise with a drill the size of the hole required or a trifle smaller. Taper the end until there is about ⅟₁₆ in. of metal round the hole, and cut away a wedge of metal as shown on the sketch. Harden the tool carefully and temper to a dark straw or brown. Taper the end to a knife edge on a grindstone, taking care not to break through the rod wall.

I have used short thin tubes which started life as cylinder base dowels as hole punches. Hollow tubes should be adequate for a paper punch, but the silver steel tool will be needed for more robust material.

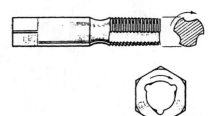

731. Home-made taps and dies

Taps and dies can be made from nuts and bolts as follows:

1. Screw the chosen nut onto the bolt until the face of the nut is flush with the end of the bolt.
2. Centre-punch three dots equidistant round the diameter of the thread, between nut and bolt, and drill three holes to the depth of the nut.
3. Remove the nut, and file a lead onto the thread segments inside it. File a similar lead and also a slight taper onto the bolt, and grind away some metal below the segmented portion of the thread.
4. Case harden by heating to a bright red and plunging into tepid water. To temper, reheat to a straw colour and quench.

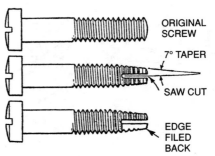

732. Clearing dirty threads

Casing threads suffer from clogging with muck, which in some instances prevents full tightening down, and in others can damage thin alloy. The sketch shows a home-made thread cleaning tap for a primary chaincase made from one of the casing screws. Ideally a spare should be adapted for use, but this design is such that the screw can still be used to tighten the casing after it has done its job cleaning the threads.

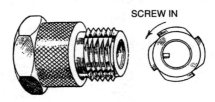

733. Spark plug tap

A suitable tap for clearing spark plug threads can be made from the lower portion of a scrapped plug. File four or five cutting edges across the threads, making sure that the cutting edges face in the same direction as the plug is screwed, and then harden and temper the tap.

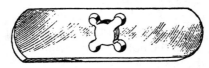

734. Home-made die from a flat file

Because of their expense, dies seem less common than taps even round the second-hand tool stalls at autojumbles. This suggestion for a home-made die comes from 1933. Take an old flat file and soften it by heating to a bright red, and cooling slowly in sand or lime. After cutting into suitable lengths, filing edges should be smoothed and rough ends rounded off. Drill a hole through the centre of the correct tapping size, and carefully tap out the required thread. Drill four small holes just clear of the thread, and then file them into the thread with a round file, leaving a sharp cutting edge. To give a lead to the die, countersink one side of the tapped hole. The die should be hardened and tempered.

735. Fork stanchion puller

A simple tool to pull fork stanchions into place can be made from an old broom handle. Cut a short length from the handle and shape it so that it can be screwed into the top of the stanchion. Screw a hook into the top of the wooden bung, and tie to it a length of wire or stout cord with which to pull up the tube.

Winter storage

The tragedy with motor cycles is that they wear out when used, and deteriorate when left idle. Avoiding the worst of the winter's salty roads seems a sensible way of preserving that expensive paint and chromework. But there are plenty of dangers lurking unseen in the garage which may make next spring's revitalization more than just sticking on the tax disc.

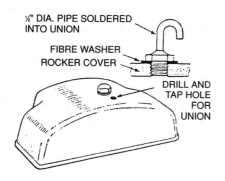

¼" DIA. PIPE SOLDERED INTO UNION

FIBRE WASHER
ROCKER COVER

DRILL AND TAP HOLE FOR UNION

736. Condensation

Condensation can cause a lot of damage to cycle parts. The best way to reduce the risk of conden-sation is to store your motor cycle in dry, well-ventilated conditions.

Keep damp out of rocker boxes and primary chaincases by tapping a hole in the cover, and screw in a plug soldered to a copper U-tube to form a breather. This may help the problem, but have the disadvantage of permanently altering the outward appearance of the machine.

737. Dust sheets

It is a good idea to cover stored machines to keep off dust, but always use a breathable material like cotton. No loose sheet will keep damp out, and plastic sheeting will trap it in.

738. Oil protection

A thin film of oil sprayed or wiped over the entire machine will keep most residual damp at bay. A wipe with an oily rag is all right as far as it goes, but it won't protect the awkward corners which seem to show rust spots first. For those spots brush on oil, or use a special spray.

739. Engine protection

One way to stop the engine from corroding internally is to turn it over at regular intervals during the winter. This prevents the moving parts from sticking and gives a chance for any residual oil in the sump to splash up the bore. Do this manually; don't start the engine unless it is going to be run long enough to get thoroughly warm. Never store the engine without oil over winter; even if the oil is old, it is the best protection for the crankcase bearings.

740. Tyres

Ideally let the air from the tubes and support the machine off the ground. If this is not possible, occasionally turn the wheels so a different part is taking the weight. If your motor cycle is stored over winter standing on its tyres, they will deteriorate.

741. Battery charging

Batteries suffer most from lack of use, because even the newest will lose its charge eventually. It is best to take the battery off the bike at the beginning of winter, and store it near the battery charger. A trickler charge every six weeks will keep it fit for the spring.

742. Battery storage

If charging facilities aren't available, another storage method is to empty out the electrolyte, swill out the battery thoroughly several times with tap water, and swill it out finally with distilled water. The battery should be stored full of distilled water, because if the plates are allowed to dry deterioration may be rapid. But keep the battery where the temperature won't drop below freezing, or a cracked casing may result.

Uses for an inner tube and acetylene rubber tube...

743. To secure tools and spares tins in the toolbox.

744. Cut cross-ways as rubber bands.

745. Cut length-ways for packing small spares or protecting a new spare inner tube.

746. Cut spirally for endless length for winding round handlebars, steering wheels, cricket bat handles or golf clubs.

747. As a rough temporary patch for a puncture.

748. Use an old Schrader valve cut from an inner tube to keep a new valve core safe.

749. To make rubber washers for acetylene generators.

750. To secure a tyre pump to the frame and prevent losing it over rough ground or in trials.

751. To keep in place a loose or temporary float chamber lid.

752. To keep in place a loose carburettor body top.

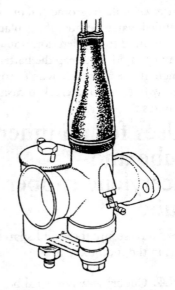

753. To render a carburettor top waterproof.

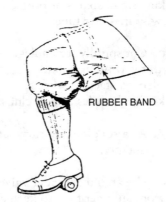

RUBBER BAND

754. To protect plus fours.

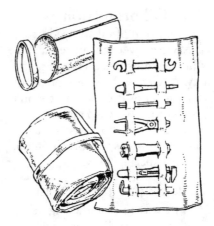

755. To make a tool roll.

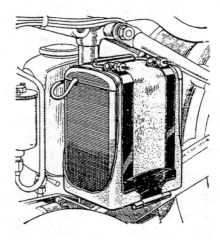

756. To make a protective cover for a battery.

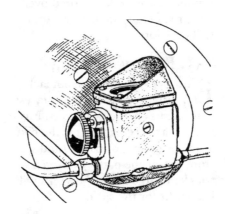

757. As an all weather sight feed shield for a Pilgrim oil pump.

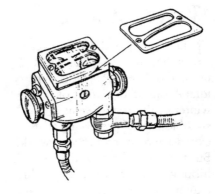

758. As a gasket under the sight feed of a Pilgrim oil pump.

759. As a waterproof boot for an Ariel Four distributor.

760. To make a spout for an oil can.

761. To repair split footrest or handlebar rubbers, or to protect new ones.

762. To protect handlebar grips while carrying out oily maintenance.

763. To take the jerkiness out of a tow rope.

764. During wartime was used to slip over a cylindrical tail light to meet black-out requirements.

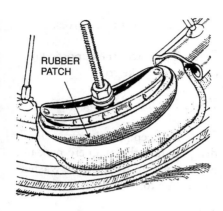

765. To make an oversize patch to stick onto the plates of tyre security bolts to prevent them from chafing the tube.

766. As emergency overshoes.

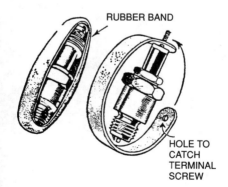

767. As a spark plug protector.

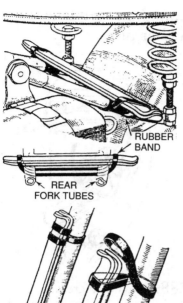

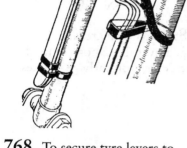

768. To secure tyre levers to the frame.

769. To pack between the springs and cover of a saddle-type seat for extra comfort and to prevent the spring outline eventually showing through.

770. To stop water running down the magneto pick-up or carburettor, cut a circle from the inner tube, punch a hole in it, and slip it on the high tension cable or throttle cable.

771. To wrap round the padlock chain to protect chrome and enamel.

772. To make a headlamp peak.

773. To make saddle spring covers.

774. To make rear suspension unit gaiters.

775. As sidecar leaf spring protectors.

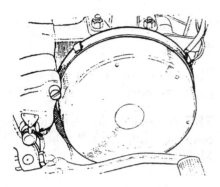

776. To form a waterproof joint at the back of a flywheel magneto.

777. To strap parcels to the inside of leg-shields.

778. To make cushions for a sidecar.

779. To make jacket cuffs and trouser legs draught-proof.

780. As a waterproof sleeve for a Magdyno contact breaker housing.

781. As a waterproof sleeve for the connections on handlebar control levers.

782. To protect chrome rims when fitting snow chains.

783. To link tent guy ropes to their pegs in wet weather to avoid the effect of shrinkage.

784. To lock the front brake on a sidecar outfit when parked.

785. As a brake light switch protector.

786. As a frame-mounted tyre pump protector.

787. To prevent the Magdyno coupling rattling on a Panther M100.

... and an acetylene rubber tube

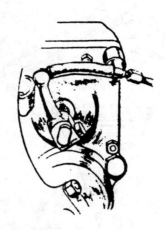

788. Filled with grease and slipped over the exposed end of clutch cables on early gearboxes.

789. To protect tyre valves.

790. To protect the exposed end of the rear brake rod.

791. For lining to goggles.

792. To keep petrol from dripping into the magneto pick-up, in conjunction with a fibre washer to seal the top.

793. To prevent clip-up rear stands from rattling in their fixings.

794. As a protecting sleeve for a cluster of electric cables.

795. To syphon petrol from one tank to another.

THE ROAD

It is impossible to cater for every eventuality which may occur on the road, short of being followed all the way by a friend in a back-up van (don't laugh; I know some who are). But it is easy to provide some insurance against roadside emergencies by foreseeing the most likely problems which can ruin a perfect day.

Many older machines, suffering from more than their fair share of worn threads and poor maintenance, will tend to loosen their nuts and bolts. So will Velocettes and all parallel twins. One tipster checked his machine by coasting over rough ground with a dead engine, listening for rattles. For most of us, regular checks at home will reduce the chance of unwelcome roadside stops and avoid losses and damage.

Be prepared

796. Tools to take

Take particular care over maintenance straight after a rebuild; the machine will be bound to suffer from minor teething troubles over the first few hundred miles. New items such as clutch plates and brake linings will bed in and go out of adjustment, and the contact breaker bolt you didn't want to strip will shake itself loose. A sensibly compiled toolkit should be carried even for short trips at this time.

797. Toolkit

If the machine is a new acquisition, make sure that the spanners in the kit actually fit the nuts on that machine, particularly inaccessible nuts which, though of a standard size, may require a specially shaped tool. It is often better to build up a toolkit just for road use, made up of smaller items than would normally be used in the workshop. For example, a folding plug spanner, a small adjustable spanner, a short screwdriver, a penknife, and so on. Only one pair of pliers is needed, and many have found that the thin-nosed variety have more roadside uses than the standard bull-nosed ones. If space can be found, a small pair of variable pipe pliers can be invaluable.

798. Tool recognition

A band of paint – preferably of the same colour as your machine – applied to the tools normally carried in the toolkit serves a twofold purpose. After maintenance in the workshop it enables the tools taken from the machine to be easily distinguished. And it prevents a mix-up occurring when helping someone on the road.

799. Spares

Even for short trips it is a good idea to carry a small tin of useful oddments, such as a chain split link (make sure it is the same make as your chain; they may be the same nominal size but different makes vary in the thickness of the plates), assorted nuts and bolts, split pins, and solderless nipples. The tin can be packed tightly with a rag to avoid rattles and damage, and held closed with a band cut from an inner tube. Other useful items are spare spark plugs, a roll of soft iron wire, insulated electrical wire, and insulating tape.

800. Toolkit and spares for touring

Invariably, the longer the journey the more tools will be wanted, even if only for peace of mind. What to take depends on the space available and your confidence in the particular machine. Generally useful, though, is a tyre pressure gauge, as those at many petrol stations are inaccurate, and some don't have gauges at all.

Spares, too, will multiply on a longer trip. A magneto or distributor points assembly; flexible tubing for petrol and oil pipes; a spray can of chain lube and maybe a spare chain; an inner tube complete with valve, and a puncture repair outfit. If much night riding is envisaged, a complete set of bulbs is a good idea, and a torch to see what you are doing if you break down in the dark.

A complete spare set of control cables is a worthwhile investment. Many old hands save luggage space, and time in the event of a breakage, by pre-routeing the spare cables beside those in use, just leaving the ends to be connected.

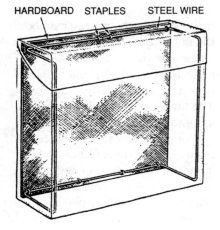

HARDBOARD   STAPLES   STEEL WIRE

801. Pannier bags

Some pannier bags, such as those fitted to ex-military mounts, are made of loose material which fail to keep their shape. One solution is to construct a pair of formers from hardboard and wire. The hardboard is cut to the size of the back of the pannier, and the wire is bent in a configuration to hold the sides rigid and stapled to the hardboard. Any sharp points of the staples protruding through the hardboard should be removed with a file to avoid tearing the pannier canvas. The former slides easily in and out of the bag, and can be removed quickly if a bulky item needs to be loaded.

802. Be prepared

Search for awkward fixings at home in comfort, so that special tools and methods of removal can be worked out in advance of a roadside repair. And don't use power tools for tightening nuts and bolts in the workshop because you may need

to remove them at the roadside with your small adjustable spanner. Adjust the rear chain with the same tools at home as you are taking with you in your motor cycle toolkit.

803. Siphoning tube

It is always worthwhile carrying a decent length of plastic pipe on a long journey. Bits of it can serve as spare petrol or oil pipe, and its complete length can be used for siphoning fuel. For easy storage, slide it up the handlebar and save valuable space in the toolbox.

804. Engineering glue

Engineering glue, such as Loctite, has many uses on an engine, but use the right product for the right job. Nutlock, Studlock and Screwlock will prevent fasteners coming loose, but never use Loctite on a plastic to metal contact; the plastic part may not survive removal.

805. Spanner leverage

To remove a stubborn nut when a tommy-bar or socket set is not available, extra leverage can be obtained by fitting one open-end spanner into the end of another.

806. Tyre levers

Tyre levers are often too long to fit inside toolboxes, and the suggestions for their storage are as various as the makes of motor cycle. On rigid machines they can be placed up the seat tube, across the rear forks under the seat, along

the rear carrier, along the top tube under the petrol tank, always secured with the ubiquitous old inner tube band. One suggestion was to bolt them to the under-side of a rear-mounted toolbox.

807. Stubborn cap

To shift a stubborn cap off an oil can, make a tourniquet from a stick and a length of string. Loop the string round the cap, push the stick through the spare end of string and turn it until it is tight. Now unscrew the cap using the stick as a lever.

808. Overnight protection

If, on holiday, no cover can be found overnight for your machine, a few strips of insulating tape over the exposed carburettor inlet, float tickler, and petrol tank cap vent hole will keep out unwanted moisture.

809. Route finding

Route card holders are commonly available nowadays, even if it's only a plastic map case dangling round the neck. But have you ever thought of decorating the windscreen? One rider, fed up with stopping to look at the map, used to write the names of the major towns en route on the inside of the screen with a chinagraph pencil (the type that rubs out). Once the idea caught on he used it for shopping lists and weekend maintenance tasks. He claimed it didn't impede his view, but it sounds like a dangerous precursor to the car phone to me.

810. Quick-fit cover fastening

For many machines overnight protection is limited to a plastic sheet, even if it's only on holiday. A quick method to attach and remove the sheet is to sew four dog lead spring clips onto the corners; these can be snapped onto the spokes. If the sheet has eyelets, a better method is to attach the spring clips to the corners with four key split rings, or slip bands cut from inner tubes through the eyelets.

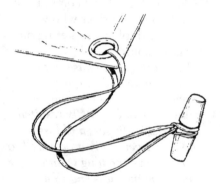

811. Cover fastening – the secure way

Another method of securing a plastic cover to the machine is to make up some bands from ½ in. elastic by threading them through the corner eyelets and sewing the ends together. Then loop them round a wood or plastic toggle (similar to a duffle coat fastener). These are just as quick to release as dog lead clips, but can be fixed to bulkier parts, thus avoiding the problem of the clips riding up the spokes in a wind.

812. Petrol weight

The weight of one gallon of petrol is approximately 7 lb 4 oz. A fully-loaded four gallon tank is therefore carrying 29 lb top

weight. In metric, one litre of petrol weighs about 723 grams; so an 18 litre tank is carrying an extra 13 kg of top weight.

813. Emergency petrol container

Rumour has it that a gallon of petrol will fit into a condom. Transfer of the fuel is easily accomplished by stretching the open end of the condom over the petrol tank filler. It must be true because of the number of motor cyclists I know who always carry one in their wallet!

Roadside emergencies

814. Here are a few tips to help in the event of an emergency, but it must be remembered that these repairs are strictly of a get-you-home nature, not cheap substitutes for the real thing. If your machine has a temporary repair, keep your speed down, pay extra attention to other road users, and fix whatever it is properly at the earliest opportunity.

When broken down beside the road, dejection turns to desolation with the inevitable onset of rain, and it is difficult to concentrate the mind logically on the problem at hand. In diagnosis, always remember to check the easiest and cheapest first. Don't tear the ignition system apart before checking the spark plug or looking for a blown fuse, or the carburettor before looking for fuel in the tank. Rumour has it that 80 per cent of breakdowns

are electrical, so that is where we'll begin.

Electrics

815. Removing a hot plug

To remove a hot spark plug by the roadside without burning fingers, carry a short length of rubber tubing in the toolbox. Once the plug has been loosened with the spanner, the tubing can be slipped over the insulator, and the plug spun out.

816. Testing for a spark

Back in the days when boys were men and motor cyclists were giants (1923 to be precise), the usual way to test a magneto was to put one finger on the plug terminal and kick the engine over. 'If a shock results, the magneto is working properly.' No doubt considered enjoyable then, it could still have its uses. To check an ignition fault it is best to start at the plug and work backwards.

1. Take out the plug, re-attach to the high tension (HT) lead, and resting the plug thread on a cylinder fin, kick over the engine. If there is a visible spark there is nothing wrong with the ignition – you've probably run out of petrol. If there is no spark, exchange the plug for a proven spare.

2. If still no spark, you could try to get an electric shock like they did in 1923, but that has to be your decision – I am not recommending it. If you do try it and there's no shock, replace the HT lead with a new length of cable, and try again.

3. If still no go, have a look at the magneto pick-up. Check the screw fixing the HT lead to

the pick-up, that the carbon brush moves freely in its holder and is clean of oil, the condition of the brush spring, and the cleanness of the slip ring. Clean the carbon brush with a rag dipped in petrol. To clean the slip ring, push the rag through the pick-up hole and turn the engine over. Do not use a graphite pencil or uninsulated screwdriver for the job.

4. Check that the contact breaker points open and close. If they are stuck open, the fibre rocker arm bush (rocker arm points assembly) or fibre tappet (face cam points assembly) may have swollen in the wet, or picked up grit. Clean it and ease the fibre with emery paper. Re-gap the points to the recommended setting – usually 12 thou.

5. Check that the contact breaker points are not burnt or covered in oil, or that you have not left a piece of cellophane between them from when you timed the engine.

6. If still no sign of life, hard luck; it's the magneto windings.

817. Testing ignition – a short cut

On a battery and coil ignition system, one way to isolate the fault as lying between the contact breaker points and the spark plug (that is, not so major or expensive a fault) is to short the contact breakers with a screwdriver. If they spark, at least there is life that far up the system.

818. Testing a spark plug

Holding a spark plug for testing is made safer, for those who don't like shocks, by inserting it in one end of a ring spanner and wedging the other end gently between vertical cylinder head fins, or between the magneto body and cylinder barrel.

819. Twin plug check

If a spark plug has packed up on a twin, and you don't know which cylinder, touch each exhaust pipe. The duff plug will be behind the cooler one.

820. Foul plug

Though it is common practice to check for a spark by coupling the HT cable to a spare plug, it could bring trouble. That single confirmatory kick could be enough to foul the plug left in the head. Play safe, even if it does take a few seconds longer, by whipping out the in-use plug and checking the spark with that.

821. Clearing a fouled plug

A tip for clearing a dirty plug on a multi-cylinder engine is to detach the HT lead and hold it ⅛ in. from the plug terminal. When the engine runs on the other cylinder(s), the fouled plug will often clear without having to be removed.

822. Short reach plug

If, in an emergency, a short-reach plug has been used in a head intended for a long-reach version, it is important to clean the thread in the cylinder head before refitting the correct long-reach plug. Ideally a 14 mm tap should be used with the flutes smeared with grease to collect the carbon.

At a pinch, an old long-reach plug can do the job, with longitudinal grooves filed in the threaded portion.

823. Cure for a misfire

Misfiring and uneven running caused by dirt in the carburettor can be cured by slamming the throttle open and shut two or three times in quick succession. This works particularly well on cold mornings.

824. Whiskered plug

This tip from 1954 comes from a two-stroke rider who was plagued with plug whiskering on short fast spins:

'The subsequent pause to take out the plug and remove the metallic particles bridging the plug electrodes usually resulted in scorched fingers and loss of temper. Eventually it occurred to me to leave the plug in situ, place the business end of a screwdriver against the case of the plug (not against the insulating material) and administer a few sharp taps on the screwdriver handle with a spanner. The jarring effect never fails to shake the particles free.'

825. Retaining the high tension lead

If no plug cap is fitted to the HT lead and the spark plug barrel nut is lost, the HT lead spade terminal can be kept on top of the plug either by pulling it tight and taping the lead to a frame member, or by putting a couple of twists in the HT lead itself. Copper wire wound into the exposed thread at the top of the plug may also work, or try cutting a disc from a tin, punching a hole through it with a nail, and pushing it on the threaded plug terminal.

826. Plug lead droop

Even with modern waterproof caps, the best arrangement for the HT lead is to droop down away from the plug cap. This will stop water running into the area of the plug connection and causing a short.

827. Magneto misfiring

A magneto may start to misfire in wet weather through water getting into the body. A temporary remedy is to take off the brush holder and dry out the slip ring as far as possible. Before replacing the brush holder, put a few drops of oil onto the slip ring. This will prevent further water being picked up by the ring from the base of the magneto as the armature revolves.

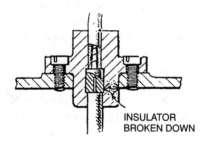

INSULATOR
BROKEN DOWN

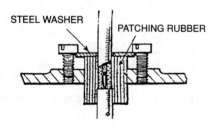

STEEL WASHER   PATCHING RUBBER

828. Maglita repair

If the insulation cracks at the HT terminal on an ML Maglita, the spark will go to earth there and not reach the plug. A temporary

repair can be effected by packing the HT lead in place with rubber (such as a patch from a puncture repair outfit). This can be held in the Maglita body by nipping up a washer between the two existing HT terminal screws.

829. Broken magneto pick-up

If the magneto carbon pick-up brush breaks up, the broken pieces can be removed from inside the mag by dipping a length of wire in the rubber solution of your puncture repair outfit (don't say you left it at home!). Afterwards the slip ring must be cleaned with a petrol-soaked rag. A get-you-home brush can be made out of a roll of silver paper.

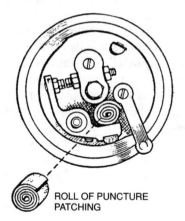

ROLL OF PUNCTURE
PATCHING

830. Broken contact breaker spring

A broken contact breaker spring can be repaired temporarily by wedging a rolled up rubber puncture patch between the contact breaker centre, the pivot spring standard, and the rocker arm. The pivot spring will hold the roll in place, and the rubber's elasticity will close the points.

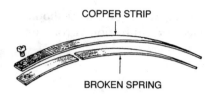

COPPER STRIP

BROKEN SPRING

831. Broken contact breaker spring – ring cam type

This tip was used to repair a contact breaker of the ring cam type. A strip of thin copper was cut the same size as the spring, and two holes bashed (literally) in it to coincide with those of the spring. This strip was placed on the contact breaker over the broken spring, and held it firmly enough to allow it to function satisfactorily.

832. Wipac switch switch

Many 50s and 60s lightweights use Wipac electrics, with a plug and socket connection of the wiring loom to the ignition and lighting switches. These switches are identical and, should a faulty switch be suspected, it is easy to check by swapping the socket connections in the headlamp shell.

833. Dynamo repair

If the copper-strand wire attached to a dynamo brush breaks too close to the brush to permit the two ends to be rejoined, a temporary repair can be made by twisting the wire round the brush-retaining spring.

834. Dynamo belt slip

To prevent dynamo belt slip when all slack has been taken up, a good temporary tip is to wrap insulating tape round the groove of the dynamo pulley. Any overlap in the tape joint should face in the direction of rotation of the pulley.

835. Dynamo cure for battery failure

If the battery fails on a six-volt system, it is possible to get home by substituting 12-volt bulbs in the lamps and disconnecting the battery leads. All that remains is to join the positive and negative battery leads, and not to rev the engine too hard.

836. Voltage regulator out of control

This example of a faulty lighting system and its temporary repair comes from 1948:

'With an ammeter showing no charge a piece of wire was held across the terminals of a two-brush dynamo; a 20 amp charge was then indicated. The problem was to reduce this charge to a reasonable level, so a lamp was connected across the terminals with a 24 watt bulb in the holder. The indicated charge dropped to 10 amps, and the lighting system worked well enough to get home.'

837. Coil ignition – flat battery

If the battery fails on a machine fitted with coil ignition, it is possible to start the engine by using a dry cell battery (from a torch if it's only six volt) connected to the coil, or by push starting until the dynamo voltage control unit cut-out cuts in. Those with later 12-volt systems,

don't risk jump starting from a car battery; the smaller motor cycle battery probably won't stand the shock.

838. Alternator anecdote

One Sunday an RAC patrolman came across a solo towing another, and found that the broken-down machine was equipped with an alternator and a flat battery. The model doing the towing had a magneto – and neither rider had thought of swapping the perfectly good battery from that to the other, so making both machines mobile again.

839. Cleaning battery terminals

Sulphated battery terminals are easily cleaned with a toothbrush and boiling water. Grease the terminals with petroleum jelly only after refixing the wires to prevent any grease acting as an insulator. To prevent acid spilling on cycle parts from a black rubber battery, run a bead of petroleum jelly round the rim of the battery and set the loose top in it, before tightening up the straps.

840. Fuse failure

If a fuse blows and no spare is available, a roll of silver paper can be inserted in the fuse holder as a temporary measure. A check should be made first as to why the fuse blew, and the fault rectified. Otherwise the component the fuse was protecting may be damaged.

841. Bulb law

United Kingdom regulations state that a machine over 500 cc must have a rear bulb of at least six watts. This rule also applies to sidecar mudguards. If a rear bulb blows, it is possible to get home with a rewired stoplight, but this should only be temporary because the hotter brake light filament may damage the plastic lens if left on permanently, and the extra wattage can blow a fuse.

842. Bulb lore

Even if it still gives a reasonable beam, the headlamp main bulb should be renewed occasionally. The reason for this is that regular heating and cooling of the filament when switching on and off causes it to stretch and sag – upsetting the beam focus.

For those who've converted to a halogen system, pick up the bulbs by the base not the glass as the natural oils in the skin will cause the bulb to overheat and the filament to blow. If you do touch the glass, clean it with methanol before use.

843. Temporary rear light

When a rear light bulb fails, the stoplight can be used as a temporary substitute. The forward end of the spring running from the stoplight switch to the rear brake lever should be detached from the lever and connected to an adjacent part of the frame. The spring should be fixed under tension to keep the stoplight switched on. Otherwise, if bullet connectors are used for the stop and tail light leads, simply swap the leads over.

844. Carrying a spare bulb

One of the best ways to carry a spare bulb is to slide it into a length of rubber tube and push a cork in both ends. Photographers may choose to use empty plastic film cannisters.

845. Broken electrical wire

If a wire pulls out of a sprung terminal, such as a single pole tail lamp, a thin bolt can replace the central plunger and the wire tightened to it by the correct thread nut. Alternatively, a shirt sleeve button can be used in place of the soldered ferrule, by poking the wire strands through the two button thread holes and twisting them together to form a connection for the bulb.

846. Spare wiring diagram

A photocopy of your wiring diagram pasted inside the toolbox lid is invaluable if an electrical fault has to be traced at the roadside.

Carburettor and controls

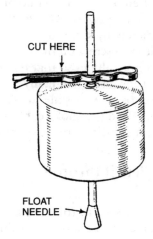

CUT HERE

FLOAT NEEDLE

847. Carburettor repair

Never poke a carburettor jet clear with a piece of wire; always blow any dirt out. A compressed air jet is the best for stubborn grit. On the road that means the air line at a filling station, or press the jet onto the core of a tyre valve. A broken float needle clip can be replaced by a ladies' hairpin cut to length.

848. Punctured carburettor float

If a carburettor float should puncture miles from anywhere so that it cannot be repaired by soldering, it may be substituted by a large cork. The needle should be pushed through the centre of the cork (the tight fit will hold it firmly in position), and the petrol level controlled by the height of the cork on the needle.

849. Locating a float puncture

A puncture in a float can be located by placing it in hot water. The petrol vaporizes and, together with the air, expands so that bubbles emerge from the leak. Ensure all petrol and water are drained from the float, by enlarging the leak if necessary, and repair with solder applied sparingly.

850. Substitute Bowden cable nipple

In case a solderless nipple is unavailable, a substitute for the soldered nipple can be made up in 10 minutes with nothing but a pair of pliers and a bit of wire. First shorten the outer casing by about an inch. Then cut off a length of three coils of the casing, and slip it on the cable. Cut a piece of wire ⅛ in. long. Double back the end of the cable, place the bit of wire in the fold, and wedge the three coils of casing over the turned back cable end. The cable does not snap off when doubled back, if carefully done.

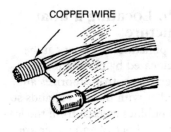

COPPER WIRE

851. Copper wire nipple

If the cable nipple has come off, and a workshop is available, bind copper wire round the broken end of the throttle cable and coat with solder.

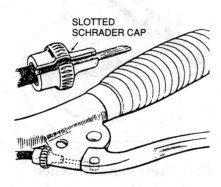

SLOTTED
SCHRADER CAP

852. Schrader ferrule

A Schrader valve cap can make a handy replacement cable ferrule in an emergency. Punch out the inside, cut a slit up one side, wide enough to slide over the inner cable, and push firmly onto the outer cable. Correct adjustment of the cable will hold it in position.

853. Lost twistgrip ferrule

The ferrule which seats the throttle cable on some twistgrips can be easily lost during a roadside repair. One idea suggested in the 50s was to make up a replacement out of aluminium kitchen foil, pressing it into the twistgrip's collet space. The arrangement worked

adequately until a new ferrule could be obtained.

854. Broken throttle cable

It is often possible to get home in spite of a broken throttle cable merely by screwing the throttle stop screw on the carburettor fully in so that the engine runs faster. On many carburettors the air slide can be removed, and the choke cable used as a substitute throttle cable.

855. Pencil throttle control

Another scheme to get you home when the throttle cable breaks is to strap one end of a pencil to the handlebar with a rubber band, and tie the broken end of the cable to the other end of the pencil. Working the pencil to and fro with the thumb gives acceptable throttle control. The rubber band is yet another bit of old inner tube, always useful to keep in the toolbox.

856. Ring-pull throttle control

There are other ways of fixing a throttle cable. If the cable breaks by the twistgrip and you don't have a screwdriver, but you do have a bit of wire, a key ring and a solderless nipple, this is the answer:

Tie the outer casing of the control cable to the handlebar; pass the end of the inner cable between the coils of the key ring; lock the cable in position with the solderless nipple. By looping the thumb through the key ring and gripping and operating the twistgrip in the normal way, the thumb will automatically work the throttle.

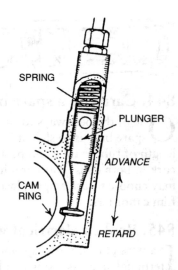

SPRING

PLUNGER

ADVANCE

CAM
RING

RETARD

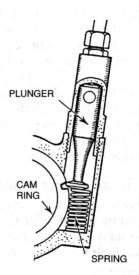

PLUNGER

CAM
RING

SPRING

857. Broken ignition cable

If the control cable breaks on a tight wire advance magneto, the small return spring will automatically retard the ignition and slow the engine. A simple get-you-home dodge is to remove the contact breaker control plunger, place the spring underneath the plunger, and replace the plunger and cam ring. Thus the spring will advance the ignition and keep it there.

858. Knotted ignition cable

A simpler method may be to tie a knot in the inner cable just above the adjuster. Screw out the adjuster to keep the ignition fully advanced.

859. Broken exhaust lifter cable

To ease starting, put the machine in gear and wheel it backwards until compression is felt. Return the gear lever to neutral, and set the other controls ready for starting. A smart swinging kick will give the engine time to spin before coming up against, and bouncing over, compression. Try that with a Velocette!

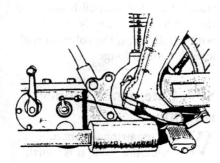

860. Sturmey-Archer clutch cable

If the clutch cable breaks, a get-you-home repair is as follows. Remove the broken wire from the outer sheath. Fit the nipple into the retaining slot in the actuating arm and thread the other end of the wire through the screwed adjuster. If the free end of the wire is now attached to the front footrest rod or an adjacent nut it will be found quite easy to use the clutch by merely depressing the wire with the heel of your boot.

861. Emergency soldering

Though rarely needed, this idea for emergency soldering may prove useful. The problem can be overcome by carrying a short length of 18-gauge piano wire and another short length of multi-core solder. By means of a lighting cable (household flex is just the job) the solder is connected to one terminal of the battery and the piano wire to the other. When the free ends are touched together sufficient heat will be generated to make the solder run.

Tyres and wheels

862. Tyre check

On a touring holiday it's a good idea to spin the wheels every night to check the tyres haven't picked up any debris. Sharp shreds may be embedded in the tread ready to puncture the tyre after a few more miles. A simple check could save a lot of tiresome trouble the following day.

863. Rear wheel removal

In cases when there is not enough clearance to remove the rear wheel from under the mudguard, the machine can be pulled onto its centre stand (or rear stand) on a kerb's edge. Even a road with a steep enough camber may give sufficient extra clearance.

864. Rear brake dodge

In one national trial, Allan Jeffries had the ill-luck to break off his rear brake pedal pivot against a large rock. Not wanting to ride all the way home without a rear brake, he fastened a length of bicycle chain from the left footrest to the brake cam lever. He applied the brake by putting

his foot on the chain part way along its length.

865. Water on linings

After going through a ford, water on the linings will render the brakes inefficient. They will soon dry out once the brakes are applied, but it is a good idea to clear the linings by applying the brakes immediately after leaving the ford, and not wait for the next emergency.

866. Tyre puncture

The method of removing and refitting a tyre is described in 'The Machine' section. However, a precaution before a long journey is to ensure that both tyres have plenty of tread and that neither tube has a patch. Everyone knows that washing up liquid applied to the tyre will help ease it back onto the rim, but most do not carry a bottle with them. A piece of candlewax is an effective substitute, and is easily tucked away in the toolkit.

867. Valve check

When stuck with a flat tyre check the valve first. Remove the dust cap, spit on your finger, and spread the spittle over the top of the valve. If bubbles appear the valve is faulty. Assuming the valve is in order, look all round the tyre to find the cause of the trouble before getting the spanners out. Mark the spot on the tyre wall in chalk to save time later in locating the hole in the tube.

868. Piston pressure

Your engine can become a tyre pump. Take 4 ft of rubber tubing from its storage place in the toolbox, and bind one end tightly to the tyre valve. After removing the spark plug, the other end is fitted into the plug hole with an adaptor made from an old spark plug. With the throttle fully open, the engine is spun with the kickstarter, and in a few minutes the tyre is fully hard.

869. Tyre pressure check

This tip from 1931 will be helpful when restoring tyre pressure accurately after a puncture:

'At home, when restoring the pressure of tyres, find out roughly how many pumpfuls it takes to increase the pressure by 1 lb. Then take the pressure of the tyre (say 15 lb); give 40 pumps and test the pressure again (say 23 lb). Therefore 40 pumps = 8 lb, or 5 pumps = 1 lb. To restore the pressure of a tyre multiply the deficiency in pounds by five, and give that number of pumpfuls.'

I'll leave it up to your conscience as to what represents the difference between an 'at home' pumpful and a 'post roadside puncture repair with machine loaded with luggage' pumpful. All I know is that constantly checking the pressure gives an excuse for a breather.

870. Removing a tyre valve

To remove an inner tube valve when a cap key is not available, place a split pin in the valve until it locates round the projection of the plunger collar, and unscrew by passing a nail through the eye of the split pin.

871. Curing a faulty valve

If a tyre is flat because of a faulty valve and a pump is available, reinflate the tyre and unscrew the rubber pump connection at the pump end. Then bend the tube double and wire it to an adjacent spoke.

872. Spare tyre valve

One of the best ways of carrying a spare valve core, collar and cap without risk of loss or damage is to use the valve body from an old inner tube.

873. Removing an old patch

If an old patch has to be removed from a tube for any reason, such as a second puncture near the first, it can best be done by pressing it against a part of the exhaust system hot enough to liquidize the glue without melting the surrounding tube. A safer method is to drip petrol under a lifted corner of the old patch.

874. Slow puncture

This tip for dealing with a slow puncture on a long journey comes from 1954:

'Recently I had the ill fortune to suffer a slow puncture in the rear tyre of my Triumph Speed Twin. Inflating the tyre at regular intervals I was losing pressure at approximately 2 psi per hour. Then I heard of the ruse of pumping milk into a damaged tube. I filled an inflater with milk and pumped in about half-a-pint. Then I spun the wheel to spread the milk thoroughly over the inner surface of the tube. Repeated subsequent checks with a tyre gauge showed that the makeshift repair was a complete success.'

875. Puncture repair?

An old trick, which some claim to have used, is to pack the cover with grass. Only the flat bit at the bottom, of course!

876. Preserving rubber solution

Ever had a puncture only to find that your tube of rubber solution has dried up? If some solution from a large tube is transferred into a small bottle, and the bottle's screw cap is sealed with candle wax, the solution will keep for much longer.

877. Emergency rubber solution

When repairing a puncture beside the road, it is worth remembering that, as a last resort, petrol can be used as a substitute for rubber solution, assuming a prepared patch is being used.

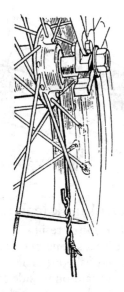

and file the end to a taper to ensure that the spoke engages easily with the nipple. Bow the spoke to insert it through the nipple hole; it will straighten when the nipple is tightened up. Deflate the tyre, and pull to one side with a tyre lever, taking care not to pinch the tube. Insert the nipple onto the end of the new spoke (using the old spoke screwed into the other end to start it), and tighten up in the normal way. The correct tension can be judged by pinging the spoke until it emits the same note as the others.

878. Repairing a broken spoke

A spoke can be repaired temporarily by bending the two broken ends over to form a pair of hooks. A piece of strong wire should be used to link the two hooks, tensioned up tourniquet-fashion with a nail. The nail should be left in place and wired up to the adjacent spoke.

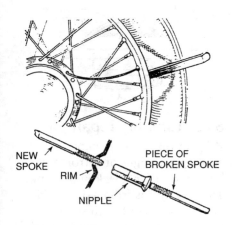

NEW SPOKE

RIM

NIPPLE

PIECE OF BROKEN SPOKE

879. Refitting a spoke

Single spokes can be replaced without removing the tyre as follows. Cut the new spoke slightly shorter than full length,

880. Collapsed wheel

For those who despair at a blown fuse on a wet night, this is a salutary tale from 1951:

'A very difficult to remove rear wheel had partly collapsed, and no rear stand was available. Seven adjacent spokes had snapped. It was a dirty night and there was no shed in which to do the job. I had some spokes of approximately the correct length, but the problem was how to get them in without puncturing the tyre. A sound spoke was removed, and seven spokes were filed off to this length. Then a further three threads were filed off. The tyre was half deflated, the nipples were held fast with a spanner, and the old spokes unscrewed. The (new) shorter ones were then threaded through the flange, and very carefully the nipples were tightened up till all the spokes were true in tone when struck. Finally the tyre was pumped up, and the journey completed. On examination later the wheel ran true within 1/16 in.'

Fuel problems

881. Blocked petrol vent

If the engine fails to start, check that the vent in the top of the petrol cap isn't blocked, causing a vacuum that prevents petrol reaching the carburettor. A dab of chrome cleaner can be the culprit – a warning against over-polishing!

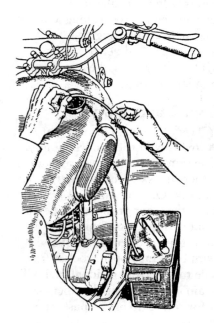

882. Syphoning petrol

Petrol can be syphoned from a petrol tank with a length of tubing, provided that the receptacle is lower than the petrol level in the tank. Many start the syphoning by sucking on the end of the tube. It works, but often results in a mouthful of petrol! A far better scheme is to pinch the tube with the left hand at the filler cap neck, and draw the thumb and index finger of the right hand to within half an inch of the end of the tube, so expelling the air. Then pinch the end of the tube tightly and release the grip at the filler cap. The partial vacuum in the tube will draw the petrol up and, when you release your grip, start the syphoning.

883. Petrol syphoning pointers

A useful emergency receptacle for transferring petrol from one tank to another is the lid of a Lucas voltage regulator or a Miller dynamo end cover, as long as they're dried thoroughly afterwards. And petrol can be syphoned by using the tyre pump as a large syringe.

884. Tank empty?

Every Scotsman knows that a whisky bottle is never empty. The same is true with petrol tanks – there is always a drop left at the bottom. On running out of petrol, push the front of the machine up a short slope (a pavement kerbstone is often enough) and, with both taps open, rock it from side to side. Any residual fuel will drain into the float chamber. Save it for riding up hills – push along the flat.

885. Temporary cure for petrol leaks

If a copper petrol pipe is broken at the olive, cut the pipe level with the soldered base of the nipple and, leaving the nut on the pipe, wrap soap-smeared fine string round the pipe as close as possible to the open end. Carefully push the temporary olive up into the tap and tighten the nut.

886. Broken petrol tap

Take the petrol tap union clean out of the tank and replace it with a cork smeared with soap.

Push a short metal tube through the cork, and wire the petrol pipe to the tube.

887. Trick or treacle

Treacle and syrup are sticky and insoluble in petrol. To temporarily stem a leak from a pipe or tank seam, a rag dressed with treacle is more effective than, say, chewing gum. Ordinary household soap, too, appears to be insoluble in petrol. If flaked and rubbed into a leaking joint, it will also provide a better cure than chewing gum. A coating of nail varnish will also work for a short time.

888. Petrol pipe repair

A broken petrol pipe can be repaired on the road with a potato, though this tip from 1960 doesn't say whether the potato or the spade to dig it up with should be carried in the toolkit. Or perhaps you could use the coin kept for opening the Dzus fastener to buy a potato at the nearest village shop. Push a hole through the potato with a pencil and insert the broken pipe ends. The joint will be leak-proof even if the break is near the fuel tap.

889. Plastic pipe repair

When plastic fuel pipes age, they tend to harden and leak where they are attached to the metal union. They can usually be put to further service, especially in an emergency, if the last inch is cut off and the pipe refitted.

890. Petrol tank leak

Goodbye epoxy resin – welcome a strong manilla envelope and fish glue. The machine was laid on its side to keep the petrol away from the crack, and the envelope was opened out, stuck down with fish glue (bought at a village shop) and rubbed flat, allowing as long as possible for it to set. Sceptics beware! This tip allowed a trade rider to claim a medal in a Six Days trial in 1923. Or perhaps they don't make envelopes like that anymore.

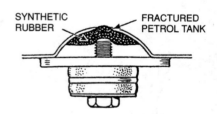

SYNTHETIC RUBBER   FRACTURED PETROL TANK

891. Tank lug repair

Over-zealous tightening of some designs of petrol tank lug can result in a leak in the tank. This example is from a 350cc BSA, but I have to confess to similar ham-fistedness in my youth on my Triumph 3TA. As a get-you-home repair the BSA owner wedged a rubber block (from the sole of a shoe!) over the hole, and held it in place with the tank bolt.

892. Reserve fuel taps

It is a good idea to use the reserve tap occasionally to keep it free from deposits, and to ensure that it is working when really needed.

893. Refuelling two-strokes

When two-strokes run out of fuel, many will be able to help out with petrol, but not the necessary oil. Don't risk it until the next petrol station; carry a small bottle of two-stroke oil in the toolbox. In summer, listen for the buzz of a two-stroke chainsaw or lawn mower for possible supplies of petroil.

Primary transmission and gearbox

894. Loose ball bearings

A dab of grease will hold in place loose ball bearings, such as for clutch adjustment and gear selection, during reassembly. On the road, when a can of grease isn't usually available, butter is a good substitute (the Greasy Spoon café won't mind, honest!).

895. Gearbox casing repair

When the kickstarter quadrant return stop on the gearbox of a Triumph Model 70 snapped off, a roadside repair was affected from a nut and setscrew, two washers and a spacer. The hole in the gearbox casing was less than an inch across, so the washers were able to bridge the gap. The setscrew was the same diameter as

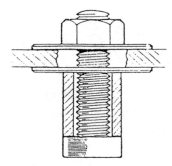

the original stop, and the spacer the correct depth. Once assembled the repair was oiltight as well as efficient.

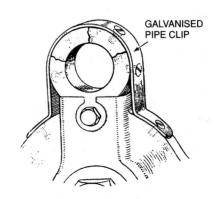

GALVANISED PIPE CLIP

896. Repairing an alloy lug

Many pre-war machines have alloy lugs on casings to take gear levers, screw adjusters and the like, and these are easily broken. A temporary repair is to drill and tap each broken section, including two holes in the main casing on either side of the lug, reassemble them in their original position, and screw them together with a metal band. The example shown is a Velocette gear lever lug, the screws used were 6BA, and the metal band a galvanized pipe clip.

897. Broken gear lever

A broken gear lever can be mended temporarily by knocking one end of a box spanner onto the broken lever, and tightening a bolt through the tommy-bar hole at the other end. Otherwise, use a pair of vice-grips on the gearbox mainshaft.

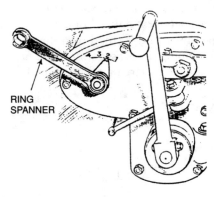

RING SPANNER

898. Temporary gearchange

Should the internal ratchet spring fail on an Albion-type gearbox the footchange mechanism is rendered inoperative. But a ring spanner placed over the indicator retaining nut and taped to the indicator makes an effective, although non-positive, temporary control.

899. Broken layshaft

Drastic problems call for drastic measures. A broken layshaft in a Sturmey-Archer gearbox was sorted out by wedging a ¼ in. tommy-bar from a box spanner set in the shaft's hollow centre. The broken off portion of the layshaft was put on the other end of the tommy-bar, pushed up tight and held in position by a length of spring cut from under the saddle cover.

900. Rear chain – missing spring clip

A missing spring clip from the split link of a chain can be replaced by a piece of wire as long as the backing plate has not been lost too. Carefully wrap it round the spindles and pull it tight into the grooves with pliers. Drive home slowly, and replace with a complete new link as soon as possible. And if you'd read the beginning of this section, you'd be carrying a spare in your toolbox!

General

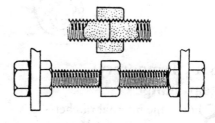

901. Finding a long bolt

It is practicable in an emergency to join two short bolts together with a nut of the same thread to create one long bolt. The two ends of the bolts should be screwed into the nut until they lock, meeting as near the centre as possible.

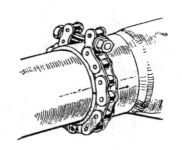

902. Broken silencer clip

A new clip can be made from a short length of old chain bolted through the links.

903. Tightening wire

Apart from in racing circles, where wiring up certain nuts and bolts is compulsory, wire fixing on motor cycles is considered a bodge. But no one can deny the usefulness of soft iron wire to hold on loose exhausts or mudguards just to get home. How many have found that the only bit of wire to be discovered in miles of hedgerow snaps under the penultimate turn of the pliers? To avoid this, it is important during the final twisting to exert a strong and even pull on the wire until the required tautness is obtained. Otherwise all the strain is put on the twist, not the wire encircling the damaged component.

904. Broken fork spring

The main spring on many girder forks will by now be weak with age, and specialist spring makers can supply an accurate copy if yours does break. This temporary repair from 1948 is only intended as a get-you-home dodge; don't drive far or fast without fitting a new replacement.

A piece of galvanized iron water pipe which fitted snugly inside the spring was slotted at the bottom to locate over the bottom fixing lug, and was ground to a taper on the outside to suit the bottom taper of the spring. Two holes were drilled and tapped into the tube for a pair of ¼ in. locking screws to clamp the coils to the tube.

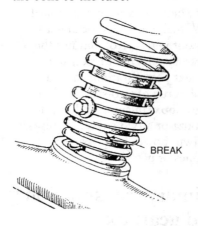

BREAK

[The following two tips are included for amusement only. Putting them into practice is highly inadvisable.]

905. 'Smoking kills'

Being stuck without a match was considered a dilemma worth taking a risk for in 1924:

'At some time or other we have all probably been caught on a deserted road with plenty of cigarettes but no matches, and longing for a smoke. A tip worth knowing in such circumstances is to remove the sparking plug, reattach the high tension wire, invert the plug and fill it to just below the point with petrol. Then, holding the body of the plug onto the cylinder, kickstart until a spark ignites the petrol.'

906. Fire stick

This tip from the 30s is slightly less dangerous, but still wouldn't get approval from your fire officer.

'When stranded without matches, soak the tip of a stick in petrol; then start the bike and rev the engine slightly. Now pull off the HT wire and keep the engine running by holding the wire about ¼ in. away from the plug terminal. The continuous spark will readily ignite the petrol-soaked stick.'

And probably the bike as well; or has our attitude to safety been blown out of all proportion?

907. Clean shoes!

During the summer of 1957 it was often too hot to wear boots. So, to protect the right shoe from damage by gearchanging, a spat was made up from the crown of an old felt hat. It was fixed in place by two pieces of elastic as shown in the sketch. It looks a good idea, but I still can't see what keeps the oil out of the trouser turn-up.

908. Engine cooling

When an air-cooled engine is running with the machine stationary it is only being cooled by direct radiation and not by means of a forced draught. The amount of cooling obtained in such circumstances is extremely small, so it is advisable not to run the engine for long periods in neutral.

909. Roadside light

Examining components such as contact breaker points can be awkward even in bright sunshine. A detachable handlebar mirror or even a polished chrome petrol cap will make a good light reflector. For night time work, some 30s machines came supplied with a little lead light mounted in the petrol tank panel. This idea can be copied on any machine by lengthening the cable inside the shell to the headlight, enabling the headlight unit to be taken out and moved to the job in hand.

910. Top dead centre reckoning

Setting top dead centre with the cylinder head off and no gauges can be troublesome. In an emergency, top dead centre can be estimated fairly accurately with a valve grinding tool as long as the piston crown is flat or only slightly domed. Attach the suction pad of the tool to the top of the piston and pull steadily upward until the piston is at the limit of its travel. The rocking which occurs when the piston is pulled up to TDC can be compensated for if a light pull is maintained until all rocking ceases. Don't disturb the valve tool until all other settings have been established.

911. Broken valve spring

Broken coil valve springs can be made to work if the two broken halves are reversed, as the flattened faces will prevent the two halves from inter-coiling.

912. Blown head gasket

This is one way in which a roll of soft copper wire can prove invaluable. Should the cylinder head gasket blow miles from anywhere, make up an overlapping ring (or rings) of copper wire and use this between the head and barrel. Though only a temporary measure, it should last long enough to get home.

913. Makeshift ring compressor

If the barrel needs lifting during a roadside repair, a leather belt can be used as a makeshift piston ring compressor. Alternatively a worm screw clip of the right size will do. It should only be lightly tightened so that it slides off the rings when the piston is introduced to the bore. If the clamp screw is undone fully, the clip can be removed from the conrod.

914. Starting first time

The classic method of obtaining a first kick start with a four-stroke single is described thus in a 60s tip:

'Ignition off, flood the float chamber, then give three gentle swings of the kick-starter to draw gas into the cylinder. Now, feel for compression and ease the pedal past this point (use the valve lifter or decompression valve, if fitted). Switch on the ignition and give one long swinging kick.

'If your machine has coil ignition and the ammeter is readily visible, watch the needle; as soon as it swings back to the zero position, that's the time for that first time, swinging starting kick.'

I can only add that if your machine is fitted with a magneto, make sure that it has been restored recently by someone competent. Money saved on the cost of magneto repair is responsible for most single's reluctance to start.

915. Starting a V-twin

This advice from 1940 could save a lot of red faces at vintage meetings. It has frequently been emphasized in *The Motor Cycle* that easy starting with a high compression single is best obtained by finding compression, raising the exhaust valve, depressing the kickstarter a further inch, releasing the exhaust valve, and giving a long, swinging kick.

This can be applied to big twins as follows: If the angle between the cylinders is, say 50 degrees, with normal direction of engine rotation there is 360 + 50 = 410 degrees between rear cylinder compression and front cylinder compression, and 360 - 50 = 310 degrees between front and rear compression. I weigh a mere nine stone and when my 990 cc side-valve is cold, I always rotate the engine once or twice, using the exhaust lifter when necessary, and set the engine just past compression on the rear cylinder; the 410 degrees round to the next compression always enables me to bump her over with ease, yet in the other position (310 degrees) I experience considerable difficulty.

916. Stripped threads

To secure a stud with a stripped thread, try winding the thread with cotton twine or plumber's white binding tape. It may hold long enough just to get home.

917. Major stripped threads

If a large nut strips its thread and a replacement is unavailable, cut a slot through one flat face of the nut, run the nut on the bolt, and then pinch it tight with a pair of vice-grips to close the slot, so gripping the thread. Arc-weld the slot up, and the nut will hold on the bolt and still be removable.

Winter riding

918. Winter oil

Engines using a heavy monograde oil need careful warming up, even in summer, to ensure the oil has fully circulated before too much load is applied. In winter this is doubly important, and it is advisable to use a thinner grade of oil. If no factory advice is available, use the next lighter grade of oil than normal.

919. Battery care

Batteries should be kept fully charged in winter, as a low state of charge may result in a freeze up, damaging plates and casing. They should be topped up immediately before taking the machine for a run; the distilled water won't mix with the electrolyte straight away, and if allowed to stand could freeze and damage the battery. If the machine is used irregularly, a

freshening charge should be given every fortnight.

920. Waterproof electrics

There is no harm in applying additional waterproofing to electrical components in winter, but no unit must be sealed up completely. Some ventilation is needed to prevent condensation developing.

921. Lazy dipswitch

During the summer the dipswitch is rarely used. Consequently, first time out in the autumn, the switch may operate slowly or, worse still, stick halfway killing all light. Keep the switch lightly lubricated with petroleum jelly (not oil or grease).

922. Rust prevention in petrol tank

To prevent the inside of a petrol tank from rusting when a machine is stored, swill it round with petrol mixed with oil. The petrol will evaporate, and should leave a satisfactory film of oil on the inner surface of the tank.

923. Woolly pully

Here is a cold weather tip from December 1936.'An ordinary pullover worn in the opposite way, with one's legs thrust through the arm-holes of the garment, keeps the lower abdomen and thighs warm. It is most effective, even in the extreme instance when one's coat-tails are flying in the air.'

924. Draught exclusion

'On cold windy rides, fold one end of a long scarf across the chest, take the other round the neck, and let the long end come right down so that it can be pulled between the legs to give protection from the wind driving down the tank.'

925. Warm clothing

Warm clothing up before putting it on for a winter ride. This particularly applies to gloves and helmet which might be kept in a cold place such as the garage.

926. Saddle tanks in rain

Rain can be prevented from running down a saddle tank and under your coat by wrapping a roll of rubber round the rear end of the tank, thus diverting the stream.

927. Wet weather goggles

To keep goggles or visor free from raindrops, stick a patch of chamois leather on the back of a glove, or make a finger stall out of chamois leather so it can be removed and cleaned. Either will dry the surface without smearing or scratching.

Other suggestions for preventing raindrops reducing visibility include wiping goggle glass with a smear of thin clean oil, or the potato cure: clean the lenses and wipe them over with a slice of potato. At first the surface will froth slightly and become opaque. Don't touch it! Leave the lenses to dry in front of the fire, and they will become clear, not only preventing rain build-up but also the starring dazzle from oncoming traffic headlamps.

The same tip was suggested using an application of 50 per cent each of water and washing up liquid. Again, allow the solution to dry, but this time polish it off.

928. A winter recipe

This advice for a hot drink comes from February 1931:
'It is seldom wise to indulge in alcohol or spiritous stimulants before a run, and the following are very effective TT drinks: hot coffee; hot beef extract (or even hot milk) with half a teaspoonful of mustard; blackcurrant tea; and good home-brewed ginger wine.'

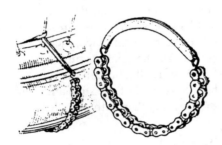

929. Snow chains

This suggestion for home made universal snow chains comes from January 1956. Cut old cycle chain into lengths of six or seven inches. Cut an old inner tube into one inch wide rubber bands and attach them to the chains with wire hooks. Space the chains at 60 degree intervals around the wheel, and hold in place with the rubber bands twisted once round a spoke. These chains worked in both soft and frozen snow, so get out there – there's no excuse now!

Pillion prose

930. Advice from a female passenger in 1950

1. Always wear goggles.
2. Insist on a comfortable pillion seat.
3. Always carry waterproof clothing.
4. Insist on fitted pannier bags for long journeys, and avoid carrying a haversack.
5. Always put your footrests up when you get off.
6. Never give signals to other traffic.

931. Keep up-to-date with the weather

No one likes to carry bulky winter clothing in the summer but, in some climates, days that turn out really warm can start and finish decidedly chilly. To avoid having to wear bulky clothing early and lug it around later, if it turns cold slide a thick newspaper under your top layer for excellent temporary insulation.

932. Smart attire

Lady pillions often don't want to spend their holiday entirely in waxed cotton and jeans, and this tip was submitted by one such in 1957.

'Permanently pleated skirts should be packed by pulling them through an old nylon stocking, from which the foot has been removed, and folding the resultant bundle in half. At the end of the journey the skirt will be entirely free of creases.'

933. A good sport?

Pillion passengers suffer enough without having to put up with this sort of advice from 1927:
'Be a sportsman. Don't expect your friend to take you to expensive restaurants and hotels every time you are out. Remember, the upkeep of the machine falls to him, also petrol, oil, and the bridge tolls and ferry

charges and cost of garaging. A canvas haversack to hold two flasks and sandwiches is all one requires; fruit and cakes can nearly always be purchased on the journey.'

I'll give him one thing – he's generous with the extra flask!

Security

In the age of the big van and bolt croppers it is difficult to give definitive advice on security, as no lock is absolutely secure. It is best when travelling not to leave machines unattended, and find a place with a secure compound or garage at night. These tips are designed to combat petty pilfering rather than full-scale theft, and they may be useful as a deterrent.

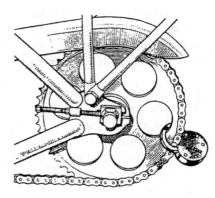

934. Sprocket lock

For machines which have the rear wheel sprocket on the opposite side of the hub from the brake drum, a padlock can be shackled through one of the sprocket holes.

935. Petrol cap lock

A spare petrol cap can be converted into a handlebar-cum-petrol tank lock. Rivet or weld a steel strip to the cap so that when the cap is in place, the bar reaches the handlebars turned to full lock. Drill a hole in the handlebar end of the strip and join the two together with a padlock.

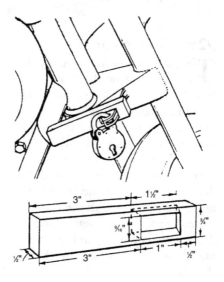

936. Captain's lock

This steering lock was devised in the early 50s with dimensions to suit a James Captain, but its method is fairly universal. Make up a steel locking bar with a slot shaped to accept the lock stop on the bottom fork yoke, and long enough when in position to butt up to the frame downtube with the

handlebars on full lock. Drill a hole in the lock stop, and secure the bar with a padlock.

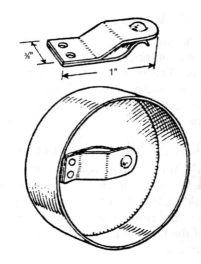

937. Anti-theft device

Many machines equipped with magneto ignition are not fitted with an ignition switch or steering head lock to act as a deterrent to thieves. The metal cap covering the contact breaker of the Lucas face-cam magneto or Magdyno can be adapted quite simply to render the engine lifeless in your absence. A springy brass strip is rivetted to the inside of a spare cover so that it touches the spring which supports the moving contact. The contact breaker is thus earthed and the ignition is dead. The modified cover can be carried in a pocket and exchanged for the usual one in a few seconds.

938. Secret switch

Many machines with coil ignition either had a spade key or a switch clearly mounted on the headlight shell. Neither were secure from theft or from vandals running the battery flat. An alternative two-way switch can be wired into the circuit and positioned out of sight. When parked it can be left in the off position.

I knew somebody who fitted a mercury switch inside the headlamp shell because his Royal Enfield only had a side stand. If the bike was lifted to an upright position with this switch activated, the horn sounded.

939. Anti-theft ruse

Alternatively, a dummy spark plug cap and lead can be fixed to the top frame tube. When the machine is left, the dummy cap can be pushed onto the plug and the real one tucked out of sight under the tank.

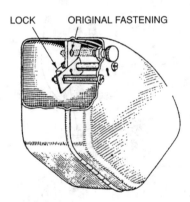

940. Locking the toolbox

This locking mechanism from 1949 will suit most pre- and post-war metal toolboxes with a hinged lid. The old screw fastening was sawn off, and the knob fixed to the toolbox lid with a nut. The door was drilled to take two fixing screws, and two tubular distance pieces were cut to size. The lock (an ordinary cabinet lock) was bolted in position by the two screws and nuts as shown, and the ends of the screws were hammered over to prevent them being undone. A keyhole was cut in the lid in line with the lock.

941. Luggage – an illustrated guide

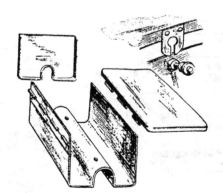

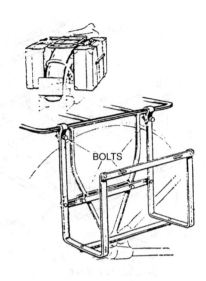

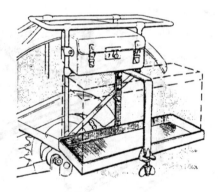

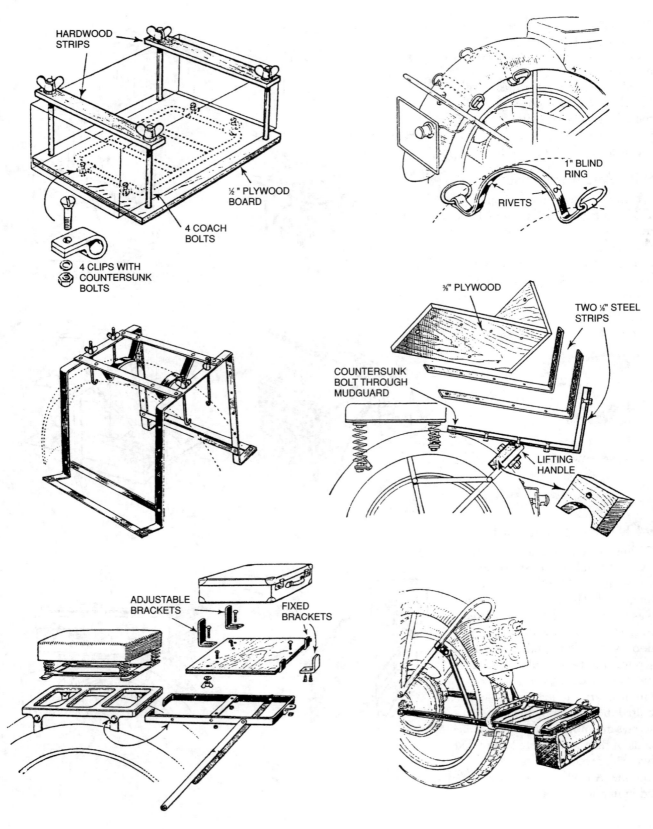

HARDWOOD
STRIPS

½ " PLYWOOD
BOARD

4 COACH
BOLTS

4 CLIPS WITH
COUNTERSUNK
BOLTS

1" BLIND
RING

RIVETS

⅜" PLYWOOD

TWO ⅛" STEEL
STRIPS

COUNTERSUNK
BOLT THROUGH
MUDGUARD

LIFTING
HANDLE

ADJUSTABLE
BRACKETS

FIXED
BRACKETS

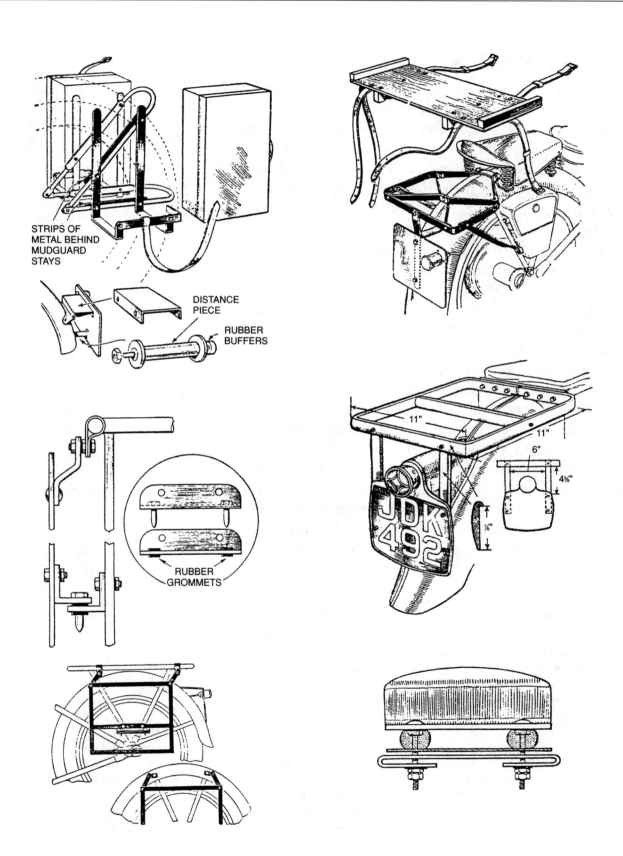

STRIPS OF
METAL BEHIND
MUDGUARD
STAYS

DISTANCE
PIECE

RUBBER
BUFFERS

RUBBER
GROMMETS

JDK
492

11"

11"

6"

4⅜"

⅞"

THE GOLDEN AGE

Searching back through *The Motor Cycle* for 'Hints and Tips', there was a point beyond which the advice was no longer relevant for the majority of classic machines on the road today. No specific date could be ascribed to it (one of the tips in this section comes from 1954), it certainly wasn't veteran or vintage, but the period loosely covers design details permanently outdated sometime after the First World War. Let us call it The Golden Age.

Much advice given in the earliest days involved the basics of acquiring and riding a machine. This is natural enough at a time when not only was the science of the internal combustion engine relatively new, but so was the concept of personalized transport. Before long the borders of everyday experience would exceed the neighbouring village, and day trips to the coast and distant holidays would become a practical reality. Topics would be limitless when directed at those whose experience was a blank sheet of paper.

Most of the tips are too dated for inclusion, such as how to carry a camera, tripod and developing equipment on the rear carrier for those holiday snaps. Some technical advice is still pertinent for owners of veteran machines, and this is included but, to start with, here is a flavour of the problems our predecessors faced and how they coped with them.

Have things really changed so much since 1908?

942. Insurance

Insurance is expensive, and forms an over large item in the modest finances of a motor cyclist. The prudent rider will insure against third party risks, as these may be cast upon one by the fault of others and a coroner's jury, and the expense may be very heavy. An insurance policy should be chosen which does not contain a speed limit clause.

943. Housing a motor cycle

A motor bicycle may be safely kept in the hall if the petrol tap be closed and does not leak, and if a plug be put in the air vent of stopper to tank. But inform the insurance people.

944. Dogs

Swinging the arm up as if to hurl an imaginary stone is a certain safeguard. Do it when close to the dog, and shoot past before he discovers there is no stone.

945. On tour

When the big car sweeps derisively by as you sit and tinker on the shadeless road, remember your humiliation is not to be ascribed to the fact that the car is more reliable than your bicycle, but to the fact that the chauffeur gave it a clean up and look over last night, when you were idly buying picture postcards. Make it a rule when on tour to glance over the machine every evening and specially see that the batteries are charged, the belt and fastener in good condition, and the tyres free from cuts and holes.

946. Counterfeit lubricating oil

The lubricating oil is the soul of the engine, therefore never buy oil of unknown makes, or from previously opened cans, or from unnamed 50-gallon drums. Many unscrupulous oil retailers refill the standard cans of responsible oil firms with cheap common rubbish, so it is as well to be constant to firms who either seal their cans hermetically with tin stoppers, or who use a wire and lead disc. Bad oil leads to mysterious overheating, loss of power, and bad running.

947. Trailers

Users of trailers were criticized in 1908, though for towing passengers rather than motor cycles, for whom this advice is of only limited value:

'A trailer is an unsatisfactory method of conveying a passenger, and under no circumstances should any trailer not specially built for motor work by a reliable firm be

attached to a motor bicycle. They are very shaky, and the passenger gets the full benefit of all the dust, noise, and smell. It is prudent for the driver to shout once in every mile, 'Are you there?"

948. Traffic

Traffic manners haven't changed much either. Under the heading 'Driving a Motor Bicycle' clubmen of 1908 were advised to:

'always be prepared for the unexpected', such as:
A child's dart out of an alley.
A cyclist's wobble.
A block in the traffic round the corner.
Traffic entering at speed from by-roads.
Vehicles in front stopping suddenly.
Vehicles behind not stopping when you stop.
Cap throwing by small boys.
Attempted suicide by dogs, cows, sheep, pigs, old ladies and children.'

'And don't forget: Never drive with the silencer cut-out open, except on lonely moors.'

'Use the hooter as little as possible; when used, give two or three firm, imperious hoots. Behind carts in narrow lanes where there is no room to pass shout 'ay-y-y-y!' to awaken the driver.'

'Never overtake and pass a driver who is not obviously aware of your presence unless you have three times as much room as you need. This is specially applicable to motor cars which you overtake.'

949. Driving a motor bicycle

There's quite an art to riding a veteran. Not only are there more control levers, they don't follow any standard layout. And though they may have the same function in theoretical terms as on later machines, their practical application is often very different. These paragraphs are quoted verbatim from advice given to novices in 1908, but will still help veteran novices of the 1990s.

950. Control of the engine

For any given speed of the road wheels there is one right position of the spark lever when battery ignition is used, and several wrong ones. These correct positions are soon learned by practice, and are the secret of good hill-climbing. When they are known and used the engine runs more smoothly, quietly and economically than with any other setting of the spark for the same road speed. (With magneto ignition the lever is generally placed nearly fully advanced and only slightly retarded on very steep hills.) Most of the following remarks apply to magneto or battery ignition, but it must be borne in mind that with magneto ignition the spark lever cannot be retarded in the same way that it can with battery ignition.

Example: 20 mph desired speed, engine 3½ hp, gear 4.5:1, road flat. The desired speed may be attained in two following ways:
1. Spark two-thirds retarded, throttle wide open, half extra air. Dull heavy explosions, pounding sensation, uses a lot of gas, heats engine.
2. Throttle almost shut, spark

nearly fully advanced, air nearly fully open. Gives light, smooth, quiet, purring explosions, keeps engine cool, economical on gas.

Or tabulate control levers thus:
Throttle – hot, noisy and expensive.
Spark   – cooler, quieter, and very cheap.
Air   – coolest, quietest, and costless (thank goodness).

For any given speed we want the spark as far forward as possible, provided there is no knocking. The throttle as nearly shut as possible, and the air set to suit the other two, but as wide open as it will go without lowering the speed below the desired point.

Therefore, first set the spark lever with the throttle well open; put it so that the machine travels a little over the desired pace, then close the throttle until exact pace desired is attained. Then open air until to open it further would slow the machine or cause misfiring.

951. Starting out

Starting out to average 20 mph along a deserted road I should set spark two-thirds forward, open throttle wide, and shut off the air. Push machine along until a fair pace is attained, drop the exhaust valve and, if inclined to take risks, mount instantly the engine fires. If not, the moment the engine fires, raise valve, mount instantly, and drop valve the moment the foot is safely on the pedal. Arrive in the saddle, instantly give a little more air to prevent engine stopping for want of it, and the speed should immediately rise to over 20 mph, the throttle being too far open. Closing this down the speed would fall to 20; I should then carefully adjust the air to that point at which the engine gave most power, and perhaps open it just one notch farther than this for the sake of coolness and economy.

952. Downhill

On arriving at a down grade that is sufficiently steep, lift the exhaust valve, switch off ignition, and freewheel down; if a very long freewheel is in prospect, half open the throttle and open air fully to scour and cool the engine. If no switch is fitted, have the throttle one eighth open and air fully open; this should weaken the mixture sufficiently to make it non-explosive in the silencer while the valve is lifted. It is inadvisable to close the throttle entirely.

If the grade is too easy to coast at a reasonable speed, fully advance the ignition, and close the throttle nearly down, giving air to suit.

If the grade be dangerous, approach summit slowly, lift valve and coast, arresting with brakes as appears wise. If very steep, close the throttle at the top, or switch off, so that engine compression may be used as an extra brake by dropping the valve at intervals.

953. Hill climbing on motor bicycles

The point in driving which takes longest to learn, and is most pleasurable in learning, is the setting of the spark in hill-climbing. This comes slowly in ordinary riding, and the best method is to spend an afternoon on a hill which is almost beyond the powers of the machine. I have more than once failed low down

on a hill by sheer bad driving, and 10 minutes later roared up to the top at a good speed. There is a great deal in knowing the machine.

The spark can never be safely advanced on steep up-gradients; therefore, start every steep hill at maximum road speed, or at a speed sufficient to carry you up. Remember that the full power of a 3½ hp engine is developed at 1500 to 1800 revolutions per minute. At 500 rpm it may only give ½ hp. When the power of the engine is insufficient to allow the climbing of steep hills with the spark fully advanced all the way up, the art lies in the judicious retardation of the spark. Sudden and violent alterations of its setting are fatal and ensure failure. As the engine slows, retard the spark a notch or so at a time, and discover by experiment whether it is helpful to cut off some of the extra air simultaneously.

The points are, therefore:
1. Start a steep hill at full speed – that is, full spark advance, throttle two-thirds open, air set to match.
2. Correct the first almost imperceptible slowing by opening the throttle to its full extent.
3. When the machine slows further, retard the spark a notch at a time.
4. If the machine is seriously slowed, some of the extra air must be cut off.
5. On a level or almost level patch halfway up, re-advance the ignition a notch at a time, and if necessary assist the pick-up by pedalling sharply.

954. Difficulty in starting

A motor cycle should never be pushed more than six yards to start it; if it will not start in six yards on the level, something is wrong, and effort will be better expended in search than in propulsion.
1. Verify setting of levers, switch, and petrol tap.
2. Is the piston really free in the cylinder? If not, inject paraffin.
3. Is there a good spark? If with HT magneto, are the plug points not more than half a millimetre apart?
4. Is the carburettor jet clear, and well provided with petrol?
5. Are the valves working, especially automatically operated inlet valve.

Imagining that the carburettor is known to be perfectly clean, and the engine was put away in perfect order, the commonest reasons for sluggishness in starting are:
1. Petrol level too low in jet.
2. Piston gummy in cylinder.
3. With coil ignition, too light a pressure between engine contacts, dirty or rough contacts, stuck trembler on coil.
4. With magneto ignition, a motor cycle engine is always easily started provided sparking plug points are set closely together.
5. Stuck up inlet valves of the automatic pattern.

A motor cycle is always as easy to get away as a push cycle if its owner takes the trouble to keep its working parts clean, and to adjust them occasionally.

955. Misfires – fault finding

For misfires occurring at all road and engine speeds persistently, check the following:

◇ Cracked or broken sparking plug.
◇ Batteries running down.
◇ Loose or dirty connection.
◇ Trembler in need of adjustment.
◇ Water in petrol.
◇ Dirt in carburettor.
◇ Magneto wants cleaning.

For misfires at speed:

◇ All the previous mentioned troubles will be noticed most at speed. Mixture can now be tested by altering air lever.
◇ Trembler needs firmer adjustment – most probable solution.
◇ Valve sticking.
◇ Wiper of contact maker jumping its segment.
◇ Sparking plug sooty or too wide a gap at points.
◇ Carburettor drained dry of petrol.

For occasional misfires:

◇ Pre-ignition through hot particle in cylinder.
◇ Moving some part of machine, such as timing lever, sets up a short circuit in a particular position.
◇ Small particle of dirt in carburettor.
◇ Exhaust or inlet valve momentarily sticking up.
◇ Loose dirt or dirty oil in contact breaker.
◇ Swinging wire or loose packing of coil and batteries.

For misfires soon after starting:

◇ Plug developing fault when warmed.
◇ Batteries running down.
◇ Valve distorted with heat, or too tight a fit in guide, and so sticking.

Note: with a high tension magneto always suspect the sparking plug as the most likely culprit for misfires; with a trembler coil, suspect the coil trembler first; with a plain coil, suspect the make-or-break contacts.

956. Acetylene lighting

Few people nowadays would be prepared to rely on acetylene lighting but, unlike obsolete electrical equipment, an acetylene system cannot be updated by carving out battery cases or concealing solid-state miniaturization. If your veteran machine has acetylene lighting, you're stuck with it, and if you want to keep it in working condition the experience of our Edwardian ancestors is still valid. Here is some more contemporary advice.

957. Cleanliness

Cleanliness is the one sole factor of success with acetylene lamps. Riders new to them should burn a charge in them at home before the first night ride, and note the effect of temporarily feeding too much water to the generator.

Given a clean lamp, gas should be obtained in 30 seconds from turning on the water. Turn it on say a full turn, and when the pipes have blown clear and the flame settles down to burn steadily, turn the water feed back to the minimum which provides a bright light. When the carbide gets sodden, a generous supply of water is necessary, but this should not be for four hours with a fair sized generator.

958. If no gas comes

If no gas comes, and the carbide and water reservoirs are filled, there is dirt either in the water valves or the central drilled tube of the carbide container, or in the burner. Most probably it is in the water valve. Do not take the valve out but, putting your lips to the water filling orifice, or round the top of the valve needle, blow vigorously till clear. If the tube or burner is dirty, you will have to detach them, and will remember to clean them next time. In case of leaks and flame bursting from the body of the lamp, smear with soap, white lead, or sealing wax; if round carbide container, renew washer and tighten it up.

959. Never leave acetylene lamps to burn out, but blow out the flame. Their expiring exhalations are full of impurities and apt to choke the burner. Detach container and leave it to exhaust itself on the garden wall.

960. Always turn off water during stoppages.

961. Much unspent carbide may be retrieved by riddling a half used charge but it seldom pays to relight a charge that has a lot of dust and sediment mixed with it from the previous night's burning.

962. Always either clean or detach the carbide container after use. The vibration of running throws the dust into the valve of the lamp, and any waste will disseminate into the gas passages after a time.

963. To clean the carbide container quickly, sludge it in a bucket of water, and gouge with a big screwdriver. The best lamps have dummy bottomless cups or inner skins in the containers; these greatly facilitate cleaning.

964. Remember carbide expands considerably when wet, therefore never fill the container more than two-thirds its volume.

965. The filter pads should be kept dry and clean or be frequently renewed. Silicate cotton is the best material.

966. The piping should be routed so that the gas is continually rising from the generator. This will prevent water collecting in the tubing, causing intermittent stoppages.

967. If there are two points of flame in the burner, the burner is all right. If not, check for blockages in the burner, water valve, or carbide container.

968. An acetylene gas purifier

Added efficiency from acetylene lamps is gained by the use of a gas purifier consisting of a tube 1 in. in diameter, containing a mixture of bleaching powder and quicklime (calcium oxide), held together by two wire gauze discs. The tube is sealed simply by a cork in each end with a brass tube inserted.

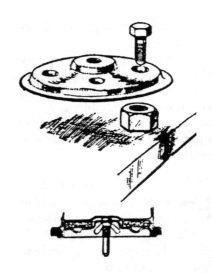

969. Improving a generator

This tip from 1923 solved the problem of a generator which worked well for half-an-hour before flickering out. It was discovered that the steaming carbide was saturating the felt pad at the base of the water container, and so the gas could not pass through the two small holes in the brass plate supporting the pad. Enlarging the holes, and even making two more, did not improve matters. Nor did the substitution of cotton wool for felt.

A complete cure was effected by bulging the plate from above, using a round-ended ⅜ in. bolt and nut as a punch and die respectively, forming a little well at each hole. This modification prevents contact of the plate and pad and so exposes a larger area for the passage of the gas through the filtering medium.

970. Acetylene generator repair

To replace a broken water container bracket-bolt on an acetylene generator, tin the end of the new bolt and solder a short length of wire to it. Pass the wire through the filler cap hole and out of the bolt hole, drawing the bolt with it. This tip can be used in any situation involving closed containers.

971. Acetylene rear light

If the rear light flame is apt to jolt out, stretch a steel wire across the inside of the lamp so that it passes through the flame, keeping it white hot. It will then usually relight the gas once it has been jolted out.

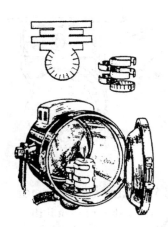

972. A one-candle-power light

This suggestion for short rides or as a get-you-home tip comes from 1924. A piece of tin is cut and bent to shape. This fitting will hold a short length of candle and grip the acetylene burner inside the headlamp shell. Extensive tests proved that the candle didn't blow out once inside the lamp, or smoke up the glass. Who needs quartz-halogen?

973. Trembler coil ignition

Even in veteran times, trembler coil ignition was regarded as a cheap substitute for an HT magneto, and soon became entirely obsolete. Here are some tips on trembler coil adjustment:

Trembler coils should always be set with the engine running. A trembler coil will fire on almost any adjustment, but if the electrical points are set too close, the platinum of one point will be deposited on the other to a greater extent than usual, and the engine will not run fast.

974. Tightening the locknut is apt to alter the adjustment on any trembler coil. Therefore, set the trembler with the engine running, so as to obtain as high an engine speed as possible, combined with as wide a setting of the points as allows the engine to run its fastest; that is, with a high shrill note as opposed to a low buzz from the trembler coil. But if the note is set too high the engine will not start easily.

975. The points of a make-and-break contact breaker must be set much closer for a trembler coil than for a plain coil.

976. Lettering of coils: SP or B = sparking plug; M, F, or E = frame; C or T = contact breaker; P, B, A, or plus sign = positive terminal of accumulator.

977. Trembler blade lost spring

In time, any trembler blade may lose its temper or acquire a set, and so cause very sluggish running of the engine. If no spare is available, a piece of whalebone or clock spring, rather less in length than the erring blade, may be drilled to slip over the holding screw, and put behind the blade to stiffen it.

978. Converting fixed to variable timing

Complaints about fixed ignition timing were being made as early as 1922, particularly by owners of susceptible two-strokes. A Belfast rider converted his 211 cc single gear Levis to variable timing as follows. On examining

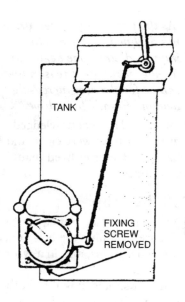

the EIC magneto he found that the contact breaker cam ring was the standard type with a slot underneath, which would permit movement if the extra stop screw fitted in the magneto end-plate to fix the timing was removed. (The screw to remove is the one which prevents the ring moving in the same direction as the armature revolves.) A control lever, rod and tank mounting were set up on the machine, and the blank timing lever on the contact breaker was drilled to take the rod. As a result the Levis was much more controllable in town, and hill climbing and acceleration improved considerably.

979. Belt driven transmission

Belt driven transmission also faded with the end of the first era of motor cycling, and choice of procuring a new belt now is probably limited to the best of what was available then. By 1923 *The Motor Cycle* considered belts to be very good:

'As the popularity of belt drive has declined, so have belts improved, until one begins to wonder what good reason there can be for the ever-increasing demand for all-chain drive.'

'Hints and Tips' acknowledged that rubber belts were clean and reliable, but shorter-lived than leather ones.

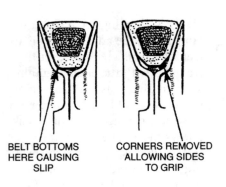

BELT BOTTOMS HERE CAUSING SLIP   CORNERS REMOVED ALLOWING SIDES TO GRIP

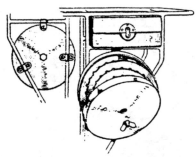

980. Belt slip

Belt slip has two principal causes: running the belt under wrong conditions, and in a wrong condition.

The belt should sink into both pulleys so that its top edge is just flush with the top edge of the pulleys, and its bottom edge well away from the bottom of the groove. This gives the sides of the V their full contact area, and any modern belt will run well under these conditions, if its section is the same angle as the pulley. Lots of pulleys are turned at an angle of 30 or 40 degrees, and a 28 degree belt gets no grip on them. Also, a correct pulley wears gradually.

As for the other condition, a rubber belt must be kept clean, and a leather belt must be kept dressed with lubricant, free from grit and wet. Don't leave a paste of grit and mud inside the pulley groove for weeks together; you'll find some there, if you look now! These two conditions being fulfilled, beltslip is a very rare occurrence.

To run habitually with a very tight belt is hard on the pulleys, and strains the engine (or countershaft) bearings as well as the hub bearings.

981. Belt surgery

A bad case of belt slip was suffered by a reader in 1924. He diagnosed the problem as the corners of the belt bottoming on the pulley flanges. As the belt was generally in good order, he ground away the lower corners of the belt to lift it up in the flange. Incidentally, all belts form a V of 28 degrees, and worn flanges should be trued on a lathe to avoid constant slipping and rapid belt wear.

982. Belt maintenance

In fitting a new rubber belt it is a good idea to put a thick coating of rubber solution on both ends, also to squeeze some through the bolt holes and screw the fastener up before it is dry. This will add to the life of the belt.

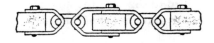

983. Roadside belt repair

A spare belt fastener should be included in the toolkit of a belt-drive machine. If a repaired belt is too short for use, and no link is available, one can be made up from the spare fastener. A piece of broken belt is inserted in the fastener to protect the pulley flanges.

984. Spare belt carrier

Not wishing to spoil the appearance of a new machine, one reader converted an old shortbread tin into a spare belt carrier. The back of the tin was fixed to frame tubes with metal pipe clips, and a hole was drilled through tin and lid to accommodate a bolt and wing-nut. To save a lot of effort, the tin was painted black to match the bike, rather than paint the bike tartan to match the tin.

985. Dummy belt rim brakes

Performance of dummy belt rim brakes depends not only on the quality of the brake block, but also its relation to the rim. If the brake block bottoms in the rim the effect is the same as for belt slip, with the same loss of grip. A remedy is to cut a small section from the lower side of the block. Check also that the rim is running true, and that it is not clogged with oil or grit.

986. Veteran valve tappet adjustment

A tip from 1910 makes clear that because of modern metals used in valve manufacture, valves *'scarcely expand at all under heat'* so '*the old rule that* ¹⁄₃₂ *in. should be left between valve and tappet does not necessarily hold good.*' Turning this tip on its head, it is useful to know that suggested valve clearances for machines before 1910 seems to be ¹⁄₃₂ in.

By 1924 the advice had been updated as follows:

'*Engines having overhead valves (OHV) differ from those of the side-by-side valve type, in that the former require practically no tappet clearance when cold, since the expansion of the cylinder as the engine warms up increases tappet clearance. Therefore, never adjust OHV tappets when the engine is warm. When cold the tappets should be just free, and no more, in the case of an OHV engine. Whereas a side-by-side valve engine requires that there should be sufficient clearance for valve expansion, say six thousandths of an inch, or sufficient to give a decided up-and-down movement between tappet and valve stem without excessive clatter when the engine is running.*'

When checking the clearance of the exhaust valve tappet, make sure that the lifter control isn't holding the tappet in any way. If there is any possibility of this, disconnect the control altogether, as the setting of the lifter may make the tappet clearance appear correct when in reality it is considerably out of adjustment.

987. Exhaust spitting with valve lifted

Using the exhaust valve lifter as one of the means of controlling speed is common practice on veteran machines. If the exhaust spits back through the silencer with the exhaust valve lifted, it usually denotes wear in the valve-lifting mechanism which is not releasing sufficient compression. And these 'give the public a bad impression and frighten horses'. Adjustment of the mechanism or a new cable should solve the problem.

988. Piston removal and replacement

On some older machines with a non-detachable cylinder head and insufficient clearance under the tank, it is necessary when reassembling the engine to insert the gudgeon pin with the piston already started in the cylinder. It is difficult to hold these in position and locate the small-end of the connecting rod. A locating tool can be made from six inches of wooden dowel the same diameter as the gudgeon pin, tapered to a point at one end. It is then a simple matter to hold the cylinder and piston in position, locate the small-end with the pointed end of the dowel, and push it through followed closely by the gudgeon pin.

989. Valve removal and replacement

To remove a valve from a side-valve engine without using a valve lifter or detaching the cylinder, proceed as follows:

1. Turn the engine over until the valve is fully opened, and then insert a strip of metal of appropriate width underneath the valve collar (in such a way that the collar will not twist sideways), so that when the tappet descends the spring remains compressed.
2. Remove the valve cap and press down the valve from above, whereupon the cotter can be drawn out.
3. Tap or pull the metal strip out of position, which will allow the spring or collar to fall off the valve stem, and the valve to be removed.

To replace the valve:

1. Reassemble all parts except the cotter, and then compress the spring by means of the upward pressure of the tappet on the collar, first interposing a nut or other spacer so as to give sufficient lift to enable the metal strip to again be inserted.
2. Turn the engine over farther until the tappet descends, freeing the spacer, and allowing the cotter to be reinserted.
3. Removal of the metal strip will leave the valve fully assembled.

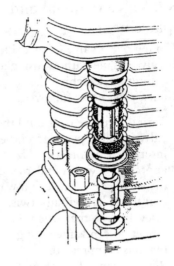

990. Valve stem lubrication

This tip is ideal for vintage side-valves. Older side-valve engines have no automatic oiling for valve stems and guides, but this drawback can be improved to a degree quite simply by applying this tip from 1954. Soft felt circles were cut ¾ in. in diameter and ⁷⁄₁₆ in. thick, and a hole punched in the centre. Three felt rings were then fitted over the exposed portion of each valve stem between the lower end of the guide and the spring bottom collar. These were saturated with oil. Every time the valve is raised the felt rings are compressed, releasing the oil. The felt rings can be kept moist with a few drops of oil every so often.

991. Two-lever carburettors

With the old type two-lever carburettor, where movement of the air lever makes a considerable difference to the running, the method to determine whether the jet is too large or too small is to ride the machine at full throttle with the air lever three quarters open, and then gradually close it. If an increase in speed or power is noticeable, the jet is too small. On the other hand, if fully opening the air lever increases the speed or power, the jet is too large. The correct jet on these early carburettors will give the maximum speed and power on full throttle with the air lever three parts open.

992. Splash lubrication by hand-pump

When these veteran and vintage machines were new, manufacturers advised that the oil hand-pump should be operated so that one pumpful was given every so many miles (depending on the model and hilliness of the country). It was proven preferable to give the engine oil in small dollops, rather than the full charge. *The Motor Cycle* recommended that if the booklet says one pumpful every eight miles, give half a pumpful every four miles instead; increase the supply when the machine is being driven hard, or climbing, and decrease it when it is running light.

993.

It is easy to check whether the engine is being adequately lubricated. When the throttle is closed for a short distance and then opened suddenly, there should be a puff of blue smoke from the exhaust. Should injecting oil make the motor cycle speed up, even though the throttle remains constant, the engine is being starved of oil and the friction is sapping power.

994. Sight feeds

There are various possible causes of a sight feed filling up with oil instead of passing it to the engine.

1. Air leakage at the sight feed glass because of the cap working loose or through faulty washers. There should be a washer each side of the glass.
2. Air leakage between the sight feed and the tank (or crankcase, if mounted on the crankcase). These faces and any washer should be dressed with a suitable sealant on assembly.
3. Loose regulating screw gland nut, allowing air bubbles to come through with the oil.
4. Loose or leaky pipe connection.
5. Drip-feed lubricator or pipe feeds blocked (assuming drip-feed is fitted).
6. Dirt under the oil pump disc valve.

995. Pilgrim pumps

One problem with worn Pilgrim pumps is that oil builds up in the sight feed chamber and eventually overflows. This can be caused by the spring pressure on the plunger wearing a hollow in the face of the operating cam, the result of which is a slight reversal of motion when the plunger nears the end of its stroke, (that is, when oil is being drawn from the sight chamber, the reversed motion blows a small portion of the charge back again). The face of the cam is actually a flat plane formed at an angle to the axis of the plunger. The hollow can be removed by carefully touching up the face of the cam with a smooth flat file. Be careful not to remove too much metal, or the port timing might be upset.

996. Lubricating hub gears

Thin cycle oil is recommended for lubricating hub gears. Thicker oil, such as ordinary engine oil, will tend to clog the delicate mechanism and cause the gearchange to become sluggish.

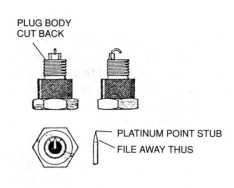

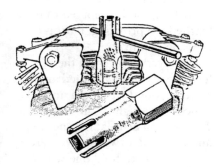

997. Plug spanner

Often good quality plug spanners are too cumbersome to fit on a plug without removing the petrol tank, especially on vintage machines where the plug may be located in a valve cap. A box spanner reduced in length and slotted to take a tommy-bar should fit between tank and plug.

998. Renovating spark plugs

This tip from 1941 was designed to combat the shortages of war. An electrode can burn back so much that by obtaining the correct gap, the points are shrouded by the plug body. It may be possible to cut away the plug body down each side of the earth electrode to the

depth of the step. The re-exposed points will be recessed in the cylinder head, but not enough to affect combustion.

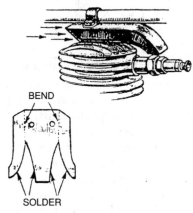

999. Cooling the plug

Some early two-strokes had the spark plug at the rear of the cylinder head. In cases where the plug overheated this suggestion for an air deflector was submitted. Clamped to the frame tube, the deflector directs cool air onto the plug body. Experiments proved that, to be successful, the downward slope of the rear part of the deflector should not be too abrupt.

1000. Plug radiators

Another idea for central plug cooling was this plug radiator made from a selection of dished copper discs. The top disc includes a tag to which the HT

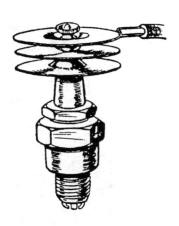

lead can be attached. Though they may dissipate heat, they look like a fairly efficient water collector as well!

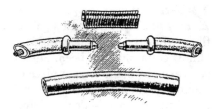

1001. Pre-war electrical connection

Pre-war electrical fittings can now be bought from specialist suppliers, but if you just need one or two and you want to keep the appearance in period, this tip from 1935 might help. Solder a clutch nipple the wrong way round on the end of each wire to be joined. Connect the nipples with an inch of Bowden casing from which the waterproof covering has been removed. The casing should be just too small to slip over the nipples, with each end opened out slightly. Twisting to the left, push the casing onto the nipples. The casing will be momentarily sprung open, but will grip tightly directly it is released. The joint can be insulated by a short piece of rubber tubing.

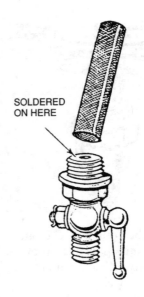

SOLDERED ON HERE

1002. Petrol tap filters

Pattern vintage-style petrol taps may not be fitted with a gauze filter, while the originals would almost certainly have been. Filters can easily be made from a piece of thin metal gauze shaped round a pencil to form a cylinder, soldered up the seam and soldered onto the top of the tap.

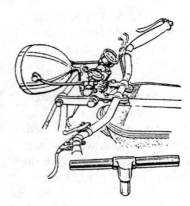

1003. Instrument bar

Many vintage machines have handlebars fitted into a central clamp in the steering column, bicycle fashion. If these have been removed at any time to fit adjustable sports bars, the empty column can be tidied up with a short length of tube and T-piece. Once fitted this will make an ideal instrument mount for speedometer, rev counter or headlight brackets.

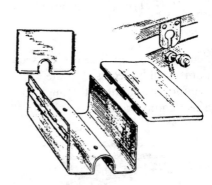

1004. Top tube toolbox

Amateur metalworkers will find this suggested design for a top tube toolbox simple to construct. The overall size is 8 in. x 6 in. x 3½ in. in 22 gauge sheet steel. Sides and bottom are in one piece, and the tunnel for the top tube of the frame is formed over a broom handle. The ends are made a ¼ in. oversize on the sides and bottom to form a flange, and they are riveted in place with the flanges inside and soldered to make a neat job. The lid has a flange all round, and the hinge is formed by rolling one rather longer flange round a spoke. The other half of the hinge is made from a separate metal strip riveted to the box. The catch illustrated was made from a length of stud, two locknuts and the terminal nut from a spark plug.

1005. Secret switch for electric horn

Though I was always brought up in the belief that street crime was non-existent in the days of the local bobby, little boys seem to have caused our predecessors quite a few problems. The heinous offence of cap-throwing has already been mentioned. By the 20s there was regular correspondence as to how to combat meddling with parked machines. Many ingenious ideas were submitted for temporarily immobilizing machines and shorting electric components to prevent the battery from being flattened. This horn switch comes from 1923, and is reputed to have 'baffled the prowling, button-pressing urchin'.

The inverted lever on the handlebar was dismantled and a piece of round wood obtained which was a tight fit inside the bar. This was planed flat on one side, and on the flat two screws were inserted, one to hold one wire of the horn flex, and the other to hold a small length of clock spring (fitted with a wood or ebonite button) and the other wire.

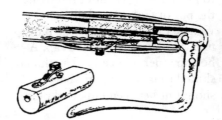

Underneath the handlebar grip a hole was drilled, and the block, wired up, was driven into place so that the ebonite button (that made the horn work when pressed) peeped unobtrusively through the hole. The flex was run up the inside of the handlebar to emerge through a hole further along. A hole was drilled down the length of the block to accommodate the existing control cable.